Family Therapy
with
Ethnic Minorities

SAGE SOURCEBOOKS FOR
THE HUMAN SERVICES SERIES

Series Editors: ARMAND LAUFFER and CHARLES GARVIN

12

Man Keung Ho

Family Therapy with Ethnic Minorities

SAGE SOURCEBOOKS FOR THE HUMAN SERVICES SERIES
VOLUME 5

SAGE PUBLICATIONS
The International Professional Publishers
Newbury Park   London   New Delhi

RC
451.5
.42
H62
1987

For information address:

SAGE Publications, Inc.
2455 Teller Road
Newbury Park, California 91320

SAGE Publications Ltd.
6 Bonhill Street
London EC2A 4PU
United Kingdom

SAGE Publications India Pvt. Ltd.
M-32 Market
Greater Kailash I
New Delhi 110 048 India

Printed in the United States of America

Library of Congress Cataloging-in-Publication Data

Main entry under title:

Library of Congress Cataloging-in-Publication Data

Ho, Man Keung.
  Family therapy with ethnic minorities.

  (Sourcebooks for the human services; v. 5)
  Bibliography: p.
  1. Family psychotherapy—United States.
2. Minorities—Mental health services—United States.
I. Title. II. Series.
RC451.5.A2H62   1987   616.89'156   86-29717
ISBN 0-8039-2677-4
ISBN 0-8039-2678-2 (pbk.)

FIFTH PRINTING, 1991

Contents

139445

"I wish to dedicate this book to my father, Ho Cheuk Yuen, who has taught me the value of family."

Preface

Different terms and definitions have been applied to describe Asian/Pacific Americans, American Indians and Alaskan Natives, Hispanic Americans, and Black Americans in the United States. Examples of such terms include *people of color, Third World people, racial minorities, linguistic minorities, culturally different, oppressed minorities,* and *ethnic minorities.* In this book, the term *ethnic minority* is used, because it encompasses three elements that are important in providing effective service to this specific population. *Ethnicity* denotes cultural distinctiveness, which supplies meaning to the cross-cultural encounter between the therapist and the clients. *Minority* refers to a group of political and economic individuals who are relatively powerless, receive unequal treatment, and regard themselves as objects of discrimination. Finally, the *therapeutic encounter* requires that the therapist learn from the clients about their cultural values, signs, and behavioral styles. Hence "ethnic minority" is more than a categorical description of race, culture, or color. It is the boundaries of separation and, in particular, how these boundaries are managed, protected, ritualized through stereotyping, and sometimes violated that is of primary interest and concern for family therapy.

Family-centered approaches to problem solving and treatment of emotional disturbances, including marital stress and difficulties of children, have recently gained wide acceptance in the the helping professions. This is evidenced partly by the increased number of books and articles on the subject published in social work, counseling, psychology, and related health and mental health fields. Not surprisingly, a majority of these publications deal with problems concerning the generalized White middle-class American family. Family problems of ethnic minorities often are treated by using the same White middle-class American family as a frame of reference. Consequently, cultural and ethnic insensitivity of family therapists and the agencies employing them has emerged as a primary factor contributing to the overall ineffectiveness and underutilization of social services and family therapy by ethnic minority families.

The rapid acceptance of the family-centered approach to problem solving has resulted in a proliferation of treatment models and approaches. The philosophical orientations and techniques employed by some of these therapeutic approaches diametrically oppose the indigenous cultural values and structures of ethnic minority families. Additionally, the interactive patterns of the ethnic minority family, like the White family, have undergone structural changes over the past decade. As a result, ethnic minorities in the United States are often faced with adopting new roles, such as those of the single-parent and step-parent, that conflict with traditional cultural norms.

The helping professions, despite their frequent contacts and emphasis upon work with culturally different families, have done little more than address from a general and peripheral perspective the problems that ethnic minority families face. Moreover, existing literature relating to day-to-day living problems of ethnic minorities in the United States and their struggle as a family unit is usually vague and scattered (Pedersen, 1985). There are few publications that provide organized, systemic, theory-based data relevant to helping these families resolve their problems.

Four ethnic minority family groups are represented in this book. They are (1) Asian and Pacific Americans, (2) American Indians and Alaskan Natives, (3) Hispanic Americans, and (4) Black Americans. The book provides theory specification, integration, and systematization for ethnic minority families. Six important features frame the organization of this book. (1) It introduces a culturally relevant theoretical framework from which appropriate assessment and therapeutic guidelines in work with different ethnic minority families are derived (Chapter 1). (2) It provides family therapists and students an up-to-date resource of the political, social, and economic problems that each ethnic minority family group faces, and the unique strengths and contributions each ethnic minority family group possesses. (3) It gives family therapists and students a clear picture of the distinctive cultural values of each ethnic group and describes the changing family structure and interactive patterns. (4) It provides a theory-based "how to," that is, specific guidelines and suggestions on culturally relevant family therapy models, strategies, skills, and techniques. (5) These cover work with the single-parent family and with the reconstituted family, and in marital therapy and divorce therapy. (6) Chapters 2, 3, 4, and 5, which discuss therapy with each ethnic group, follow the same standard outline. This prevents duplication, repetition, and content unevenness. Adherence to a single outline also facilitates comparison and integration of common core knowledge and differences in ethnic minority family therapy, which are covered in Chapter 6. It is hoped that the organization of this book not only provides students and practitioners with a comprehensive, up-to-date examination of family therapy with ethnic minorities, but that it also provides an analytical and functional format that lends itself to the scientific ordering of information and a promising challenge of quality for practice theory with ethnic minorities. Specification of family therapy knowledge should facilitate the learning process of both undergraduate and graduate students. Practicing family therapists will find that the book also presents practical information that they can readily use in their work with ethnic minority families.

Because this book focuses on an ecological family systemic approach, psychodynamic and psychoanalytic theories have received only scant attention. Such unevenness should not be construed as meaning the intrapsychic world of ethnic minorities is unimportant or irrelevant. Given that this is a book for family therapy, the interpersonal resolution of inner conflict is examined because it forms the basis of most marital and family dysfunction. None of the family therapy models or approaches for ethnic minorities was adequately "tested" according to prevailing paradigms of social science and practice research. However, they relate closely to existing family therapy theories. Furthermore, all interventive approaches and principles suggested represent *supplements* to existing family therapy theories, not alternatives.

It is generally recognized that there is not only considerable interethnic group diversity, but that there is also marked and significant intraethnic group heterogeneity. In an attempt to delineate and systematize knowledge about ethnic minority family structures and practice principles, the possibility of stereotyping, obviously, is great. Aware of this danger, I tried to avoid it and even consulted a panel of distinguished ethnic minority practitioners and educators. Yet, I, undoubtedly, have not been totally successful. If I have presented incorrect or stereotypical information, I apologize and invite reader's corrections. The lack of satisfactory gender neutral pronoun in the English language has prompted me to use "he" or "she" throughout the book without any idea which has been favored. The book is infused with case examples, almost all of which come from my own practice. The few that do not are "gifts" from colleagues, trainees, or students at the Moore Transcultural Family Study Center. All of the identifying information has been changed or omitted to protect client confidentiality.

Finally, I wish to thank the individuals who have helped me with this book. I wish to thank Charles Garvin, editor of the Sage Sourcebooks Series, who provided me with invaluable suggestions and continued support and encouragement. I owe particular thanks to Leon Chestang, Joe Walker, Paul Keys, Ella Euwing, Ronald Lewis, John Red Horse, Toni Dobrec, Guadalupe Gibson, Herman Curiel, Terri Petrikin, Sophia Lam, and Muriel Yu, who read and critiqued parts of the manuscript pertaining to each ethnic minority group. I want to express my appreciation to Leona Huffaker for editing an early draft of the manuscript and to the secretarial staff of the Information Processing Center of the University of Oklahoma, who typed the manuscript. Finally, I want to thank my wife, Jeannie, for her understanding, patience, and support, and my sons, Christopher Yan-Tak and Stephen Yan-Mong, who excused me when I locked myself up in a room to work and entertained me whenever I took a break from writing.

—Man Keung Ho

1

Theoretical Framework for Therapy with Ethnic Minority Families

The wide acceptance of the family-centered approach to problem solving has generated many treatment theories and models. The philosophical orientations and the techniques employed by some of these theoretical approaches may diametrically oppose the indigenous cultural values and family structures of an ethnic minority family (Mizio and Delaney, 1981). Tseng and McDermott (1975) warn that the client's orientation to the process of help-seeking and the "fit" between traditional paradigms and those utilized by providers may be critical to successful process and outcome. Judging by the overwhelming underutilizations of mental health services and high dropout rates by ethnic minority clients (Jones, 1977; Fujii, 1976; Barrera, 1978; Jackson, 1973), a wide gap clearly exists between the unmet needs of the ethnic minority clients and families and the therapists' ability to provide for their needs successfully. It is also clear that family therapy with ethnic minorities requires an organized culturally sensitive theoretical framework. From such a framework, existing family therapy principles and techniques and innovative emic-based (cultural-specific) therapy principles and techniques can be utilized.

The following discussion focuses on the conceptual framework for therapy with ethnic minority families. Emanating from such a conceptual framework that considers the ethnic minority's reality, culture, biculturalism, ethnicity status, language, and social class, the traditional social work "person-in environment" focus of the ecosystem theoretical framework is introduced. The application of family system communication theory and family system structure theory in therapy with ethnic minority families will also be presented.

At this time, there is no single integrated theory upon which therapists practicing family therapy can rely. This problem is accentuated when therapists deal with ethnic minority families. Furthermore, as Gurman and Rice point out, family practitioners "have generally failed to deal with common themes running through each other's work" (1975, p. 36). As a result, many concepts that address the same family phenomena or processes are identified by different names.

This book takes the stance that there are important common themes among theories and therapies, particularly those used in family therapy with ethnic minorities. Two criteria are used in this book to ensure an organized, common, systematic format for analyzing, discussing, and presenting family therapy theories: (1) Theories used are rooted in and derived from the field of *family* therapy; and (2) practice experience that this author and other ethnic minority practitioners have acquired through direct work with ethnic minority families (emic-approach) is used. A discussion of each of these important criteria follows.

This book applies primarily theories that have developed within the field of family therapy. A large portion of the theory of family therapy today derives its underlying conceptual framework from the systems theory and developmental tasks (Levande, 1976). Family therapies differ in their points of emphasis within the systems of theory itself. Two groups of family therapy theory have emerged: one group emphasizes the "bits and pieces" communicative-interactive framework represented by Virginia Satir (1967) and Jay Haley (1976). The other group emphasizes "family-environment transactions, intergenerational dynamic order" structure-functional framework represented by Salvador Minuchin (1974) and Murray Bowen (1978).

Although there are other theoretical approaches to family therapy—for example, behavioral, psychodynamic, task-centered, problem solving, family life cycle developmental framework, and strategic family therapies—they do not advance new theories about family dynamics. New "tactics" may be attached, but the focus of these theories is, nevertheless, on the actual structure and communication styles within the family system. As a result, they are subsumed under the communicative-interactive and structure-functional theories.

The second criterion this book uses, as mentioned earlier, is the emic-approach. "Emic-based" ideas, although not widely known or utilized by family practitioners, offer considerable promise for enhancing the understanding of ethnic families and enlarging interventive repertoires. Pike (1954, p. 8) defines emic-approach as "an attempt to discover and to describe the pattern of that particular culture in reference to the way in which the various elements of that culture are related to each other in the functioning of the particular classification derived in advance of the study of that culture." The emic-approach is relevant to the immediate social and physical nurturing environment of the "dual perspective" advanced by Norton (1978). According to Norton, every ethnic minority individual is embedded simultaneously in at least two systems: that of his immediate social and physical nurturing environment and that of the larger major society. The nurturing environment defines the various elements of each particular culture and it determines an individual's need and a sense of identity. Practice experiences derived from direct work with ethnic minority families, in turn, helps to generate practice principles that are particularly relevant to each ethnic minority group.

In an attempt to systematize and to integrate theories with ethnic minority families, each chapter (2, 3, 4, 5) pertaining to therapy with specific ethnic family group will first identify relevant principles of family behavior and, second, identify relevant principles of practice. A major assumption is made here that theories of family behavior that are at a high level of abstraction are appropriate for ethnic minority families, but the manner in which they may be translated into principles of therapy is ethnic-specific. The general and specific application of these theoretical perspectives for therapy with each ethnic family group is contained in each chapter under "Part 2: Culturally Relevant Techniques and Skills in Therapy Phases." A *technique* here refers to the specific means or procedures through which a particular aim mutually agreed upon by client/family and therapist is implemented and accomplished. A *skill* refers to the unique fusion of aptitudes and knowledge or capabilities essential to performing a professional task or activity (Barlett, 1958). Unique aptitudes that are part of skill may include a therapist's warmth, sensitivity (to own ethnic background, client's ethnic background and reality, and adaptation of skills in response to client's ethnic reality), flexibility, positive regard and respect for client/family. Therapists' capabilities that are part of skill include therapeutic procedures responsible for accomplishing a task. To demonstrate the close relationship between theoretical perspectives and actual practice, case illustrations are presented in Part 2 and specific treatment modalities are explored in Part 4 of each chapter.

The Conceptual Framework for
Therapy with
Ethnic Minority Families

The development and selection of a culturally sensitive theoretical framework for therapy with ethnic minorities must take into consideration five major factors that distinguish minorities from the mainstream middle-class White American families. These factors include (1) ethnic minority reality, (2) impact of external system on minority cultures, (3) biculturalism, (4) ethnicity difference in minority status, (5) ethnicity and language, and (6) ethnicity and social class. The following discussion aims to define these concepts and factors as they relate to the theoretical framework for therapy with ethnic minority families.

Ethnic Minority Reality

Racism and poverty dominate the lives of many ethnic minorities. Racism as it is practiced in the unequal distribution of income, goods, and services among the ethnic minorities is made more obvious by the election in 1980 of a president who reversed more than 50 years of development in social welfare. In a 1982 editorial entitled "Milking the Poor," the *Wall Street Journal* points out that programs benefiting the poor—rather than programs reflecting the interests of the middle class, such as social security, Medicare, and certain business subsidies—had been successful targets for the Reagan administration's budget cuts. As a result of perpetuatory racism and discrimination, the socioeconomic status of ethnic minorities degenerates. For example, the median 1980 income for White families was $21,900; for minority families it was $13,470. Unemployment was a major factor that lowered the income level of the ethnic minorities. From 1970 to 1981, the unemployment status of ethnic minorities increased from 8.2% to 14.3%; for Whites, the increase went from 4.5% to 6.9% (U.S. Bureau of the Census, 1981). The rise in single-parent and no-earner families obviously has had a bearing on the increase in the number of ethnic minorities living below the poverty line. Racism and poverty have a negative effect on the lives and structure of an ethnic minority individual and family. These factors also affect the minorities' help-seeking behaviors that include underutilization of family therapists who generally are monolinguistic, middle-class, and ethnocentric in family problem diagnosis and treatment (Acosta et al., 1982).

Impact of External System on Minority Cultures

In addition to coping with racism, poverty, and societal constraints, ethnic minority families must also adjust tensions created by conflicting value systems of the White society. In contrast with the middle-class White American cultural values, which emphasize man's control of nature and the environment, most ethnic minority groups emphasize man's harmony with the environment. While the mainstream society is future-oriented, worshipping youth and making sacrifices for a "better" tomorrow, ethnic groups reminisce about the past and take pleasure in the present. In the relational dimension, while middle-class Americans prefer individual autonomy, ethnic minorities prefer collectivity. Because the "doing orientation" is basic to the middle-class White American life-style, competitiveness and upward mobility characterize their mode of activity. Asian/Pacific Americans prefer self-discipline, Black Americans adopt endurance of suffering, and both American Indians and Hispanic Americans may prefer a being-in-becoming mode of activity. Finally, the sociological structure of the mainstream society addresses itself basically to the nuclear family, which contrasts to the extended family common to minority groups. Constraints are imposed on minority family members to adjust. Due to differences in value systems, discriminatory conditions, and societal constraints, ethnic minority members can be expected to experience significant family and individual problems and difficulties. Chestang (1976) labels minorities' shared experiences with the mainstream dominant system as social injustice, societal inconsistency, and personal impotence. Social injustice is exemplified by the overrepresentation of minorities in prison. Societal inconsistency refers to the individual's personal rejection, and personal impotence results when adequate supports are not available.

Biculturalism

Threats to survival and self-esteem require adaptation from ethnic minorities that cause "a split in the acculturative process resulting in the development of a duality of culture" (Dreyfuss and Lawrence, 1979, p. 78). A member of an ethnic minority is inevitably part of two cultures. Biculturalism demands the bilateral bringing together of items, values, and behaviors. It signifies participation in two cultural systems and often requires two sets of behavior. This characterization of dual response has both conscious and unconscious aspects. It can be

internalized as a central aspect of the personality, but does not mean
dual personality; rather, it involves two distinct ways of coping with
tasks, expectations, and behaviors (Chestang, 1976). For example, a
Hispanic man may behave according to hierarchical vertical structure at
home with his family and friends, as his culture demands, but he can
behave competitively in the work place as the White American culture
requires. In assessing an ethnic minority client's biculturalism, it is
essential to consider age, sex, and educational, economic, social,
political, familial, and linguistic factors. Familiarity with the cultural
values of each group should serve as a baseline for the assessment.
Hence family therapy theory must consider the level of acculturation
within the ethnic and mainstream culture, the degree to which the client
is able to choose between two cultures/worlds, and the level of
participation in each world that is desirable and obtainable by each
client or family.

Ethnic Differences in Minority Status

Several factors affect the status and adjustment of ethnic minorities
in this country. The status each ethnic group or subgroup experiences, in
turn, affects social adjustment and family living in a White dominant
society. Historical and governmental relationships serve as important
indicators in understanding the experiences of a particular ethnic group.
A history of slavery for Black Americans and their struggle to maintain
African cultural roots in a society that challenges and oppresses them
make Black Americans feel precarious at best and demoralized at worse.
Racism and colonialism have made American Indians "emigrants" in
their own homeland. In contrast to any other ethnic minority group in
the United States, a person is not a "real" or "authentic" Indian unless he
or she fits into categories defined by the federal government, including
blood degree and tribal status. In order to be eligible for federal Indian
programs, a person must be able to *prove* he or she has at least one-
quarter Indian "blood," as recognized by the federal government.

Immigration status also plays a vital role in the living experiences of
many ethnic minority individuals. Some Southeast Asians and refugees
realize they may never be able to return to their homeland. They often
experience emotional cutoff and wonder if and when there will be a
reunion with relatives. Such geographical disconnection and intergenerational family emotional cutoff have adverse implications for
family structure and functioning. Conversely, minority groups such as

Puerto Ricans may consider their stay in this country transitory and know that they can easily visit their families again. Whether the ethnic minority individual is a legal resident or an illegal alien is also of significance. Incredible abuses toward illegal aliens are a well known. Many aliens live in fear of being reported.

Understanding and discerning the status of a particular ethnic subgroup is important to assess their needs for family therapy accurately. For example, if the society accepts the Vietnamese who are Asians as an immigrant group, discrimination against them could be temporary. If, however, they are assigned minority status because of their race, culture, and language, discrimination against them will be the same as toward other Asian groups. Finally, skin color is an important factor in determining the experiences of an ethnic minority person or family. Because color is one of the most pervasive reasons for discrimination, many ethnic minority individuals attempt to "pass" as White. Puerto Ricans from a mixed heritage can easily be traumatized by societal pressure to define themselves as Black or White, complicated further when other family members are labeled differently.

Ethnicity and Language

The transactional definition of *ethnicity* "as an element of behavioral and cognitive participation in the decisions and symbolic construct which supply meaning to communication" (Bennett, 1975, p. 4) requires that family therapists be knowledgeable of the implications and ramifications of ethnic connections, especially language used by an ethnic individual or family. Ethnicity is experienced and persists through language. A common language provides a psychic bond, a uniqueness that signifies membership in a particular ethnic group. It is often comforting to speak one's own language, particularly when under stress. Bilingual family service should be made available to ethnic minorities given that communication is crucial to effective service delivery. Although many ethnic minority clients are bilingual—and that bilingualism is a strong indicator of biculturalism—problems of mis-communication may still occur. Many ethnic minority clients do not have parallel vocabularies or may not know various meanings of words. An ethnic minority client may need to use his native language to describe personal, intimate, gut-level issues. When forced to speak English, the same client may appear to have flat affect, when, in reality, the problem is linguistic. The use of interpreters may be limiting, for much of the state of the art in family therapy is gaining information from the way family members interact and exchange communicative pragmatics. The use of children to interpret, particularly minor ones, can reverse the hierarchical vertical structure of some families (Asians and Hispanics) and, therefore, is inappropriate. Family therapy with ethnic minorities requires close examination of the language used by each ethnic client, family, and group, for there are many variations of the language, from ethnic group to ethnic group, intergenerational and even regional, that may impede effective communication.

Ethnicity and Social Class

Social class refers to "differences based on wealth, income, occupation, status, community power, group identification, level of consumption, and family background" (Duberman, 1975, p. 34). However useful the definition of social class may be for categorizing people for some purposes, by itself it may not be adequate for a full appreciation of ethnic differences as they relate to family therapy. Individuals may act in accordance with their perceived class interest in some situations and in accordance with their cultural preferences or minority identify in others. Gordon (1969) uses the term *ethclass* to describe the point at which social class and ethnic group membership intersect. This formulation helps in examining the meaning of membership in an ethnic minority group and in various social classes. A limited number of ethnic minority members may have more income and be in the upper or middle class, work in more highly valued and rewarding occupations, and have more prestige than others. This, in turn, affects the extent of their well-being, including health, help-seeking patterns, real and perceived power to achieve desired goals, self-respect, and the degree of dignity conferred by others. For those who are in the lower social class, the ethnic reality may translate into continuing and persistent discrimination in jobs, housing, education, and into the reception received in the workplace and by health care and welfare institutions.

Members of ethnic minorities who have achieved material goals still are frequently reminded of the oppression that plagues their kindred and of their identification with the specific ethnic group. Although economically and materially successful, some ethnic minority members still experience difficulty in being accepted by the White middle-class society. At the same time, they may feel alienated from their own ethnic group (Combs, 1978). There is evidence that ethclass among the ethnic minority is positively correlated to a member's English efficiency and educational level, and acculturation rate (Anda, 1984). However, ethnic minority members' higher social class status does not imply that ethnicity plays a less important role in their life. As Mass (1976) indicates, the influence exerted by the value patterns that were acquired throughout childhood is often considerable even among those whose behavior is highly Westernized. Other studies (Native American Research Group, 1979; McAdoo, 1978; Staples, 1978) also have indicated that "successful" or "acculturated" ethnic minority families show a strong interest and need in keeping alive the folkways, arts and crafts, language, and values associated with their heritage. The ethnic minority families' retention of their traditional heritage and persistent adherence to their own ethnicity should have important implications in the conceptualization of a practice theory that addresses their needs and problems. Discussion of a practice theoretical framework for therapy with these families follows.

The Ecosystem Framework

The ecosystem perspective was selected as the theoretical framework because of its "person-in environment" traditional social work focus that takes into consideration the unique background experiences and contributions of each ethnic population. A description of the ecosystem approach as it relates to therapy with ethnic minority families follows.

While many theories of family therapy are conceived as being directed at the process of conflict, anxiety, and defense systems within the individual or the family (Feldman, 1986; Ackerman, 1958; Stuart, 1980; Satir, 1967; Haley, 1976), the ecosystem approach maintains that imbalance and conflict may arise from any focus in the transactional field. Carel Germain (1973, p. 326) defines *ecosystem* as "the science concerned with the adaptive fit of organisms and their environments and with the means by which they achieve a dynamic equilibrium and mutuality." "It [ecology] is the study of life and death in time and space," according to Auerswald (1971, p. 68).

By adopting an ecological perspective, a family therapist is focusing on adaptive (and maladaptive) transactions between persons and between the person and the environment, that is, the interface between them (Gordon, 1969). Ecological and transactional models have been "appealing to social work in that they are middle-range, operational, interdisciplinary frameworks that allow for considerable latitude in practice interventions that are compatible with social work's humanistic orientation" (Stein, 1974, p. 72).

When using the ecosystem framework, there are several practice principles that are particularly relevant in therapy with ethnic minorities, characterized as a group or groups of "politically underprivileged" individuals who interact through maintaining their own sense of cultural distinctiveness (Bennett, 1975, p. 4). Four of these practice principles are discussed below.

First, individual or family problems are not conceived as diseases; instead, problems or difficulties are understood as a lack or deficit in the environment (as in the case of migration or immigration), as dysfunctional transactions between systems (social services organizations and delivery systems), as adaptive strategies (cultural shock), or as a result of interrupted growth and development (role conflict and resource deficits in the environment). A therapist's change effort can thus focus on the interface between systems or subsystems. The goal will be the enhancement of the relationship between those systems.

Second, intervention efforts are directed to multivariable systems, and a single effect can be produced by a variety of means. The principle of *equifinality*, which means that a number of different interventions may, owing to the complexity of systems, produce similar effects or outcomes, encourages flexibility and creativity in seeking alternative routes to change. While a therapist may try to relate interventive strategies to existing theories that are Western middle-class American-oriented, innovative strategies of change based on the client's cultural background and life space (emic-approach) also are encouraged.

Third, intervention strategies make use of natural systems and life experiences and take place within the life space of the client. The family itself is a natural helping system and an instrument of change. Emphasis on the client's life space and family as a natural helping system places the therapist in a role as cultural broker instead of intruder or manipulator.

Finally, the ecological principle that a change in one part of the system has an impact on all other parts of the system allows a therapist the flexibility to function within a practice constriction without involving all family members in the change process. Thus working with one family member who is more "acculturated" or motivated than other family members may well bring about significant change in the total family. When family interactions rigidified by traditional role structure, and the family as a whole is not amenable to family therapy, the one-to-one therapeutic modality may be the only workable resolution for many ethnic minority families. In defending this therapeutic modality, Bowen writes "a theoretical system that 'thinks' in terms of family and works toward improving the family system is family psychotherapy" (Bowen, 1978, p. 157).

An ecological framework can guide the family therapist in conceptualizing and defining the "unit of attention," defined as the universe of data that provides the raw material for the assessment process. The ecological framework begins with an analysis of the structure of the field by using common operational properties of systems as criteria to identify family systems, subsystems, and environmental systems. By tracing the communications within and between the family system and other systems, the ecological framework can help clarify the structure, sources, pathways, repository sites, and integrative functions of messages. The holistic nonexclusive nature of the ecological framework minimizes the danger of excessive selectivity by the therapist in the collection and analysis of data.

During data collection in therapy, a therapist can use the ecological framework to identify the "unit of attention," defined by Germain as "a field of action in which the client—his biological and personality subsystems—is in transaction with a variety of biological, psychological, cultural, and social systems within a specific physical, cultural, and historical environment" (1968, p. 408).

When using the ecosystem framework to assess family structure and function of an ethnic client or family, a therapist should give special consideration to that family's particular cultural values. In the study of ethnicity, *culture* is defined as those things that are relevant to communication across some kind of social boundary (Barth, 1969). Such a definition also suggests where a therapist must look in order to discover cultural differences. It assumes that some factors that characterize the family background and experience of each individual are, at least at the moment of communication, more important than other external factors. According to Kluckhohn (1951), cultural orientations are distinguished from concrete values by their levels of generality: "A value orientation is a generalized and organized conception, influencing behavior of time, of nature, of man's place in it, of man's relation to man, and of the desirable and undesirable aspects of man, environment, and inter-human transactions." Such individual differences are particularly critical during the assessment phase of therapy. The ecosystemic framework is particularly helpful to a therapist in organizing and assessing data during the assessment phase of therapy. To begin, problem-solving and evaluation/termination phases of therapy with ethnic minorities, interventive techniques and skills based on *family* practice principles, and emic (cultural-specific) practice principles are offered.

Communicative-Interactive Framework

The communicative-interactive framework developed and advanced by Haley (1976) and Satir (1967) was based upon George Herbert Mead's (1934) symbolic interactionism, which places major emphasis upon the interactive processes taking place between individual family members and subsystems within the family. The contributions of the interactional framework center primarily upon changes within the family unit that are a result of interactions between members. From this framework, an analysis can be made in which individual family members act and react to the actions of others and to the meanings attached to these actions. Interactive processes that are of particular importance to therapy with ethnic minority families include communication, conflict, role relations, and decision making. Because the communicative-interactive framework is concerned primarily with change rather than with stability, the concepts of family equilibrium or family's transaction with the outside world are less important. This framework, when applied singularly, can easily shift from one that concentrates upon interactive processes between system members to one that emphasizes intervention methods that focus primarily upon individual actions or behavior (intrapsychic).

Structure-Functional Framework

Strongly committed to the systems outlook, the structuralist position emphasizes the active, organized wholeness of the family unit. Like the communication theorists, the structuralists are interested in how the components of a system interact, how balance or homeostasis is achieved, how the family feedback mechanisms operate, how dysfunctional communication patterns may develop, and other systems factors. There are also important differences between the two theories. Rather than observe the basic elements in a family transaction—what messages members send back and forth—the structuralists adopt a more holistic view, observing the activities and functions of the family as a clue to how the family is organized or structured. The focus here is on using the content of a transaction in the service of understanding how the family organizes itself. The structuralists, in general, are more concerned with *how* family members communicate than *what* they communicate. For Boszormenyi-Nagi and Spark (1973, p. 17), the study of power games, communication patterns, or rule processes is only marginally relevant and is monotheoretical because, in their view, these concepts fail to explain the complexities of human interactions.

The structure-functional framework, primarily developed and advanced by Bowen (1976) and Minuchin (1974), was based upon the anthropological and sociological work of Talcott Parsons (1f951), Robert Merton (1957), and George Homans (1964). The relevance of this approach in therapy with ethnic minority families lies with its emphasis on the family as a boundary-maintaining social system in constant transaction with environment or other social systems. The internal family system is composed of individual members who define both the family as a whole and the various subsystems within the whole, that is, the marital, parent-child, and sibling units. In transacting with the environment, individual members are viewed primarily as reactors who are subject to influences and impingement from the greater social system. The health of functioning of an ethnic minority family system can be measured by its adaptive boundary-maintenance ability following stressful situations caused by pressures from transactions with other environmental systems or with society as a whole (Minuchin, 1974; Bowen, 1978; Vincent, 1967). Hence therapy as guided by this conceptualization suggests two levels of intervention: strengthening the boundary-maintaining ability of the family for adaptive purposes that serve stability or equilibrium needs, and intervention at the broader societal level to reduce destructive influences, upon families, that emanate from the environment (Minuchin, 1974; Aponte, 1979; Foley, 1975). This model also facilitates the comparison of family structures and functions in the traditional and cross-cultural frame.

Having discussed the conceptual perspectives, ecosystemic theoretical framework, and the application of communication and structure family therapy theories, we now direct our attention to the application of this theoretical framework to understand and provide effective therapy for each of the selected ethnic minority groups.

2

Family Therapy with
Asian/Pacific Americans

PART 1: PRETHERAPY PHASE CONSIDERATIONS

The Asian/Pacific Family Structure

Cultural Values in Relation to
Family Structure

The term *Asian/Pacific* generally includes Chinese, Japanese, Korean, and Filipino Americans, and Samoans, Guamanians, Hawaiians, and other Pacific Islanders. Recent immigrants and refugees from Vietnam, Thailand, Cambodia, Laos, and Indonesia, and persons from India, Pakistan, and Ceylon, and children of mixed marriages where one parent is Asian American are also included (Morishima, 1978, p. 8). For Westerners, the differences among the Asian/Pacific group may seem minimal, but vast differences exist. In addition to the obvious language difference, the historical, social, and economic differences among these nations should not be overlooked.

Asian/Pacific groups also share some common features of family structure and function (Sue and Morishima, 1982). Application of concepts presented in this chapter should be preceded by a careful evaluation of the particular Asian/Pacific family client, including his or her geographical origin, the birthplace of family members, and generation in the United States, and the family's social class or position in both its country of origin and in the United States. The concepts and therapy skills and techniques discussed should be applicable to most Asian/Pacific American families, especially those who are recent immigrants and old immigrants with strong traditional ties. These concepts may be *least* applicable to later-generation Asian/Pacific Americans such as *Sansei* (third-generation) Japanese Americans, who are usually thoroughly assimilated into the American culture.

Traditional Asian/Pacific values governing family life have been heavily influenced by Confucian philosophy and ethics, which strongly emphasize specific roles and the proper relationships among people in those roles. According to the Confucian system, the quest for spiritual fulfillment was to achieve harmony in this world and in this life through observing the five basic relationships of society: those between a ruler and his subjects, father and son, husband and wife, elder and younger siblings, and friends (Keyes, 1977, p. 195). These five relationships demand loyalty and respect. Within the family, filial piety or the respectful love of parents, is of paramount importance. It is the cornerstone of morality and is expressed in a variety of forms. *Oya-Koko*, a Japanese's version of filial piety to parents requires a child's sensitivity, obligation, and unquestionable loyalty to lineage and parents.

Highly developed feelings of obligation (*giri* in Japanese) govern much of the traditional life of members within a family. While contractual obligations such as parent to child and teacher to pupil exist and are important, the unspoken obligatory reciprocity that arises out of human relationship, such as kindness and helpfulness, has a greater impact on the personal life of the individual. Parents are considered by their children as the greatest obligation because parents were the ones who brought them into the world and cared for them when they were helpless. Hence, regardless of what parents may do, the child is still obligated to give respect and obedience.

Closely related to obligation is the concept of shame (*tiu lien* in Chinese) and shaming, which are used traditionally to help reinforce familial expectations and proper behavior within and outside of the family. Should a family member behave improperly, he or she may not only cause him- or herself to "lose face" but also may cause the family, community, or society to withdraw confidence and support. In Asian/Pacific societal structures, where interdependence is so important, the actual or threatened withdrawal of support may shake a person's basic trust and cause him or her considerable anxiety over the thought of facing life alone. Hence the fear of losing face can be a powerful motivating force for conforming to family expectations.

Along with Confucianism, Buddhism also left its legacy in Asian/Pacific folkways. Qualities essential to harmonious living involving compassion, a respect for life, and moderation in behavior; self-discipline, patience, modesty, and friendliness, as well as selflessness are highly valued in Buddhist canons. The value *enryo* requires in a

Japanese family that an individual maintains modesty in his or her behavior, be humble in expectations, and show appropriate hesitation and unwillingness to intrude on another's time, energy, or resources. To *gaman* for a Japanese is to evince stoicism, patience, and uncomplainingness in the face of adversity and to display tolerance for life's painful moments. To maintain a harmonious family life, the Japanese family capitalizes on *kenshin*, which demands submission and devotion to group interests and purposes. The importance of these cultural values have a direct bearing upon the relationship subsystems, structure, and interactive patterns of Asian/Pacific American families.

Extended Family Ties

The individual in traditional Asian/Pacific culture is protected securely in a wide network of kinship. He or she is clearly reminded that other social relationships or friendships should be secondary to the needs of the family and other kin relationships. Extended family ties are maintained by sharing a common domicile or by frequent visits. The fact that Asian/Pacific families once settled seldom move also helps to keep extended family ties intact. Among Filipinos, kinship relationships extend beyond the set relations generally suggested by the concept of an extended family shared by other Asian/Pacific groups. Filipino families tend toward bilateral equality in family relationships by incorporating relatives of both parents into the extended family. The *compadrazgo*, a Filipino system in which trusted friends and allies can be recruited to serve as godparents to children, further demonstrates the wide scope and viability of the family network. Extended family ties help maintain a good reputation for the patrilineage in the community and play important roles in the affairs of family life and in the socialization of children (Ponce, 1977; Chin, 1982).

**Mate Selection and
Husband/Wife Relationship**

While the tradition of *omimai* (arranged marriage) is gradually disappearing among the Asian/Pacific American families, the choice of mate is still heavily influenced by the families on both sides. Within the traditional Asian/Pacific framework, marriage serves to perpetuate the continuation of the husband's family line. Through marriage, the wife is considered to have left her family of origin and to have become absorbed into the family of her husband. The marriage ceremony symbolizes the death of the wife's relationship with her natal family (Sung, 1967). Such a patriarchal system adopted from Confucianism places the wife in a low status in the family structure. A wife's position, in addition to being lower than that of her husband and her husband's parents, is also lower than that of her oldest son. Furthermore, a woman within the traditional Confucian framework was given three pathways to follow, all of which involved subservience to a man. In youth, she must follow and obey her father or uncle. In adult womanhood, she must follow her husband. In later years, she must follow her oldest son. In arguments between the wife and the parents-in-law, the husband was expected to ally himself with his parents (Yang, 1959). Because the most crucial factor of a marriage was the birth of a male progeny, barrenness was deemed more than sufficient cause for divorce.

Today, among Asian/Pacific Americans, the status of a wife in her interaction with her husband and with the family is influenced by the following factors: Was the wife born in her native country or in the United States? Is she married to a foreign-born or native-born husband? What level of education does she have? Is there a scarcity of women of marriageable age? Generally, the higher the education, the more Americanized the women are, and the higher the status of women in the family. Despite the wife's level of education and acculturation, she still has the tendency to assume the role of assistant director and helper to her husband rather than having a totally egalitarian relationship.

Parent-Child Relationship

The roles and expectations of a parent-child subsystem within an Asian/Pacific American family are well-defined. The father is the head of the family. He makes the decisions, and his authority generally is unquestioned. In addition to being the breadwinner of the family, he is totally responsible for the welfare of the family as a whole. He makes and enforces the family roles and is the primary disciplinarian. Hence the father is frequently perceived as somewhat stern, distant, and less approachable than the mother. The mother, on the other hand, is recognized as the nurturant caretaker of both her husband and children. Her energy and creativity are channeled primarily into taking care of her children. In addition to providing the children with physical care and emotional nurturance, the mother intercedes occasionally with the father on the children's behalf. She forms a strong emotional bond with her children, especially her firstborn son who later is expected to provide economic and social security for her upon her husband's death. Due to the strong emotional attachment the oldest son feels toward his mother, the wishes of the mother are frequently respectfully attended to by the son.

While the primary role of the father is to provide and enforce the rules, and the mother's role is to nurture and care for her children, the child's responsibility at home is to obey and to be deferential to his or her parents. The Asian/Pacific child is taught to behave only in ways that will not bring shame to his or her parents. The child is also reminded that the effect of his or her behavior on parents and clan must be the major consideration governing action (Ritter et al., 1965). Love and affection generally are not openly displayed in an Asian/Pacific family. When the child is an infant, both parents usually show no hesitancy in pampering the child publicly. After these early years, the child quickly becomes incorporated into his or her role in the family structure and learns to live by the more rigid guidelines and expectations of the family and the society. Generally, Asian/Pacific children grow up in the midst of adults, not only their parents, but also members of the extended family. Further, they are seldom left at home with baby-sitters or other adults (Hsu, 1972). Having been exposed to the companionship of adults, an Asian/Pacific child also is taught strict control of aggression. Sollenberger (1962), in his study, found that 74% of Chinese parents demanded their children show no aggression under any circumstances.

Sibling Relationship

Traditionally, Asian/Pacific families always favor a male child over a female child. Due to the patrilineal, patrilocal, and patriarchal principles guiding the Asian/Pacific family, the birth of a boy was a particularly joyous event. Through the boy, the parents could be assured that the family name and the memory of ancestors would continue to be worshiped in the afterworld. The birth of a daughter, on the other hand, was a liability to the family. She neither carried on the family name nor worshiped her natal ancestors (Fei, 1962).

The oldest son is the most desired and respected child in the sibling subsystem. Accordingly, he also carries more responsibilities than the rest of the siblings. He is expected to be a role model for his siblings as well as to have authority over them. He is expected to provide continuous guidance to his younger siblings, not only when they are young but throughout their adult lives. He is to inherit the family authority and leadership upon the death of his father. Conflicts among siblings arise when the oldest son fails to fulfill his responsibilities including other sibling's expectations of him. A daughter, despite greater freedom of choice in marriage and in seeking a career, is still seen primarily as the caretaker of a household.

Sibling rivalry and aggression are in general discouraged in an Asian/Pacific American family. Relationships among siblings are modeled after the Chinese concept of *jang*, in which older children are encouraged to set a good example for other siblings in gentleness, manners, and willingness to give up pleasure or comfort in favor of someone else. To show respect to the older siblings, the younger siblings use appropriate kin terms of address between brothers and sisters in different age groups. For example, one addresses siblings as "Older Brother, Oldest Sister, Second Older Sister, Third Older Sister, Fourth Older Sister." Also implicit in this addressing system is the explicit reciprocal role expectations and interaction regulating the "proper" sibling behavior.

The youngest daughter in the Asian/Pacific American family usually either came to the United States at a young age or is American born. She may resent being left with responsibility for her parents as her older siblings leave home. Because she is likely to be the most acculturated, she may be the most vulnerable to cultural value conflicts. The positions of oldest son and youngest daughter have been associated with the highest rates of psychopathology in Chinese culture, suggesting that the social roles that go with these positions may at times be highly stressful (Kleinman and Lin, 1981).

Intermarriages

With declining omimai (or arranged) marriages, early and steady dating among young Asian/Pacific Americans has become a common practice. Contracted marriage for economic and social gain and for convenience may still exist, but marrying for love based on mutual interests and compatibility has become a norm among young adults. Third-generation Asian/Pacific Americans become more assimilated, and interracial and interethnic dating and intermarriages increase.

Up until 1948, California had prohibited marriages between Asian/Pacific Americans and Caucasian Americans. In 1959, over ten years after the law had been repealed, fewer than three out of every ten Japanese American marriages were interracial (Barnett, 1963). In 1972,

Tinker (1972) completed a survey of the marriage records of Japanese Americans in Fresno, California, and found that 56% of them were interracial. Kikumura and Kitano (1973) also found that the vast majority of intermarriages involved Japanese women rather than men. Urban associates (1974) found high rates of intermarriage among other Asian/Pacific groups as well. Kitano and Yeung (1982), in their recent study, indicate that the most striking finding is the increase in Chinese intermarriage when compared to earlier studies. The rise from under 10% in the 1950s to over 40% in the 1970s indicates the popularity of intermarriage with Chinese and other groups. Such popularity was brought about by increased cultural contact and acculturation with other ethnic groups, and the decrease of racial prejudice and discrimination by other groups.

Obviously, intermarriage complicates the interaction and adjustment of couples and other family members involved. Generally, the greater the distance between spouses in cultural background, the more difficulty they will have in adjusting to marriage and family life.

Divorcing and Remarriage

Traditionally, Asian/Pacific Americans considered divorce a great shame and tragedy, especially for females. In addition to barrenness, the husband had six other classical reasons for divorcing his wife, among which were filial impiety, jealousy, and talkativeness (Burkhardt, 1960). Asian/Pacific Americans' disapproval of divorce is related to the fact that it is a serious social ostracism that few could afford to experience, even at the risk of an unhappy household. Few Asian/Pacific American males would consider befriending a woman who previously had been engaged to or gone steady with another man, let alone a divorcée. Hence the divorce rate has been relatively low among Asian/Pacific families and remains so today (Schwertfeger, 1982). For the more traditional wives, discord and unhappiness are generally turned inward toward the self and are reflected in a high suicide rate rather than in divorce statistics. Sung (1967, p. 162) notes:

> The suicide rate among the Chinese in San Francisco is four times greater than that for the city as a whole, and it is predominately the women who decide to end it all. Suicide has been the traditional form of protest for Chinese women who find life unbearable within their matrimonial bonds.

The younger generation of Asian/Pacific Americans, especially those born in the United States, may not be as conservative as their foreign-born parents, for they are brought up in a culture where individual love and happiness are more important than what other people say about the family.

Impacts of Immigration and Cultural Adjustments

The traditional Asian/Pacific American family structure has provided stability, interpersonal intimacy, social support (Hsu, 1972), and a relatively stress-free environment (DeVos, 1978) for its members. However, the process of immigration and cultural transition has been a severe blow to these families. The process of immigration necessitates a large number of life changes over a short period of time that are associated with lowered well-being (Holmes and Masuda, 1974). There are two interrelated levels of adaptive cultural transition that every Asian/Pacific American family in the process of immigration must face: (1) the physical or material, economic, educational, and language transitions; and (2) the cognitive, affective, and psychological (individual members and family as a unit) transitions. The transformations from these two levels of cultural transitions can cause dysfunction in Asian/Pacific American families.

Specifically, there are five major factors that contribute directly or indirectly to the cultural transitional difficulties that lead to the dysfunction of Asian/Pacific American families. These factors include (1) economic survival, (2) American racism, (3) loss of extended family and support system, (4) vast cultural conflicts, and (5) cognitive reactive pattern to a new environment.

Asian/Pacific Americans are known as survivors. Their need for economic security to provide the basic necessities of life such as shelter, food, and clothing, coupled with their desire to provide for their offspring, prompt the adult members of the family to begin employment immediately upon arrival in the United States. Those who lack professional skills and are deficient in the English language may only find working-class jobs with six-day work weeks, 10- to 12-hour days, subminimum wages, and no or few benefits. If the parents' earnings are low, the family can only afford to live in substandard housing. In the past, these new immigrants often were subjected to discriminatory laws. Despite their accomplishments in the professional and technical fields, they are underrepresented in managerial and professional occupations (U.S. Commission on Civil Rights, 1980). Most Asian/Pacific Americans believe that they must perform better than Caucasian Americans in order to get ahead (Loo and Yu, 1980).

The primary strength of a traditional Asian/Pacific family structure is in providing an environment for mutual support and interdependence. The process of immigration drastically changes the scene. Relatives and close friends are often no longer available to provide material and emotional support to the nuclear family. The traditional hierarchical structure and rigidity of family roles make the expression and resolution of conflicts within the nuclear family very difficult if not nearly impossible. The absence of interpersonal interaction outside of the nuclear family, in turn, forces greater demands and intense interaction within the nuclear family, leaving members with a high degree of vulnerability and unresolved conflicts.

Discrepancies in acculturation between husband and wife and between parents and children can have negative effects on the decision making and functioning of a family. Asian/Pacific American youth is more receptive to Western culture and value orientation for they wish to be accepted readily by the larger society. An individual family member's acceptance and incorporation into the Western orientation of individualism, independence, and assertiveness, especially in attitudes related to authority, sexuality, and freedom of individual choice, make the hierarchical structure of a traditional Asian/Pacific family dysfunctional.

Inherent in every immigration is a cognitive response that each family member goes through. Shon and Ja (1982) listed these responses as follows: (1) cultural shock and disbelief at the disparity between what was expected and what actually exists, (2) disappointment at what exists, (3) grief at the separation from and loss of what was left behind, (4) anger and resentment, (5) depression because of the current family situation, (6) some form of acceptance of their situation, and (7) mobilization of family resources and energy. There are many variations to this generalized schema of responses, and each family member may experience these responses in different order. These seven factors contributing to the cultural transitional difficulties also have drastically altered the structure and content (relationship) of current Asian/Pacific American families. Two subsystem relationships (wife/husband, parent/child) are especially worthy of mentioning for each has important implications for family therapy.

Wife/husband relationship. Because the wife has to work to help support the family financially, she can no longer devote equal time and energy to being a subservient wife to her husband and a nurturing mother to her children. If she still tries to adhere to the traditional roles and expectations of her as passive, accepting, and nurturing, she is bound to experience role conflict. Should her husband not accept the change and not accommodate her new role, conflict will occur. If her children experience adjustment problems, she may blame herself for not being able to stay home with them. She may displace her hostility on her husband, who fails to live up to his role as the provider for the family. Because she is asked to assume new and more responsibilities, she expects more respect, power, and freedom in decision making pertaining to herself and the family. The fact that her in-laws and other extended family members are not around enables her gradually to shift from the traditional role of passive obedient spouse to more of an equal partner.

The demands on the husband to share his primary leadership role may lead to conflict and dysfunction within the family. He may interpret his wife's wish for an egalitarian relationship as a step to undermine his authority. His insecurity is further compounded by the fact that he fails to live up to the traditional role as the primary breadwinner for the family. His failure to assume his role as provider can bring shame and dishonor, not only to himself, but to the family lineage as a whole. To reassure himself and to compensate for his inadequacy, he may demand even greater respect from his wife.

Obviously, problems confronting the couple demand an immediate and constant renegotiation of roles and expectations. Negotiation is difficult and nearly impossible due to the traditional role rigidity and communication pattern and process that emphasize indirectness and prohibition of the expression of honest and true feelings. Further, if the couple's marriage is arranged, negotiation within a marital relationship will be a totally new concept that is practically impossible to acquire during a period of emotional duress.

Parent/child relationship. A child during cultural transition also has increased demands on him or her. Placed in a strange culture about which he or she has no choice, the child is overwhelmed by the numerous unexpected obstacles confronting him or her. At a time when a child desires comfort and security, he or she finds him- or herself totally alone. The child is ambivalent about both his or her parents working long hours. He or she may also feel upset by the fact that his or her grandparents, relatives, close friends, and recreational opportunities are no longer available. The child is constantly reminded by the parents that they invest their future in their children. The child also is expected to do well in an English-speaking school, even though the child cannot speak English. When the child becomes proficient in the English language, he or she also learns to accept and assimilate the cultural and value orientations that come with the English language. The child's assimilation with the Western culture then makes him or her a total stranger in his or her own home. His or her newly learned assertiveness and freedom of choice and speech creates more conflicts and physical and emotional distance between the child and the parent. Should a child disobey, the parents, especially the father, who is the disciplinarian in the family, will feel threatened and may demand more respect and deference from the child. The child's rapid acculturation including greater proficiency in the English language can cause role-reversal in the family. Because of the child's proficiency in English, he or she may be appointed translator or spokesperson for the family in extrafamilial transactions and relationships. The status newly acquired by the child may cause him or her to have less respect for the parents who remain traditional, rigid, and uneducated in English.

Family Help-Seeking Patterns and Behaviors

To help Asian/Pacific American families successfully, we need to understand their traditional cultural values toward dysfunctional behaviors. The cultural values presented here are highly applicable to first-generation immigrants, recent arrivals, and, to a lesser but important extent, the American-born. As Mass (1976) indicates, the influence exerted by the value patterns that were acquired throughout childhood is often considerable even among those whose behavior is highly Westernized.

Most Asian/Pacific Americans do not seek psychiatric dynamics and psychological theories to account for behavioral difficulties (Lapuz, 1973). Instead, social, moral, and organic explanations are used. When an individual behaves dysfunctionally, external events such as physical illness, death of a loved one, or the loss of a job are the cause of his or her problem. The individual always is the victim of unfortunate social circumstances over which the individual has no control, and, therefore, is not to blame. *Shikata ga nai* (It can't be helped) in Japanese reflects such an attitude.

Moral explanation involves the transgressions of interpersonal duties and loyalties held sacred by a specific cultural group. Dysfunction is seen as a punishment or a direct result of immoral behavior. Hence the dysfunction or suffering of an Asian/Pacific individual may be attributed to his violation of filial piety. Community elders or family members may be expected to exhort the individual to improve his or her dysfunctioning. Organic explanations for personal dysfunction are most common in Asian/Pacific culture (Kleinman and Lin, 1981). The Chinese model of Yin and Yan, suggesting the imbalance between two basic life forces, has long been accepted as being the source of difficulty in physical or emotional functioning. The social, moral, and organic explanations to account for behavioral dysfunctioning not only maintain the individual's dignity, but also help to safeguard the honorable family name.

While an Asian/Pacific family undergoes several stages in its attempt to help its members, different families may have different service needs and help-seeking patterns. Generally, there are three types of Asian/Pacific American families in the United States:

(1) Recently arrived immigrant families. For a considerable period of time after their arrival in the United States, new immigrant families must direct most of their energy simply to adjusting to a completely new environment. Most experience the seven phases of cognitive reaction identified by Shon and Ja (1982) and listed previously in this chapter. Initial requests for services by this type of family tend to be predominantly requests for information and referral, advocacy, and such other concrete services as English-language instruction, legal aid, and child care (Kim, 1978, p. 233). Due to cultural differences and language barriers, these families seldom seek personal and psychological help.

(2) Immigrant-American families. Such families are characterized by foreign-born parents and their American-born children, and the great degree of cultural conflict between them. Younger members are usually more acculturated, Americanized—assertive, individualistic, and independent. Members of subsystems between wife and husband, parents and child, and siblings may share different values and goals conflicting with those set previously by the parents or grandparents. Some children may not know or speak their parent's native language, making communication and negotiation among family members nearly impossible. These families usually require help in resolving generational conflicts, communication problems, role clarification, and renegotiation. Biculture and bilingual workers are required to help this group effectively.

(3) Immigrant-descendant families. Such families usually consist of second-, third-, or fourth-generation American-born parents and their children. They are acculturated to the Western value orientation and

speak English at home. They usually reside outside of the Asian/ Pacific American neighborhood and can seek help from traditional human service agencies or private practitioners with some degree of comfort and little stigma.

Applying Culturally Sensitive Family Theories, Models, and Approaches

Family Communication Theory

The family communication theory has much to offer in work with Asian/ Pacific American families. The following discussion focuses on the contributions of the family communication theory and is organized into two parts. The first section describes the principles of family behavior from the perspective of the family communication theory. The second second describes practice principles derived from the communication theory.

Communication principles of family behavior as they relate to understanding the Asian/ Pacific American family. Theory about communication has been an essential part of understanding families since the early days of family therapy. This discussion of the major principles of communication relies primarily on the work of members of the Mental Research Institute in Palo Alto (Bateson, 1958; 1972; Watzlawick, Beavin, and Jackson, 1967; Watzlawick, 1976; Jackson, 1967; 1968). Watzlawick et al. delineate several basic factors that are helpful in understanding the pragmatics of communication as they relate to Asian/ Pacific families.

First, it is impossible not to communicate, as all behavior is communication. In an attempt to adjust to the cultural transitional process, an Asian/ Pacific child, due to his powerless status in the family, may choose physical symptoms to communicate his stress and resentment toward his parent's relocation. A client's consistent absence from the interview may reflect his reluctance for a formalized style of problem solving. All Asian American clients do communicate in their unique cultural ways.

Second, communication not only conveys information but generally contains a command called *metacommunication* that is relevant to Asian/ Pacific American families. To Haley (1963), every relationship contains within it an implicit power struggle over who defines the nature of that relationship. Power struggle in the past was not a major problem within a traditional Asian family, where each family member's position and status were well-defined and rigidly enforced. The process of immigration, coupled with the infusion of Western cultural influence on individuals can cause confusion and intensify a power struggle within the family. Further, the Asian/Pacific American family interaction takes into account a prescribed vertical and hierarchical role structure, which is determined by age, sex, generation, and birth order of family members. A family member's failure to identify and to adhere to a metacommunicative pattern is sure to produce role conflicts and family problems.

A third principle of communication relates to what Bateson referred to as the "punctuation" of the communicational sequences, as exemplified in a parent-child relationship between an immigrant father and an American-born child. The father punctuates the sequence of communication thus: "I have to maintain authority over my undisciplined son." The son, on the other hand, defines the relationship differently: "I must emancipate from my overcontrolling father who refuses to allow me to grow up." Such a relationship can easily lead to an impasse in the family transaction resulting in child abuse or physical impairment on the part of the father or the son.

Finally, for an understanding of the nature of communication, it helps to recognize that there are two major types of communication: digital and analogic. Digital deals with the verbal content of communication, whereas analogic deals with the nonverbal component. Under most circumstances, human communication involves both analogic and digital components, which complement each other in the message. Digital communication is more precise, versatile, and capable of abstraction and logic. Analogic communication, although imprecise and often ambiguous, tends to be a more effective and powerful way to communicate. It is essential to determine the extent to which there is congruence between the message and the way it is delivered. Incongruity may take the form of inappropriateness, invalidation, or paradox. Again, the acculturation process between members of an Asian American family has complicated these two aspects of communication. Because different family members are at a different rate of acculturation and value orientation, incongruous communication occurs more than is expected.

Other communication concepts such as *syntactics* (the grammatical properties), *semantics* (meaning of communication), and *pragmatics* (behavioral effects of the communication), also have important implications in work with Asian/Pacific families who often do not speak the same language. As a result of different periods of immigration by family members to the United States and different rates of acculturations of these family members, it is not uncommon to find older members speaking only their native language and younger American-born members speaking only English. Because family members lack a common language by which they can communicate or share emotional exchanges, inappropriate, invalid, or paradoxical communicative exchange is bound to occur.

The principle of schismogenesis (Bateson, 1958) is also helpful in understanding the marital relationship of an Asian American couple. This principle states that cumulative interaction between individuals tends to result in progressive change and that whatever the balance is in a relationship, it tends to become exaggerated over time. Bateson identified two major kinds of dyadic transaction in schismogenesis, namely the complementary (dominant/submissive) and symmetrical (similar). Due to time changes, the cultural transitional process, and lack of a social support network, an Asian couple may experience difficulty in maintaining a traditional complementary relationship with the husband being the dominant and the wife being the submissive partner in the marriage. Further, the same couple may also experience difficulty in a competitive symmetrical relationship. Such a relationship develops as the wife's financial earning power expands, coupled with her exposure to increased Western influences on equalitarian couple relationships.

Satir's classification (Satir, Stachowiak, and Taschman, 1975) of family behavior for a family member under stress has a great deal of usefulness in understanding Asian American families. The placator always agrees, apologizes, tries to please; the blamer dominates, finds fault, and accuses; the super-reasonable person remains detached, calm, super-cool, and not emotionally involved; the irrelevant person distracts and seems unrelated to anything going on. Such distraction can take the form of physical illness as is often the case with Asian-Americans. Only in the congruent way of communicating does the person appear real, expressive of genuine feelings, and send out straight (not double-binding or other confusing) messages.

Communication Practice Principles

The principles of behavior derived from communication theory can contribute significantly to understanding the dynamics and interaction of an Asian/Pacific American family. The following discussion aims to explicate the manner in which these principles can be applied to actual work with an Asian/Pacific American family.

Communication practice principles as they relate to work with an Asian/Pacific American family. Because the Asian/Pacific American family interaction takes into account a prescribed vertical and hierarchical role structure determined by age, sex, generation, and birth order of family members, infraction of such an interactive pattern is sure to produce role confusion, conflicts, and family problems. Insofar as family therapeutic goals are concerned, a therapist's first task is to engage the family members to alter the symmetrical (parallel or competitive) or paradoxical (conflicting direction) (Haley, 1963, p. 18) communication interchange and develop a complementary relationship (where one leads and the other follows) characteristic of the Asian/Pacific American culture. However, due to the immigration process and the various cognitive affective response phases each family member may be experiencing at different times, complementary communication interchange among family members is bound to run into strong resistance and conflict. The communication theory is very useful in assessing the family system and interactive pattern, yet a therapist's role in engaging the family in renegotiation and redefinition of the power relationship is not an easy task. The concept of power is too idiosyncratic, threatening, competitive, disrespectful, Western, and, therefore, foreign to the Asian/Pacific American culture. The role of the therapist—defined by Haley as that of a "metagovernor of the family system"—thus requires intense active participation and, at times, manipulation. The therapist's active leadership role may easily be interpreted by the family as an unwelcome intrusion. Further, Haley's therapeutic tactics, such as the paradoxical messages (double bind) and prescribing the symptom (encouraging the usual dysfunctional behavior), may be totally confusing and absurd to most Asian/Pacific families. The techniques of relabeling/reframing (by emphasizing the positive) should be most appropriate and relevant for it is consistent with the Asian/Pacific cultural emphasis on respect and compassion for others. While a communication therapist's emphasis on short-term time-limited behavioral change is an approach welcomed by Asian/Pacific families who operate on concreteness, Haley's singular and persistent focus on power relationship may be a bit ambiguous, offensive, and intrusive. Most Asian/Pacific Americans are taught that proper interaction should be guided by roles, duties, obligations, and deference to others.

Virginia Satir's (1967) cognitive approach to "teach" family members to recognize the family's rules so that the rules and the interactional patterns may be changed has great appeal. Her emphasis on "good feelings" within the family and among family members is consistent with Buddhist's teachings of harmonious living, compassion, selflessness, respect for life, and moderation in behavior. Satir's capitalization on family history, which she called the "family life chronology" (Satir, 1967), should be an invaluable tool in understanding the family system dynamics influenced by the intergenerational immigration process and acculturation.

The relevance and application of communication theory in work with Asian/Pacific American families depend not so much on the theory itself but on "how," or the context (environment) in which it is used. While generally it is true that effective family functioning depends on open, full, honest expressions among all family members. It will be totally insensitive and disrespectful if the therapist encourages the younger members of an Asian/Pacific American family to express openly and honestly their negative feelings in front of their parents or elders. On the other hand, open expression of positive and respectful verbal and nonverbal behavior to older members of the family is expected and accepted. Hence it also points out the importance of the use or misuse of conjoint family therapy. To express negative feeling honestly in front of others, especially those who are older, is not accepted by Asian/Pacific Americans and, therefore, is counterproductive. Instead, to learn to behave respectfully and deferentially to others will always bring honor and harmony in interpersonal interactions. A therapist's challenge then is how to promote the resistive family members to behave respectfully and accordingly. Family members' perception of the therapist as a proper role model is significant especially during the initial phase of therapist-family interaction.

Finally, the usefulness of communication theory in work with Asian/Pacific American families largely depends on the degree to which family members as well as the therapist share the same common language. Sharing the same common language goes beyond comprehending the verbal, digital, or content aspect of communication. It also includes understanding the "when" and "how" to make use of the nonverbal, analogical relationship component of a communicative interchange.

Family Structure Theory

The discussion that follows on family structure theory is divided into two sections. The first examines behavioral principles and the second looks at family practice principles of structural family therapy as they relate to assessing and working with Asian/Pacific American clients.

Behavioral principles of structural family theory as they relate to assessing Asian/Pacific American clients. The Asian/Pacific American family is deeply immersed in a family system that does not stress individuality. The immense power of the family—parents, grandparents, ancestors, and extended kin—in shaping one's destiny is taken for granted and accepted as an implicit part of life. Who we are, how we think and communicate, what we choose to do and to be, whom we choose to be with, to love, and to marry is a function of that complex system that has developed over the generations. Murray Bowen (1978) is the person perhaps most closely identified with the intergenerational perspective. The central concept in Bowen's theory, the concept that links the intergenerational and here-and-now perspectives, is "differentiation" as it relates to the intrapersonal, interpersonal, and intergenerational process. In intrapersonal terms, differentiation of self and its opposite, fusion, refer to the relationship between the intellect and goal-directed activity, on one hand, and the emotions or feeling-directed activity on the other. The well-differentiated person is provident, flexible, thoughtful, and autonomous in the face of stress. The less differentiated, more fused person is often trapped in a world of feeling, buffeted about by emotions, disinclined to providence, inclined to rigidity, and susceptible to dysfunction when confronted with stress.

In the sphere of interpersonal activities, differentiation means the ability to maintain a solid, nonnegotiable self in relationships within and outside the family and to take comfortable "I" positions, and not forsaking intellectual and emotional integrity to obtain approval, love, peace, or togetherness. Geographical or physical distances experienced by immigrating Asian/Pacific Americans is not to be equated with differentiation. The differentiated person can leave the family to build his or her own life without feeling disloyal and still remain emotionally close, or can be geographically close without being trapped emotionally in intense family relationships.

In the sphere of family relationships, differentiation refers to the family's ability to accept change and difference from its members; such a family can allow its members to become autonomous. The concepts of differentiation and fusion not only apply to the existing family system but are also linked to the past through a process of "multigenerational transmission." The level of differentiation in an individual, according to Bowen, is determined by the differentiation level of one's parents, and by sex, sibling position, quality of relationship, and environmental contingencies of developmental transition points.

Bowen's concept of "family projection process," in which parental emotions help to shape and define what the child becomes, even though these definitions have little to do with the original realities of the child, closely apply to immigrant parents of American-born children in Asian/Pacific American families. The triangle, or three-person system, which Bowen considers the basic building block of all emotional systems, has a different meaning in a traditional Asian/Pacific family. Bowen believes a two-person system may be stable as long as it is calm, but when anxiety increases, it immediately involves the most vulnerable other person to become a triangle (1976, p. 76). Due to male dominance and the unusual mother-oldest son close relationship in the Asian/Pacific family, the two-person system (especially the spouse-parental system) is seldom close and solid. Hence the process of triangulation takes on a different meaning. In Bowen's view, the identification of these key triangles is a central assessment task in "detriangulating" key threesomes. The process of assessing the intergenerational family system and the use of that system as a resource for change is presented in Parts 2 and 3 of the chapter.

Bowen's concept on "emotional cutoff" has particular application to work with Asian/Pacific American families. According to Bowen, everyone has some degree of unresolved emotional attachment to the previous generation. The lowest level of differentiation, the greater degree of unresolved dependency to be dealt with in the person's own generation, in marriage, and to be passed on to the next generation in the projection process just discussed. The "cutoff" consists of denial and isolation of the problem while living close to the parents or by physically running away as in the case of migration, or a combination of the two. Whatever the pattern, the person yearns for emotional closeness, but is allergic to it. As a rule, the more a nuclear family maintains emotional contact with the previous generations, the calmer, more orderly, and less problematic their lives will be. Conversely, the greater the degree of cutoff, the more the nuclear family becomes a sort of emotional pressure cooker with no escape valves or with attempted escape valves that are far less effective than emotional contact with the extended family could be.

Having sketched in broad strokes some of the concepts and theories about the intergenerational family, we now turn to examine the present family system.

Family Structure theory, focusing on the family system's structural (contextual) dynamics, especially the creation, maintenance, and modification of boundaries that are rules defining who participates and how (Minuchin, 1974, p. 53), is useful in work with recent immigrant families. Because both husband and wife must often work outside the home, the couple (spouse) system within the immigrant family gradually shifts toward "disengagement" where a relationship is too rigid and distant. Such is also true for the parent-child subsystem. Because most immigrant couples' marriages depend on the approval and directives of the parents, the couples usually are inadequately prepared to negotiate a series of mutually satisfying "patterned transactions." In addition, they also have difficulty in separating from their families of origin considered essential in the maintenance of a spouse subsystem. Should the couple migrate with the extended family, their long work hours, plus a strange cultural environment, will throw them into enmeshment (relationship too diffuse and close) with their parents and thus make the couple (spouse) subsystem extremely vulnerable.

Older siblings because of economic necessity may need to work. Long working hours may deprive their normal socialization and interaction with younger siblings who may acculturate at a much faster pace at an American public school. A different pace of acculturation among the sibling subsystem will tend to create conflict and unresolved cultural value differences. The enmeshment created between the spouse with their family of origin and the disengagement of the spouse's children contribute to a large degree to the problem of the immigrant families.

While normal family development is disrupted by cultural transition, most immigrant families find adaptation to stress unbearable. In particular, "stressful contact of the whole family with extrafamiliar forces" such as societal agencies (Minuchin, 1974, p. 78) is more than the family can cope with. Other stresses at transitional points in a family such as the birth of the first child, the emergence of the oldest child into adolescence, or the death of a loved one will surely disrupt the normal family functioning. Stress created by such transitional points can also be very problematic to immigrant American families (with foreign-born parents and American-born children) whose members experience different rates of acculturation.

Structure Practice Principles

Structural family practice principles as they relate to work with Asian/Pacific American families. Bowen's emphasis on differentiation of self (from the family "culture mass") as the primary goal of therapy has important implications and applications in work with Asian/Pacific families. Differentiation of self from family of origin is no easy task for it contradicts Asian/Pacific culture that places enormous value on the sensitivity of individuals to the opinions and expectations of others regarding their conduct. Externally derived evaluations become a part of one's system of self and form a significant basis for one's view of self (Norbeck and DeVos, 1972). Yet Bowen considers differentiation of self inevitable if one expects to function adequately in a rapidly changing bicultural environment.

Because of the traditional rigid family role system prohibiting free expression, and the language barrier within the family, conjoint (with every family member present) family therapy sometimes is neither feasible nor desired treatment modality. Bowen's family therapy technique of focusing upon one individual, usually the more differentiated member in the family, should be congruent with the Asian/Pacific American family structure. This technique protects the dignity of the individual and honors the good name of the family. While the therapist works with an individual, the goal is to modify the structure of the emotional system of the family through that individual's change. At times, that specific individual may not necessarily be a member of the nuclear family. Detailed description of this approach is presented in Part 2 of this chapter.

The technique employed by Bowen to help a spouse define and clarify her relationship by speaking directly to the therapist instead of the husband and wife speaking to each other is also applicable to work with Asian/Pacific Americans. Bowen's detached but interested, intellectual, calm, low-key approach to problem solving again corresponds closely to Buddhism's teaching on moderation in behavior, self-discipline, patience, and modesty. Bowen's belief in actually teaching the family members how to differentiate, clarify their values, and resolve family problems coincides with the family's expectation of the therapist as an expert. His or her effort in taking careful family history (multigenerational transmissions records) reflects sensitivity to the immigration process, intergenerational perspective, and the need for individualizing each family.

Minuchin's differential applications of "joining techniques" are especially helpful during the beginning phase of treatment with an Asian/Pacific American family. Much of the success in joining depends on the therapist's ability to listen, his capacity for empathy, his genuine interest in his client's problem, and his sensitivity to feedback. According to Minuchin, joining is not just the process of being accepted by the family, it is being accepted as a therapist, with a quota of leadership highly aspired to and expected by an Asian/Pacific American family.

Maintenance is one technique used in joining. The therapist lets him- or herself be organized by the basic rules that regulate the transactional process in the specific family system. If a three-generation Asian/Pacific American family presents a rigid hierarchical structure, the therapist may find it advisable to approach the grandfather first and then to proceed downward. In so doing, the therapist may be resisting his first empathic wish—perhaps to rescue the identified patient from verbal abuse—but by respecting the ethnic specific rules of the system, he will stand a better chance to penetrate a therapeutic impaction.

While maintenance concentrates on process, the technique of tracking allows the therapist to examine the content of speech. In tracking, the therapist follows the subjects discussed by family members like a "needle follows the record groove." This not only enables the therapist to join the family culture, but also to become acquainted with idiosyncratic idioms and metaphors that the therapist can later use to help his directive statement carry additional authority.

Minuchin's "joining techniques" are generally helpful to a therapist working with an Asian/Pacific family. His "disequilibration techniques" or family restructuring techniques generally do not share the same degree of effectiveness in working with this specific ethnic group. These techniques, including enactment and boundary-making, escalating stress (by emphasizing differences), physical movement, utilizing the symptom (by exaggerating it), and manipulating mood (by escalating the emotional intensity), are much too abstract, challenging, emotional, confrontative, and, therefore, antithetical to Asian/Pacific culture and are sometimes counterproductive to therapy.

The preceding discussions aim to provide a framework in which to understand Asian/Pacific American families of the past and the present. The two family theories presented, communication and structure, can be applied in working with these families. Part 2 of this chapter discusses how to integrate and apply the theories in therapy with Asian/Pacific American families.

PART 2: CULTURALLY RELEVANT TECHNIQUES AND SKILLS IN THERAPY PHASES

Beginning Phase

In view of Asian/Pacific American clients' unfamiliarity with family therapy, the significance of the first contact phase is obvious. If this beginning phase is not "properly" conducted, the first interview will most likely be the last time the worker will have contact with the client or family. Four skills and techniques are essential in work with Asian/Pacific Americans in the beginning therapy phase. These skills and techniques include engaging the client/family, cultural transitional mapping and data collection, mutual goal setting, and selecting a focus/system for therapy.

Engaging the Client/Family

Many Asian/Pacific Americans do not understand the role of a family therapist and may confuse him or her with a physician. Regardless, they will perceive the therapist as the knowledgeable expert who will guide them in the proper course of action. Hence the family therapist is seen as an authority figure to be more directive than passive. Being directive does not mean that the therapist will tell the family how to live their lives; rather, it involves directing the family therapy process. Minuchin's joining technique is most applicable because the therapist needs to be accepted with a "quota of leadership." A family therapist needs to convey an air of confidence. When asked, he or she should not hesitate to disclose his or her educational background and work experience. Asian/Pacific American clients need to be assured that their therapist is more powerful than their illness or family problem and will "cure" them with competence and the necessary know-how.

Some Asian/Pacific American clients may ask the therapist many personal questions about his or her family background, marital status, number of children, and so on. The therapist will need to feel comfortable about answering personal questions in order to gain a client's trust and to establish rapport. Once trust and rapport with the therapist are established, clients may form a dependency on the therapist. Such dependency patterns do not necessarily indicate transference or other psychodynamic difficulties. Given the interpersonal complexity of Asian/Pacific cultures, forming relationships that mirror those found in family groups or in friendship networks may be helpful to the client as a means of guiding the interpersonal process with the therapist (Green, 1982).

Due to the strong emphasis on obligation in Asian/Pacific culture, clients may consider keeping appointments or following directives as doing something for the therapist in return for the therapist's concern. The therapist should neither condemn nor confront such client behavior but capitalize on it to help the client resolve his or her problem (Ho, 1982).

Additionally, a therapist needs to pay attention to "interpersonal grace" and show warm expressions of acceptance, both digitally (verbally) and analogically (nonverbally). The therapist can do this, for instance, by asking about the client's health, offering a cup of tea, suggesting the client remove his or her coat, or indicating a more comfortable chair. Such semantic and pragmatic expressions serve to convey genuine concern and can add greatly to beginning and maintaining a positive relationship.

Cultural Transitional Mapping and Data Collection

Relevant personal, familial, community information and cultural mapping are extremely helpful in the assessment of Asian/Pacific American families who undergo rapid social change and cultural transition. Sluzki (1979, p. 389), working with migrant families, states categorically that "in the course of the first interview, the therapist should establish which phase of the process of migration the family is currently in and how they have dealt (as a family and individually) with the vicissitudes of previous phases." Additionally, culturally specific factors relevant to each family member's life experiences must be ascertained. Personal data such as language and dialect spoken, physical health and medical history, foreign and/or Western medication used, work roles, help-seeking behavior patterns, and other significant demographic information (years in the United States, country of origin, immigration status, and so on) are helpful in assessment. Psychological data including individual family member's process of adaptation and acculturation, past problem-solving ability, degree of life cycle interruption, and so forth can provide important clues to assessment and treatment goal formulation. Social and cultural data, which include the individual's immigration and relocation history, work hours, and environment, and extent of contact with a human service network, will help the therapist to assess the degree of support or stress from the external environment.

A comprehensive map should also include the transitional position of the multigenerational family in society. Such a map may include the position of each individual and the family as a whole in life cycle stages, cultural origin, family form, and current status relative to other family members (Hartman, 1978). The map can provide insight to family member's intergenerational perspective and levels of "differentiation" (Bowen, 1978). Moreover, Bowen's concept on "emotional cutoff" can also be assessed by cultural mapping. Whenever differential rates of adaptation are found, the influence of transitional conflict may be presumed and relevant therapy applied. Lee (1982) has suggested four criteria to determine a family member's degree of acculturation: (1) years in the United States—as a whole, the longer the client lives in the United States, the more he or she is acculturated; (2) age at time of immigration—an 8-year-old is more easily assimilated than an 80-year-old; (3) country of origin, political, economic, and educational background—a Chinese graduate student from Hong Kong (British Colony) is more easily assimilated than a young adult from mainland China; and (4) professional background—an English-speaking Japanese doctor is more easily assimilated than a Japanese cook.

Techniques in data collection require more than the usual question and answer mode of interaction. The use of family photographs, albums, paintings, and native music can facilitate interaction and generate meaningful information (Ho and Settles, 1984). While sharing feelings and family secrets with the therapist (who is an outsider) can provoke feelings of guilt and uneasiness, many Asian/Pacific American clients are yearning for a close relationship with someone who is understanding and supportive.

Mutual Goal Setting

Asian/Pacific Americans, especially those who are from immigrant families and immigrant-American families, find it difficult to admit they have emotional or psychological difficulties, because such problems arouse considerable shame and a source of having failed one's family. Here again, the therapist's use of semantics relevant to Asian/Pacific American culture is important. They will respond more favorably should they perceive the treatment goal as an obligatory means to meet their concrete basic needs such as employment, food, and shelter. Their acceptance of such a treatment goal is consistent with their traditional social explanation of disorienting events. This type of explanation allows the individual to see him- or herself as a victim of some unfortunate but uncontrollable event, a result of nonpersonal determinants. Therapeutic goals emphasizing the rehabilitation of physical or organic illness also are acceptable to Asian/Pacific American clients.

The client's preference for "impersonal" physical illness excuses him or her from moral failure and familial irresponsibility. Minuchin's "maintenance technique" of following the client's basic rules in the transactional process greatly facilitates the mutual goal formulation process of therapy.

Most Asian/Pacific clients find loosely targeted and abstract long-term goals incomprehensible, unreachable, and impractical. They prefer structured and goal-directed work with clear, realistic, concrete, and measurable objectives (Murase and Johnson, 1974; Ho, 1976). A family therapist should not rule out the possibility, however, that some Asian/Pacific American families, especially the immigrant-descendent families, may respond well to highly personalized insightful therapy related to emotional cutoff or focusing on psychodynamic functions and difficulties. Families receiving this type of therapy should be carefully screened and such therapy should not be attempted without a strong therapist-client or therapist-family trusting relationship.

Selecting a Focus/System Unit for Therapy

Prior to determining the focus of therapy, the therapist needs to access the readiness of family members to communicate as a group. Minuchin's "maintenance" practice principle is helpful at this stage. The hierarchical and vertical structure of Asian/Pacific American families does not allow all family members to share their true thoughts and negative feelings together. For parents to express fear or sadness openly in front of children indicates in Asian/Pacific culture that parents are losing control and "losing face," thus abdicating their authoritarian roles. Open expression of negative feelings by children might be interpreted as lack of respect and deference to parents. Such behavior might inflict shame on parents and guilt on the children. The therapist's decision of which family member to see and on which subsystem to focus must be based on the nature of the family problem(s), data derived from cultural mapping, and, perhaps most importantly, the readiness of the family for problem solving in a group or conjoint context.

Realistically, there are situations when the therapist will have access to only one family member, preferably the one who is most acculturated, self-differentiated, and respected. Such cases reflect the usefulness of Bowen's (1976) family theory, which focuses on self-differentiation in actual application to Asian/Pacific American families. Regardless of who is seen and what the focus of therapy may be, the therapist's beginning efforts must be directed toward resolving the external stress of the family. Further, the therapist's efforts have to be respectful but structured and active. Once the family experiences immediate concrete success, all family members develop more trust in the therapist and hope for the family's ability to regain a harmonious life-style.

Most frequently, in an Asian/Pacific immigrant-American family experiencing multigenerational conflict, the respected subsystem in the family is the parents, who usually are least acculturated. In such cases, the parental subsystem usually is the focus selected by the therapist for therapy. According to Satir (1967, p. 71), the parental subsystem is the axis around which all other family relationships are formed. The mates are the architect of the family. The traditionalist attitude on the part of the father seldom allows the therapist to enter into the family system for therapy or restructuring. Hence help is often needed from a respected extended family member who is acculturated. The actual application of this "therapist-helper" technique will be discussed more fully in the following section.

Problem-Solving Phase

Because Asian/Pacific American families often define their problems in terms of social, moral, and physical illness, resolution of personal or family-oriented problems takes on a particular form and direction that requires different techniques and approaches than those usually used by family therapists. Five skills and techniques of particular importance in the problem-solving phase of therapy include using indirectness in problem solving; social, moral, organic reframing/relabeling; promoting filial piety, obligation, and self-control; restructuring the social support system; and employing a therapist-helper. Each of these five techniques and skills is discussed below.

The Use of Indirectness in Problem Solving

In view of the Asian/Pacific Americans' sensitivity toward others, especially authority figures (including the therapist), the communication behavioral principle of complementarity needs to be observed. Direct confrontational techniques such as "Do you ever care about your family?" or "Tell your wife what you really think of her!" should be avoided. Most Asian/Pacific Americans view confrontation as disrespect and lack of moderation, and take criticism as a personal attack, an unacceptable insult, and an interpersonal rejection. Whenever an

Asian/Pacific client needs to be challenged with his or her impasse or persistent resistance responsible for his or her personal or familial functioning, the therapist is advised to use an "indirect" means. For instance, "Do you ever care about your family?" (direct confrontation) could be changed to "We all have different ways to care about our families—I wish to learn from you about your ways of caring about your family" (polite, respectful, but indirect). Similarly, "Tell your wife what you really think of her" (direct) can be rephrased as "Please comment on the things your wife does that contribute to the family" (accentuating the positive indirectly).

Social, Moral, and Organic Reframing/Relabeling

Haley's and Minuchin's reframing/relabeling technique is extremely helpful and applicable in working with Asian/Pacific American families. Using this technique, the therapist capitalizes on the pragmatics of Asian/Pacific American culture by emphasizing the positive aspects of behavior, redefining negative behavior as positive. Regardless of the nature and intensity of the conflict, Asian/Pacific Americans do not cause indignity for themselves personally and do not deface their family's name and reputation. For a therapist to hold a client directly responsible for the cause of the problem would alienate the client and cause him or her to terminate therapy prematurely. Therapists should focus on alleviating the Asian/Pacific client's anxiety of blame for the problem by capitalizing on the ecosystem transactional conception of family problems. With reduced anxiety, the client can devote more energy to obligatory problem solving within the family. During the course of a parent-child conflict, the therapist can relabel the problem "socially" by pointing out to the clients that the immigration process can be unsettling for every family involved. In the case of an unresolved interpersonal relationship manifesting itself in physical illness or physical symptoms, the therapist can "morally" relabel the illness to put it beyond everybody's prediction and control. To perform an obligatory role or function as a means to eradicate the present problem should be the therapists' main emphasis, rather than searching for a consensus as to the cause of the problem. The role of a therapist as a teacher (Satir) or coach (Bowen) is highly applicable at this stage of the therapeutic process.

During the process of relabeling, the therapist should be sensitive to complementary roles within an Asian/Pacific family. For example, a child's accusatory remark to his father "You don't care about me" can be relabeled (to the father) "Your son is wondering what he can do to help you be proud of him?" The meaning or interpretation resulting from relabeling may not be accurate or exact, but the important message relabeling can help convey to the family is that all family members respect and value interrelationships with each other. Through the pragmatics of traditional teachings of filial piety, mutual respect, and obligation, the family can resolve its own problems.

Promoting Filial Piety, Obligation, and Self-Control

Despite acculturation, most Asian/Pacific clients greatly value what others, especially family members, think of them. An individual's worth is dependent upon how well she or he gets along with other family members. As a child, one is expected to comply with parental and social authority; so does the parent who has the responsibility and obligation to perpetuate the family's "good" name. By capitalizing on Minuchin's technique of family restructuring, a therapist can challenge the family's obligation to maintain the family as a unit. By doing so, the therapist further challenges family members to exercise their power of self-control inherent in Asian/Pacific American culture. In the case of a husband and wife conflict, the communication dynamic of "schismogenesis" (constant state of change) (Bateson, 1958) can be explained, and the therapist can challenge both spouses to refrain from expecting favors from each other. Instead, they are challenged to render good deeds or favors to each other. They can be encouraged to do this as a means to fulfill their obligatory duties to make the family a harmonious place for the children and themselves to live.

Authority figures in the family may have difficulty in understanding the value of a therapist's directive. Guided by the communication principle of pragmatics and Minuchin's disequilibration technique of "boundary-making," the therapist can gently remind the parents or other authority figures that their familial role as elder also carries with it the educative duties for younger family members. Unless they can practice self-control, they may fail as a positive role model (obligation) to the younger members of the family.

The therapist's warm acceptance of the client can make the client feel he or she should be mutually accepting of the therapist. The therapist can use the clients' feeling of obligation to return favors to challenge the client to follow instructions or directives and to help the family resolve its problem.

Restructuring Social Support System

The Asian/ Pacific American family paradigm, defined as family's construction of reality (Reiss, 1981), consists of strong and close-knit extended families and support systems. Members of the nuclear family or extended family sometimes are forced to interact to the extent they become "fused" (Bowen). As a result of fusion, family members demand too much from each other and at times fail to meet their own individual needs and to resolve family problems. This is more characteristic of newly arrived immigrant families than other Asian/ Pacific American families. As soon as possible, the therapist should assist the family or the newly arrived members of the family in establishing a social support network whereby the family or the individual can reestablish a greater sense of "differentiation of self" (Bowen), but at the same time fulfill the family paradigm need for social belonging. A social support network can also provide the family or the individual a place to bridge the ecological deficit, to form friendships, ventilate frustrations, learn acculturated social skills, and recreate. Upon realizing one's situation is not unique, an individual can view his or her her family problems from a more objective, less emotional, and more hopeful perspective. When the therapist tries to link the family with an existing social network, the concept of "balance" is vital. Factors essential for balance include matching the family or family member's (or members') age, origin of birth place, length of stay in this country, socioeconomic class, formal education, language, and religion with existing resources. In some instances, especially where there is a scarcity of Asian/ Pacific American families, the therapist may need to identify, recruit, and organize such a social support network.

Employing a Therapist-Helper

In view of cultural shock, language difficulty, Asian/ Pacific American families' unfamiliarity with the concept of family therapy, family members degree of undifferentiation, and the families' overall resistance to therapy, the traditional therapist-family therapeutic approach may not be feasible. Instead, the strategic use of a therapist-helper who is a family member, or an extended family member, or a trusted family friend may be required to helping the family solve its problem. The therapist-helper approach is indicated when the family is persistently uncooperative and too emotional and when there is a definite language barrier between the therapist and the family. In addition to being the last resort by which some Asian/Pacific American families can be helped, the therapist-helper approach provides the family with a normal course of problem solving, and an acculturation direction not influenced by the therapist. In view of the hierarchical male-dominant culture of Asian/ Pacific Americans, the therapist-helper normally is a male. He should not be clearly identified as a traditionalist or as a Westerner. He needs to have the respect of both parties in conflict. For example, in the case of a father-son (youngest) conflict, the ideal therapist-helper would be the oldest son. In the case of a husband and wife conflict, the therapist-helper may need to be an uncle or an individual whom both spouses respect. In some instances where extended family members cannot be found, an individual who has a bicultural background and reputation (someone who is foreign-born but is adjusting well in the United States) can be asked to be a therapist-helper.

For the therapist-helper approach to work, the family in conflict needs to agree that the therapist-helper will be visiting with them for the purpose of problem solving. Additionally, the therapist-helper needs regular coaching and supervision from the therapist.

Evaluation and Termination

The pragmatics of Asian/Pacific American culture need to be considered during the evaluation process. It is unrealistic to expect Asian/Pacific clients to provide a spontaneous and honest feedback to their therapy because of their cultural orientation and deference to authority figures. An innovative method of assessment that takes into consideration the family's cultural background is best for Asian/Pacific clients. Such evaluative methods should be systematic but anonymous, focusing on the worker's employment of relevant means or procedures in helping the clients resolve relevant individual and family group goals or problems (Ho, 1980).

In view of Asian/Pacific client's reliance on social, moral, and physical illness to explain their interpersonal and psychological problems, the therapist should not emphasize the dysfunctional state of the family's problem in attempting to help family members evaluate their progress. Asian/Pacific clients' adherence to modesty and moderation in behavior will not allow them to credit themselves individually or publicly. Instead, they may attribute family improvement to their ancestors who continue to look after them. As a means to honor their ancestors and the therapist, the family may invite the therapist for a feast. The therapist should feel comfortable in complying with the family's obligation.

Considering Asian/Pacific client's capacity for self-control and their unwillingness to be of burden to others, especially to the authority figure, the therapist needs to guard against premature termination initiated by the clients. Hence evaluation depending only on clients' self-report may be inaccurate and inappropriate. Instead, the therapist needs to make home visits and engage in a variety of informal activities and rituals such as a tea party and festival celebrations within the client's own home environment and community. Through informal interactions with the client and the family, the therapist can obtain firsthand information pertaining to the overall functioning of the family.

The process of termination should take into consideration the Asian/Pacific client's concept of time and space in a relationship. The client may regard the therapist as a family member and may want to maintain contact with the therapist even after the successful achievement of treatment goals. For many Asian/Pacific Americans, a good relationship is a permanent one that is to be treasured. If a good relationship is allowed to continue in a natural course, the traditional psychodynamic therapeutic concept of separation anxiety during the termination phase may not apply in work with Asian/Pacific clients.

The preceding discussion applies to existing family theoretical perspectives and emic-based practice principles in therapy with Asian/Pacific American families. Part 3 of this chapter will further explicate and delineate how these family theoretical perspectives and emic-based practice principles can be integrated in actual therapy with an Asian/Pacific American family.

PART 3: CASE ILLUSTRATION

Mental health service is totally new to Mrs. Chan.

Mrs. Chan, a 65-year-old Chinese widow from Hong Kong, was referred to me by a community mental health treatment center worker. The worker declared that she was no longer able nor willing to work with the patient, who spoke very little English and had displayed *limited cooperation*.

According to the mental health worker, Mrs. Chan was first referred to her by a

Emotional problem manifests itself in physical symptoms. Problem related to husband's death, immigration process, and present rejection by son's family. An ecosystem conception of presenting problem.

Social isolation and disengagement; desire for contact.

Therapist being Chinese caused Mrs. Chan to "lose face," but to gain hope and understanding.

Mrs. Chan's deference to authority (therapist).
Therapist's deference to Mrs. Chan (her age). A mutual practice of ritual.

To establish family ties and obligation, to convey social grace, and to apply joining technique.

Her analogic communication conveys her acceptance of me as a helper.

An indirect signal to the mental health worker that I needed privacy with Mrs. Chan.

To convey social grace and to create natural atmosphere for sharing.

Therapist exercises ritual to show respect for and deference to the client.

Indirect means to vent hostility toward son and emotional cutoff.

Therapist's ritualistic behavior consistent with Chinese practice. Use of analogic communication as a means to "track down" client's problem.

family physician, who had been unable to correct Mrs. Chan's *insomnia* and *weight loss* through medication. In addition to her physical problems, Mrs. Chan's symptoms included depression and lack of appetite and energy. She spent her time *gazing motionlessly out the front window* of her apartment.

When the mental health worker first introduced me to Mrs. Chan, Mrs. Chan's reaction was mixed with *shame* and *hopefulness*. She remarked that she feared "losing face" because of her situation and regretted greatly that she had been a "*burden*" to me. I replied that I considered it a *privilege* and rare opportunity to be of assistance to her.

I added that my deceased *mother's maiden name* was the *same as her last name*.

Mrs. Chan relaxed and remarked that my mother must be very *proud of me*. I thanked her for the indirect compliment.

I then *thanked* the mental health worker for introducing me to Mrs. Chan.

As soon as the mental health worker departed, Mrs. Chan began to *prepare tea* for me.

I *immediately volunteered* to help her.

Mrs. Chan sighed and remarked that she *wished* her son was as *respectful* as I was toward her.

To help Mrs. Chan ease her pain and disappointment, I intentionally avoided *looking her in the* eye; instead, I helped her with her tea.

Mrs. Chan volunteered that the last several months had been very painful for her.

Country of origin.

Eight months ago, her husband died in *Hong Kong*, where she used to live.

Five months ago, her *only son* had invited her to live with him and his family in the United States.

Implication of close mother-son dyadic relationship.

It is considered a disgrace for a widow to live alone.

To protect her son's reputation and to save face for herself. Revelation of family paradigm.

Mrs. Chan first was apprehensive about leaving her home, close friends, and relatives in Hong Kong, but due to Chinese social *pressure and customs*, she yielded to the idea of living with her son. She did not wish her relatives and friends to *suspect* that her son *did not want to take care of her*.

Different rate of acculturation and generational conflict. Family subsystem boundary is threatened.

Unfortunately, living with her son and his family did not work well for her. Mrs. Chan and her daughter-in-law, an *American-born Chinese*, never seemed to get along with each other. They had *open conflict* about the *role* of a wife and the proper manner in which young children should be disciplined.

Example of triangulation; intergenerational conflict manifests in physical symptom. Problem caused by transactional dysfunctioning.

Mrs. Chan's son, *caught in the middle*, developed a severe case of *sleep disturbance*.

To protect her son's health, Mrs. Chan agreed to live in an apartment by herself. Mrs. Chan explained that the idea of living away from her son was *difficult* for her. She would never have conceded to his idea if she still *lived in Hong Kong*.

Her difficulty was conceived as deficits in the environment and adaptive strategy.

Interventive effort was directed to multivariable systems, an ecosystem practice principle.

I then visited Mrs. Chan's son at *his home*. He and his wife seemed most uncomfortable in my presence. To put the couple at ease, I empathized by saying that I could easily understand the potential conflict the couple might have with a mother *they hardly knew*. Mr. Chan responded that he really had no choice, for his primary *responsibility* was to his wife and two children.

To ease guilt. To join the spouse system. To relabel the problem socially, emphasis on nuclear family and an indication of Western values.

I commented that I could appreciate the dilemma he was in, but that I *suspected*

To "track down" and to promote filial piety sentiment.

His mother is perceived as external threat. Nuclear family becomes "enmeshed."

Treatment goal responsive to cultural orientation—harmony within the family.

Capitalizing on Mr. Chan's wife's egalitarian role in mutual goal formulation. Using the family as a resource for problem solving.

Negotiating and stabilizing the new structure based on redefined roles of family members.

Individual therapy is used to assist self-differentiation and to augment family transaction.

To reestablish social support system as a supplementary intervention effort.

To satisfy her altruistic need and obligation (social). To complete therapist's effort in enhancing relationship between systems.

that he was not *totally satisfied with his mother living alone.*

"Not at all, not at all," Mr. Chan continued, shaking his head, "but I cannot let her [his mother] *disrupt my family!*"

"It would be *ideal* if both your *immediate family* and your *mother* could be *taken care* of equally well," I challenged.

"It would be nice, but I don't know how," Mr. Chan responded despondently.

I *asked Mrs.* Chan (Mr. Chan's wife) if she had any suggestions.

Mrs. Chan first responded by regretting the situation. Then she suggested that perhaps her mother-in-law could have *limited visits with the family* and the children. We all agreed to give this idea a trial.

In the next two months, Mrs. Chan enjoyed her *regular visits with her son* and his family. Between regularly scheduled visits, Mrs. Chan had several opportunities *to baby-sit* for her grandchildren, who had grown fond of her.

During this two-month period, I visited Mrs. Chan weekly and assisted her in her *adjustment* to her husband's death, to a new culture and environment, to her son, whom she had not previously seen for ten years, and to her son's wife and children.

To encourage Mrs. Chan to be a part of the community, I *introduced her to* several Chinese families. On several occasions, she *participated* in activities of the Chinese foreign students' organization. She assumed the role of an "*away-from-home mother*" to some of those Chinese students from Hong Kong. Mrs. Chan's ailments subsided. Her son and his family planned soon to invite her to live with them again.

PART IV: CULTURALLY RELEVANT TECHNIQUES AND SKILLS FOR SPECIFIC THERAPEUTIC MODALITIES

Marital Therapy

Traditionally, when a couple experiences marital discord to a degree that requires outside help, the extended family, especially the husband's parents, are the ones to provide assistance. The process of immigration often separates the couple from the extended family. Similarly, the process of acculturation and the changed roles and status of both husband and wife make marital adjustment extremely vulnerable. While the principle of schismogensis (Bateson, 1958) offers some explanations, the couple's unfamiliarity with and distrust of mental health services leave them with practically no resources for securing help with their marital conflict. In the couple, usually the wife, discord and unhappiness are generally turned inward toward the self and are reflected in frequent psychosomatic complaints and a high suicide rate. Marital discord can be reflected in parent-child conflicts, with the child bearing the parental marital symptoms (Satir, 1967). Asian/Pacific couples seldom seek marital therapy. Usually it is only when medication has been proven inadequate to correct the client's chronic physical symptoms or when a child's behavioral problem reflects a clear marital discord between the couple. The following guidelines are suggested while providing marital therapy to an Asian/Pacific couple.

Assessing the Couple's Readiness for Conjoint Marital Therapy

Asian/Pacific clients, especially the male, often need to safeguard respected roles and to save face. A husband may be unwilling to admit publicly both to his wife and the therapist that he fails as the responsible head of the family. He usually will not disclose intimate information about their sex life or potential physical spouse abuse. Likewise, a traditional Asian/Pacific wife will not express openly how she actually feels toward her husband. If either spouse is not ready for a conjoint session, marital therapy can best be conducted by a therapist assisting the husband and wife privately and individually to understand and gain empathy for each other. Bowen's calm, unemotional, but interested approach can be most effective in assisting the individual spouse to gain a cognitive understanding of the problem. Through new insight and understanding, the couple may alter their stereotyped roles and expectations toward each other.

Emphasis on the Social Moral Explanation of Marital Disharmony

Focus on the affective aspect of the couple's relationship, which generally is emotional in nature, is discouraged. The therapist should emphasize the new role or behavior each spouse needs to assume in order to solve its problem, whether it be disciplining a child, financial management, or taking care of the couple's parents. Again, understanding the etiology of the presenting problem should be employed as a means to motivate the couple to modify their behavior in order to remedy the current situation. The concept of family is very important to Asian/Pacific clients. Most of them are willing to try almost anything to comply with their new role expectations if they believe it will improve family relations.

Challenging the Couple's Willingness and Ability to Collaborate

A couple experiencing marital discord usually feels confused, frustrated, and shameful because of their inability to improve the situation. The couple may feel worse if they attribute the present difficulty to their selfishness and inconsideration of others. The therapist's task is to relabel the presenting power-struggle problem to a system transactional problems, and to provide the couple with the opportunity and know-how to regain feelings of obligation and self-worth. Should a couple continue to argue defensively, the therapist can use Minuchin's "maintenance technique" to gently remind the couple of the advice their elders or ancestors might suggest to resolve their problem. As the couple begins to list self-sacrifices as a means to end conflict, they regain "good feeling" toward self and toward each other (Satir, 1967). The therapist should assess each spouse's sacrifice to determine if it is too great or unrealistic.

Teaching the Couple Skills for Negotiation

The key to problem solving in marital conflict is full and open communication and skill in negotiation. However, negotiation in a marriage is a Western concept most foreign to traditionalist Asian/Pacific couples. In addition to their lack of knowledge and experience in negotiation prior to marriage, most Asian/Pacific couples are plagued by their rigid role expectations and dyadic complimentary style of communication. When assisting the couple in learning to negotiate in a symmetrical fashion, the therapist may run the risk of having the couple, particularly the husband, contend that the therapist is trying to influence them to adapt to a Western style of behavior. The therapist should gently remind the couple of the presenting problem that brought them in for therapy. Without engaging in further debate or intellectualization or the wisdom of Western or Eastern life-styles, the therapist can redirect the couple to focus on the immediate problem and the common goal of re-creating a harmonious home environment that will benefit the couple's children and honor their ancestors. The concept of biculturalism is applicable for use during therapy, for it provides the couple with a tool by which to negotiate privately in an egalitarian fashion. At the same time, the couple can interact with each other in a more traditional way when they are with others within their ethnic community. While the focus in marital therapy generally is interpersonal, the presenting here-and-now couple conflict may not be resolved if one spouse or both partners remain "undifferentiated." Bowen's approach to differentiate the individual can be most helpful to emotion-laden couples.

Divorce Therapy

The divorce rate among Asian/Pacific Americans is relatively low. In addition to the cultural values that prohibit the breakdown of a family in general and divorce in particular, most Asian/Pacific Americans with traditional orientation are not familiar with legal divorce proceedings. Those who decide to end their marriages may not wish to discuss it with a therapist whose expertise is unknown to them. Hence divorce therapy usually is indicated after the client has exhorted medical treatment for physical symptoms, or after the client has established a trusting relationship with the therapist through different presenting problems. Because divorce is a very serious step for an Asian/Pacific client, the following recommendations are suggested to ensure clients receive appropriate help and services.

Exploring Divorce Consequences

Given that divorce is regarded as socially *unacceptable* within the Asian/Pacific culture, a therapist needs to help the client anticipate the possible ostracism that he or she will face. Despite an individual client's unique need and reason for the divorce, other relatives and close friends may view the client's behavior as immature and impulsive. The client may be labeled as lacking compassion, tolerance, and self-control. The therapist needs to assess the client's strength to withstand the painful and punitive consequences without resorting to physical maladies or suicide. In cases of constant physical abuse or prolonged emotional sufferings due to unresolved conflicts, the therapist may introduce an analogous concept such as temporary separation as a means to dilute the tension between a husband and wife. Only as a last resort should the idea of divorce be discussed as a possible alternative. The untimely and premature introduction of the idea of divorce may hasten the termination process of therapy or it may render disservice to clients whose problems would be compounded by the lack of familial and social support resulting from divorce.

Providing the Client with Legal and
Social Support at the Time of Divorce

If divorce is the alternative chosen by the client, the therapist's role is to provide the client with the best possible legal assistance through securing a matrimonial lawyer who is not only proficient in divorce proceedings but also is sensitive to the client's cultural orientation and background. In addition, the therapist should help the client secure a support system consisting of the client's relatives and close friends. The client may also need additional help with child care or other daily tasks during the critical unsettling period. Again, the ecosystem approach to divorce along with the concept of family equilibrium should be considered. Other precautions against a client's potential suicide attempt also need to be considered at this stage. In attempting to provide the client with rationalization and emotional support, the therapist needs to help the client understand that the decision to divorce is not necessarily a result of immaturity or lack of self-control and self-discipline. The divorce can be interpreted as the client's desire to discontinue indignities and defacing the family's name. It is sometimes helpful to use the moral explanation that the wife and husband were not meant for each other in the first place.

A husband or wife's decision to endure suffering inherent in divorce can also be explained as their devotion to the children who no longer need to be subjected to the disharmony of an unending marital discord. The therapist's respect and acceptance of the client's decision to continue the marriage or divorce can be most comforting to the client during a very emotionally upsetting period.

Employing Social/Moral Explanations to Help Clients Cope with Postdivorce Adjustment

Considering the relative nonromantic involvement in most traditional Asian/Pacific marriages, emotional termination and adjustment toward the previous spouse after divorce may not be as traumatic as in romantic marriages. However, for some clients, divorce can trigger previous unresolved multigenerational emotions and problems. Bowen's intergenerational perspective and rational objective role on the part of the therapist can be used effectively with many divorced clients. The client's ability to assume new roles after divorce, especially that of the breadwinner and disciplinarian for the children, may present difficulties · for Asian/Pacific female divorcées. Haley's hierarchical theory and Minuchin's restructuring perspective should help the divorcée cope with the moment after crisis. To compensate for their guilt and to save face and reaffirm their decision to divorce, most Asian/Pacific female divorcées are reluctant to seek and receive help from relatives and close friends. Furthermore, they may decide to put their stoicism to real tests, rationalizing their suffering as a natural and fair consequence of their "misbehavior" (divorce). Further, relatives and close friends may not agree with the client's decision to divorce. They may withdraw support and sympathy for the client. The therapist's role is to be a systems broker between the client and her relatives and close friends. In some instances, when relatives and close friends of the divorcées choose not to be involved with the client, the therapist's task is to help the client secure new support systems, preferably with other divorcées who share similar experiences. Asian/Pacific clients who choose divorce usually consider it the last resort and are quite resourceful in adjusting to postdivorce problems. As discussed previously, most Asian/Pacific American males are highly prejudiced against divorcées, especially those who have children by a previous marriage. As a result, some female divorcées may choose to intermarry; others may elect to remain single and devote full attention to their children. The latter decision can potentially produce enmeshment in the mother-child relationship. A therapist's task is to assure the divorcée that she does have options after divorce and that divorce, despite being a critical moment, consists of both the danger (*Ngi*) and opportunity (*Gee*), components of the Chinese character for crisis. The therapist's task in postdivorce counseling is to help the client focus upon the opportunity component of the crisis.

Single-Parent Therapy

Asian/Pacific American culture's objection to divorce and the strong kinship support system make single-parenthood a new phenomenon. Special considerations are recommended in working with this client population.

Mobilizing the Support System

In view of Asian/Pacific American close-knit family ties, a divorcée seldom finds herself taking care of children without at the same time receiving some means of assistance from relatives or close friends. For recently arrived immigrants, support systems may not be as readily available as for second- or third-generation clients. The therapist's primary task in single-parent therapy is to assess the extent to which the client is utilizing or underutilizing the existing support system.

Liaison Between the Client and Her Relatives

In situations when divorce is too much a stigma for the relatives, the therapist's task it to be a systems broker between the client and her relatives. The therapist needs to clarify for the relatives the reasons for the client's divorce. Again, the therapist's use of social, moral, and physical explanations for divorce help to reduce the relative's misunder-standing, guilt, and resentment toward the divorcée. Additionally, the therapist needs to sensitize the relatives to the various needs of a single parent who may be reluctant to seek help from them actively. The needs of a single parent obviously are the primary concern, but a therapist should never lose sight of the fact that the single parent's relatives also feel ambivalent and may have unmet needs. The therapist needs to be supportive and patient with the relatives who may choose to ventilate their disappointment, anger, and resentment toward the single parent. Should the relatives persist in rejecting the single parent, the therapist then can gently remind the relatives of their responsibilities for and obligation to the single parent and her children. The therapist's accepting attitude toward the single parent can be a consoling force to the relatives who may have feared the stigma others would attach to their divorced family member.

Assisting the Single Parent to Restructure the Family

Due to past rigid social parental roles and responsibilities, coupled with guilt and embarrassment, some Asian/Pacific American single parents refuse to seek help from outside the family or from their older children. Thus a single parent may expect to function both as father and mother to the children without support from relatives. Many parent-child conflicts occur as the single parent "burns out" physically and emotionally. The therapist's task is to assess the single parent's level of differentiation, motivation, and knowledge of parenting, and to support the single parent's desire to be a responsible parent whose duties include assuring that the children get the best possible care. With trust and a positive rapport, the therapist can gently guide the single parent to restructure and divide tasks, responsibilities, and functions within the family. To be the head and authority figure of a family is a totally new concept to many female Asian/Pacific single parents. The therapist's task is to educate the client to assume the dual role of disciplinarian and nurturer in the family.

The relationship between the mother and the oldest son traditionally is very close. The father's absence due to divorce may further reinforce this natural "enmeshment" or "fusion" between the mother and her oldest son. The therapist needs to be cognizant of such cultural familial structural phenomenon. While constructive suggestions usually are welcome to ensure both the mother's love and the oldest son's developmental needs, any criticism regarding the potential enmeshment between them will be rejected as culturally insensitive.

Assisting the Single Parent to Define and Meet Own Needs

To assume the role of a single parent successfully, the client may need help in defining and meeting her own needs. Her failure to meet her own needs may be related to her level of differentiation and it can be detrimental to her physical and mental health as well as jeopardize her children's freedom and opportunity to meet their developmental needs.

Yet, the single parent may not be receptive to suggestions to meet her own needs at a time when she perceives her problems were caused by her egotism and selfishness. Hence a therapist should employ the ecosystem approach by capitalizing upon community resources such as educational and recreational opportunities for the children. As the children are constructively and productively occupied, the single parent can take pride in her accomplishments as a responsible parent. She then may relax her guilt feelings about the divorce. Subsequently, she may come to realize she is a competent person and that she also has individual needs.

Whether a single parent can successfully meet her needs or not also depends on her children's cooperation and acceptance of her needs. Because most children of divorced parents harbor feelings of ambivalence, they fear their inattention and insensitivity may further alienate their mother. As a result, they become overly attentive and protective toward their mother. Their inability to let go also limits their mother's opportunity to be free and to attend to her own needs. A therapist's task then is to assist the children to understand their mother's needs and to help facilitate these needs whenever possible. Again, Bowen's theoretical perspective on family organization and structuring are very applicable in work with a single parent and her children.

Therapy with Reconstituted Family

In view of the relatively low divorce rate among Asian/Pacific families, therapy with reconstituted family is not expected to be in great demand. Should such therapy be needed, the traditional role rigidity on the part of most Asian/Pacific families make negotiation and final accommodation within the reconstituted family extremely difficult. The following suggestions are recommended in providing family therapy with a reconstituted family.

Focusing on Parental Coalition

Problems in a reconstituted family may manifest themselves in parent-child conflicts in a child bearing the symptoms of the family. The therapist's initial and primary focus should be on assessing and repairing the parental subsystem (Satir, 1967). In a study of reconstituted families by Lucille Duberman (1975), one factor identified as important for the success of these families was that the parental coalition be viable.

A mutually supportive couple relationship seemed to influence the success of the relationship with the children. As a means to repair the parental subsystem, the therapist needs to sensitize the couple to the structural concepts such as new boundaries and roles that are required in the functioning of a reconstituted family. Should the couple experience an impasse in their negotiations, the therapist may need to capitalize on existing resources by introducing the couple to a well-functioning reconstituted Asian/Pacific American family. By exposing the couple and their children to another well-functioning reconstituted family, the problem family is provided an accepted role model to emulate.

Help the Family to Change Existing Mythology Through Relabeling

Asian/Pacific families are culturally bound and filial piety toward one's natural parent cannot be challenged. For a child to respect another adult as a natural parent is disloyal and, therefore, forbidden. Moreover, many of the social definitions of the stepparent roles have traditionally been derogatory, and myths about wicked stepparents abound. The therapist's task is to encourage the children to vent and to dispel such myths. While some children may never love or respect their stepparent as they do to their natural parent, they have a responsibility to honor their mother or father and to make the home environment a harmonious setting. In view of the Asian/Pacific clients' emphasis on blood ties and ancestral worship, the therapist should never attempt to persuade the children to replace their natural parent with their stepparent.

Work with the Relatives and Grandparents of the Reconstituted Family

The work of the reconstituted family in boundary definitions will never be complete if the network of relatives is uninvolved. The degree to which the kin network needs to be involved varies with different families. The reconstituted family needs to be cognizant of relatives and grandparents' impact on their interaction with each other. The ecosystem approach can be useful to the therapist at this stage.

During the period of single parenthood, many Asian-Pacific grandparents assume a major role in the family, especially if a parent and children returned to the parental home. Some grandparents retain the parent-child roles with their own children, despite the fact that the child is now a parent. This often results in grandparents usurping the authority of the natural parent or stepparent with their grandchildren (Weiss, 1975). Structurally, grandparents and relatives of both former spouses need to reestablish new boundaries for themselves with the family members of the new marriage so that they can serve as a source of support rather than pose potential conflict. If the parents of a reconstituted family are willing to express their concern directly to their children's grandparents, the therapist's task is to be a liaison person who can tactfully convince the grandparents that their best assistance to their children and grandchildren at the present time is noninterference.

PART V: CONCLUSION

The family is the central unit of social organization for Asian/Pacific Americans. Due to cultural orientation, English-language limitations, separation from friends and extended kin, and other isolating environmental factors, the family often provides the only means of interaction, socialization, validation, and stabilization. The Asian/Pacific American family is shaped not only by past traditions and current life experiences, but also by the ongoing political and economic events in the Asian/Pacific countries and the United States. Many environmental stresses, such as poor housing, underemployment, discriminatory laws, and individual and institutional racism, exert a disorganizing influence on the Asian/Pacific American family system.

The continued underutilization of mental health services indicates Asian/Pacific Americans' tradition and strong reliance on the dictum that personal/interpersonal problems or issues should be kept within the family and solved there. Hence family therapy remains the most pertinent problem-solving approach and modality for Asian/Pacific American clients. Therapy with Asian/Pacific families requires taking a holistic view of health and an interactive and contextual perspective of behavior. This chapter has focused on the holistic view and the integration of social, psychological, physical, and cultural phenomena during different phases of therapy with Asian/Pacific families.

3

Family Therapy with American Indians and Alaskan Natives

PART I: PRETHERAPY PHASE CONSIDERATIONS

Understanding the American Indian and Alaskan Native Family Structure

American Indians and Alaskan Natives are racially as differentiated as the Europeans and far more diverse culturally and linguistically. For example, just in the North American region, there are 13 distinct language groups, 130 major tribal groupings, and an undetermined number of subgroupings (Josephy, 1971). The 1980 U.S. census indicates that the total population of American Indians and Alaskan Natives in the United States reaches 1.8 million. Because American Indians and Alaskan Natives share the similar cultural background and family structure, for simple reference and easy reading, the term *American Indian* will be used in the rest of this chapter to refer to this population.

There are more than 400 tribes in the United States today and approximately 280 reservations (Edwards and Edwards, 1977). About half of the more than 1.8 million Indians live in urban areas. Many Indians are very traditional, live in isolated rural areas on reservations, and know little English; many others have been raised in urban areas and have had little or no contact with their Indian heritage. Many American Indians experience continual struggle and conflict in attempting to achieve a balance between their Indian values and those of the dominant society.

Contemporary social service and health data on American Indians reflect a multitude of problems plaguing American Indian families. For example, the average life expectancy for an American Indian is only 44 years. Infant mortality rates are such that 32.2 Indian babies out of 1000 die in their first year of life. This is approximately twice the rate for Blacks and four times the White rate (Cahn, 1979). The average level of annual income for an American Indian family of four is $1500 (Edwards and Edwards, 1977, p. 948). Their death rate from tuberculosis is seven times the national average, and the suicide rate is triple the national average (Cahn, 1979, pp. 55-56). American Indian unemployment is approximately five times the normal rate (Josephy, 1971, p. 359) and their average length of schooling is five years, with a dropout rate of 50%, or almost double the national average (Wax, 1970, p. 27).

In contrast to any other ethnic minority group in the United States, a person is not a "real" or "authentic" Indian unless he or she fits into categories defined by the federal government, including blood degree and tribal status. In order to be eligible for federal Indian programs, a person must be able to prove he or she has at least one-quarter Indian "blood," as recognized by the federal government.

American Indians are generally perceived as a homogeneous group, a composite of certain physical and personality characteristics that have become stereotypes reinforced by the media. As Deloria acclaimed, "People can tell just by looking at us what we want, what should be done to help us, how we feel, and what a 'real' Indian is like" (Deloria, 1969, p. 9). Obviously, the idea that there is an "Indian" stereotype that could fit all or even most American Indians today is naive and simplistic. Like other clients, the Indian client wishes to be recognized as a person, a human being, not as a category. To recognize the American Indian client as a person, the family therapist must understand and respect the unique cultural family background and rich heritage of the client.

Cultural Values in Relation to Family Structure

Although no Indian tribes are identical in their cultural beliefs and practices, there are some unifying concepts that set them apart from the dominant society. The following list is not meant to be exhaustive, but rather illustrative of some of the ways American Indian values differ from values of White Americans. Neither is it meant to apply rigidly to all Indians because of the individual differences noted previously.

Table 3.1 summarizes and contrasts cultural values between the

TABLE 3.1

Cultural Value Preferences of Middle-Class White Americans
and American Indians: A Comparative Summary

Areas of Relationship	Middle-Class White Americans	American Indians
Man to nature, environment	Control over	Harmony with
Time orientation	Future	Present
Relations with people	Individual	Collateral
Preferred mode of activity	Doing	Being-in-becoming
Nature of man	Good and bad	Good

dominant society (Anglo-Caucasian, middle class) and American Indians. Data on middle-class American values are based upon the work of Papajohn and Spiegel (1975); whereas American Indian cultural data are taken from studies and observations of Zintz (1963, p. 175), Bride (1972), Attneave (1982), Lewis and Ho (1975).

Harmony with nature. American Indians hold nature as extremely important for they realize that they are but one part of a greater whole. There are many rituals and ceremonies among the tribes that express both their reverence for nature's forces and their observance of the balance that must be maintained between them and all other living and nonliving things. They believe that growing things of the earth and all animals have spirits or souls, and that they should be treated as humanely as possible—with respect and appreciation for the contributions they make to the people's life-style. American Indian's need in keeping harmony with nature has often been misinterpreted as "laziness" or "inactivity."

Present-time orientation. The American Indian is very much grounded in what is happening in his or her life at the moment, rather than making specific plans for future endeavors. They are busy living their lives rather than preparing for them. In contrast to the general belief that they have no concept of time, American Indians are indeed time-conscious. They deal, however, with natural phenomena—mornings, days, nights, months in terms of moons, and years in terms of seasons or winters (Tracks, 1973, p. 33). While this time orientation may be partially related to the nature of traditional Indian economies and the need to focus on daily survival, it is also related to the Indian's worldview of events moving through time in a rhythmic, circular pattern. Artificial impositions of schedules disrupt the natural pattern.

The contemporary American Indian family may have maintained

some of this naturalness of rhythm. Hence Indian time can be both a passive-aggressive resistance to mechanistic inhumane ways, and it can also be a way of expressing contrasting priorities. In the course of family therapy, concrete immediate problems and their solution may be more relevant than future-oriented abstract philosophical goals.

Collateral relationship with others. American Indians believe in working together and getting along with each other: the family and group take precedence over the individual. This concept of collaterality reflects the integrated view of the universe where all people, animals, plants, and objects in nature have their place in creating a harmonious whole. In emergencies, but only for a brief period, an authoritative leader, who usually is an elder with demonstrated expertise and problem-solving skills, may be permitted to take charge, but this is clearly the second choice. The impatient solution of majority vote revered by democracies seldom takes place; instead, long and arduous discussions are generally held until a group decision can be reached.

Closely related to the concept of collaterality is the traditional practice of "giveaway" that still persists in almost all tribes. All forms of belongings are given ritually to honor others for their help or their achievement or to acknowledge kinship ties. The practice of "giveaway" serves as a means to recycling the good of honored dead and as a means of showing respect to the living (Momaday, 1974).

American Indian adherence to collaterality is sure to conflict with the dominant cultures' stress on individuality and competition. Indian children in public schools are often mistakenly seen as "unmotivated" due to their reluctance to compete with peers in the classroom or on the playground. Indian workers also are mistakenly labeled as "lazy" or "unproductive." However, their cooperative spirit can be revitalized and capitalized on in problem-solving process during a family crisis or imbalance.

Being-in-becoming as preferred mode of activity. The dominant culture has repeatedly demonstrated a value system that seeks to control, to be in charge, and that often destroys the balance of nature. This is done with the view that human beings are superior to all other forms of life and have, therefore, the right to manipulate nature and situations for their comfort, convenience, and economic gain. Contrarily, the American Indian is taught to endure all natural and unnatural happenings that he will encounter during his life. He believes that to attain maturity, which is learning to live with life, its evil as well as its good, one must face genuine suffering. Hence he may present himself as pessimistic, downtrodden, low-spirited, unhappy, and without hope for the future. However, as one looks deeper into his personality, another perspective is visible. In the midst of abject poverty comes "the courage to be"—to face life as it is, while maintaining a tremendous sense of humor (Huffaker, 1967).

An American Indian's courage to be may also be misinterpreted as his being stoical, unemotional, and vulnerable. He is alone, not only to others but also to himself. He controls his emotions, allowing himself no passionate outbursts over small matters. His habitual mien is one of poise, self-containment, and aloofness, which may result from a fear and mistrust of non-Indians.

The American Indian, as he values his right to be, also values and respects other's right to be and to do their own things. Traditionally, American Indians are raised not to interfere with others (Tracks, 1973). From childhood, they learn to observe rather than to react impulsively to situations. They learn to respect the rights of others to do as they will and not to meddle in their affairs.

The nature of man is seen as good. The main orientation of the American Indian toward human nature is that it is generally good. Human misbehaviors are thought to result from lack of opportunity to be and to develop fully. There are always some people or things that are bad and deceitful. An Indian believes, however, that in the end, good people will triumph just because they are good. This belief is seen repeatedly in American Indian folktales about Iktomi the spider. He is the tricky fellow who is out to fool, cheat, and take advantage of good people. However, Iktomi usually loses in the end, reflecting the American Indian view that the good person succeeds while the bad person loses (Bryde, 1971, p. 15).

Indian tribal and Christian religions. Both Indian tribal and Christian religions play important parts in the lives of American Indian people. Religion is incorporated into their being from the time of conception, when many tribes perform rites and rituals to ensure the delivery of a healthy baby, to the death ceremonies, where great care is taken to promote the return of the person's spirit to the life after this one. In view of the diversity of American Indian tribes, considerable variation in the practice of Indian religion is to be expected. It is not unusual for American Indians to participate in ceremonies and rituals within their native religions and also to attend and hold membership in Christian religions. American Indians who speak native language tend to maintain their religious ceremonies, customs, and traditions. They also have more trust in their native medicine people for physical and mental health needs than in the Anglo medical doctor or family therapist. Solution of some family problems may require both services of dual cultural perspectives. With the knowledge of the above, selected cultural values, a family therapist can be expected to understand and appreciate the traditional family structure and the contemporary scene of the American Indian family.

Traditional Family Structure and Extended Family Ties

The failure of providing effective family service to American Indians lies primarily within the therapist's misuse of the nuclear family conceptual framework in organizing service delivery. Consequently, the American Indian family may become a unit of analysis with specific household parameters. As household units, both nuclear and extended family models can be found in American Indian family systems (Red Horse, 1980b). Miller et al. (1977) points to a decline of vertical generations in a single household as an indicator of Indian extended family deterioration.

American Indian family systems are extended networks, characteristically including several households. It is an active kinship system inclusive of parents, children, aunts, uncles, cousins, and grandparents (Wahrhaftig, 1969). In addition, nonkin can also become a family member through being a namesake for a child. This individual then assumes family obligations and responsibilities for child rearing and role modeling.

Due to historical tribal mobility and the force of American governmental policy, many family systems extend over broad geographical regions and assume interstate dimensions (Red Horse, 1980b, p. 463). The multiple family household framework provides family members with a strong sense of belonging along both vertical and horizontal extensions. Grandparents and older namesakes serve as role models for younger family members. They provide examples for spousal interaction and child-rearing guidelines.

Thomas (1969), in an attempt to illustrate how the vertical family structure is reinforced with horizontal organization, describes the important role functions of uncles and aunts in Oklahoma Cherokee families. As to the authority structure of the extended family system, it could be arranged in a variety of ways, with an administrative focus on the oldest man or women. A specific patterning of an extended family again varies according to different tribal differences, yet in each the basic outline follows the structure of three or more generations in each household.

American Indian family networks adhere to what has been identified as an open family-closed community pattern (Mouseau, 1975). Outsiders, including the family therapists, do not gain entrance easily. The extended family network represents a relational field characterized by intense personal exchanges that have lasting effects upon one's life and behavior (Speck and Attneave, 1974).

Mate Selection and Husband/Wife Relationship

In view of the important influence of extended family ties, many tribes strongly encourage their young people to marry within their tribal group. Contact between young men and women was controlled by the clan mores and systems. Traditionally, most marriages were arranged and couples entered into the marital relationship with some feelings of apprehension. In the Apache tribe, male relatives of widows were expected to marry the widows. If this could not be done, the widow was free to marry whomever she chose (Brown and Shaughnessy, 1982, p. 8).

The traditional marital practice of American Indians basically is monogamous. Men join their wives' households and economically support their wives but retain ritual, leadership, and disciplinary roles in their natal households (Brown and Shaughnessy, 1982). Thus a husband may discipline his sister's children and play only a passive role in his wife's household. The Hopi say that "the man's place is on the outside of the house." The disharmony created in these contrasting roles contributes to a high divorce rate among the Hopi (Eggan, 1966, p. 126).

Partly due to the extended family system household and partly due to the man's role as a hunter whose work took him outside of the home, open display of emotions and affection between the husband and wife rarely existed, although the mutual bond may in fact be close, affectionate, and satisfying. Traditionally, Eskimo men treated their wives as inferior and were reluctant to have close interpersonal contacts (Hippler, 1974). Couples rarely went visiting together or entertained friends together, and nonkin adult social gatherings were usually of the same sex only. Within the Navajo tribe, traditionally, the sons-in-law were not permitted to speak to or to look at their mothers-in-law (Brown and Shaughnessy, 1982, p. 7). Such practice as regarded as a sign of "respect" for the mother-in-law/son-in-law relationship.

American Indian women, independent for the most part, played a submissive, supportive role to the husband (Hanson, 1980). The wife would constantly observe her husband, looking for signs and opportunities to please him. In some instances, it was customary for the Lakota husband to take additional wives to assist in the homemaking chores.

Although traditionally, American Indian wives had a position of low prestige, they had far more freedom and latitude in their roles than men. As observed by Spindler and Spindler (1971, p. 398), "the disruptions created in rapid cultural change hit the men more directly, leaving the women less changed and less anxious—Menomini women continue to play the affective, supportive, 'expressive' role of wife, mother and, social participant in a more or less traditional fashion, unhampered by rigid role prescriptions." Today, American Indian women have two primary chores: to survive and to keep their families intact (Medicine, 1978). Their experience at hard seasonal labor has made them more employable than their husbands. This sometimes causes conflict in the marriage.

Parent-Child Relationship

Traditionally, the parents' role in an American Indian family was occupied with basic survival needs such as hunting, providing shelter, gathering or cultivating crops, preserving food, and so on. Because the basic parental disciplinary role was shared among relatives of several generations, biological parents were afforded the opportunity to engage in fun-oriented activities with their children. Hence the American Indian parent-child relationship is less pressured and more egalitarian than that of the dominant culture. When the child was an infant, he experienced intense, warm maternal care from the mother. He was carried in a parka hood on the mother's back with skin-to-skin contact much of the time. This kind of extreme nurturance generated a strong sense of security in the child who is egocentric but optimistic, friendly, but ambivalent about violence (Hippler, 1974).

Among all tribes, children are of utmost importance for they represent the renewal of life. An Indian child is not seen as an entirely dependent being, but rather, as an individual who can, within a short time after birth, make the most important decision regarding the identity he will assume. Traditionally, this afforded Indian children a rightness of choice. Because of this, ordering and physical punishment to force a behavior are discouraged (Lewis, 1970; Morey and Gilliam, 1974). Children are disciplined and taught by numerous caretakers other than the biological parents. It is expected that they will respond to the appropriate behavior passed on by generations. American Indian children are not taught to have guilt, for parents believe they have no control over others or their own environment (Attneave, 1982).

In some tribes, the mother and the daughter may be referred to by the same term (Brown and Shaughnessy, 1982, p. 30). A daughter would properly address her mother as "mother-sister," the mother would properly address the child as "child-sister." This again emphasizes the high status that the child is afforded in American Indian families.

Because Indian parents are only one of the "instructors" in the child's life, their instruction usually takes the form of observation and participation. A child is seldom told directly what to do and he is often left to his own device and decision. This freedom, however, is not experienced in a vacuum, but rather in concert with the felt expectations from many significant adults including the grandparents (Red Horse, 1980a). The felt expectations serve as an important support to make the right choice.

Parent-child interaction among American Indian families is often determined by sex role. For example, it was common for Lakota women to instruct their daughters and granddaughters in proper conduct throughout adulthood. Sons, on the other hand, after the age of ten, were the primary responsibility of the father. Unfortunately, in fatherless homes, young sons are often without guidance due to the mother's unwillingness to assume this responsibility for fear of creating a "winkle" or sissy (Hanson, 1980, p. 479). Further, the traditional parent-child interaction is greatly diminished by the fact that about 20%-25% of American children grew up outside of their parents' home (Brown and Shaughnessy, 1982).

Sibling Relationship

The strong extended family ties and the clan system of American Indian culture provide a child with many siblings. In addition to biological brothers and sisters, an Indian child traditionally was brought up with many cousins. They had close interactions with each other through early childhood. The particular supportive patterns between brothers and sisters usually began in adolescence when they were expected to help in the material support of the tribe and in religious activities. The similarity of cousins and the brother-sister relationship allowed an Indian child the nurturance and support she or he needed to grow up as an adult (Blanchard, 1983).

Because observation and participation were a major part of an Indian child's socialization and development, younger siblings received encouragement from their older siblings to behave appropriately. Often, the older siblings provided the first demonstration and it was part of their responsibility to assist in the formation of certain behaviors.

Due to the different matrilineal and patrilineal patterns among the tribes, there was no distinct favoritism afforded to the sexual identity of a child. The particular economic and social system dictated the more desired sexual identity of the child for the tribal group. For example, in the Southwest Pueblos, girls were often preferred over boys, but in other tribes, boys were preferred. Similarly, cultural traits of noninterference, noncompetition, and interdependence rendered the ordering position of siblings less of a significant factor within the American Indian families. However, American Indian's cultural emphasis upon sexual identity and development strongly encouraged the child to participate in sex-role appropriate activities. Hence at the age of 8 or 10, siblings of the same sex formed a closer relationship with each other than with siblings of the opposite sex. Such close relationships perpetuated and lasted until adulthood.

Intermarriages

Traditionally, American Indian marriages were more in the nature of a contract between kin groups. With the influx of Europeans in the early 1800s and the more recent Relocation Act (Stuart, 1977) endorsed by the Bureau of Indian Affairs to assimilate the Indians into the mainstream of the population in the cities, there was a gradual increase in intermarriages among American Indians of different tribes, as well as between American Indians and other racial groups.

Differences between Europeans who arrived in the New World played an important role in determining the nature of Indian-European intermarriage. For example, the French, Spanish, and Portuguese were more tolerant of intermarriage with the natives then were northern Europeans. Thus since early historical times there have been significant populations of Spanish-Indian "mestizus" and French-Indian "métis," but few British-Indian "half-breeds."

The exact number of intermarriages between American Indians and other races is difficult to ascertain. Among other factors, national data on intermarriage after 1977 are not available due to the civil rights movement, which discourages racial and ethnic identification in public records. However, according to Canadian Indian statistics (D.I.A.N.D., 1975), 585 Indian women, or 29% of all those marrying, lost their Indian status in 1974 as a result of their intermarriage to nonstatus Indians. This example not only dictates the high incidence of intermarriages of American Indians, it also reflects the political discrimination and social obstacles the intermarried are experiencing. Similarly, in the United States, Jones (1974, p. 27) reports that Bureau of Indian Affairs welfare aid was refused in Anchorage to Indian women who had married Whites, even though the marriage partners had separated.

Divorce and Remarriage

In view of the diversity of tribal cultures and customs and the vast cultural differences between the American Indian and the dominant culture, marriages between tribes and races are destined to run into great difficulties. Marriages within the tribe also are negatively influenced by the dominant societal value of individualism and competitiveness. Although data on divorce among American Indians are unavailable, one can expect that it will be as high or higher than other racial groups. The rate of divorce and remarriage can be expected to be higher among urban American Indians who intermarry and lack the support of the extended family system.

Divorce and remarriages are more acceptable within the American Indian family than the dominant culture family (Price, 1981). Such acceptability may be related to American Indian cultural traits of collaterality, being-in-becoming, right for choice, and noninterference. The strong support system consisting of extended family ties and multiple households reaffirms the place of the divorced person in his or her the family. As an example of the permissiveness of remarriage, some Indian tribes of the Great Plains and North West coast still practice polyandry, or plural husbands. This was brought on by special circumstances, such as the crippling of an older married brother with the subsequent additional marriage of the younger brother to the older brother's wife. This tolerance of diversity within American' Indian societies tended to be greater than in the dominant society, which has a rather limited set of familial rules that emphasize permanent monogamous marriage.

Impacts of Political, Migration,
and Cultural Adjustments

The breakdown of American Indian cultural traditions and family customs began in the early 1800s. In 1815, the United States government coerced tribal leaders into signing treaties they could not read, and thus not understand (Costo and Henry, 1977, p. 209). These treaties opened the doors for greater influx of European homesteaders and miners. As the influx of Whites continued, and they eventually become a political dominant group, Indians became restricted to reservation areas. By 1849, the Bureau of Indian Affairs was given full authority to oversee the activities of the Indian people. The Sacred Black Hills were taken by an illegal treaty, the buffalo were destroyed, and the language and religious practices were forbidden by the missionary schools (Merian, 1977, p. 14). It was during this period that Indian children were taken away from their parents with the intention of educating them in the White man's mold. These children's placements later included boarding schools, religious institutions, foster care, and adoption. These practices severed the links of the support system that centers on children and thus encouraged the destruction of the basic tenets of tribal life.

The Dawes Act of 1887 (Merian, 1977, p. 22), which divided the reservation land into allotments and individual ownership, forced Indian men and women to become farmers and ranchers. With the shift of occupational skills and requirements, Indian men were no longer recognized as brave warriors or hunters. Indian women were also traumatized as they painfully watched their children taken away and as they witnessed the gradual psychological deterioration on the part of their husbands.

Following World War II, the unemployment rate for Indians returning to their reservations soared. In 1952, the Bureau of Indian Affairs sought to relieve the high unemployment problem by finding jobs for Indians in urban areas (Stuart, 1977). This program was considered as yet another attempt by the government to destroy the Indian culture and family structure by encouraging assimilation into the urban environment rather than attempting to strengthen Indian ways of life by developing more work opportunities on reservations (Farris, 1973, p. 84). Between 1952 and 1968, some 67,522 Indians who were the heads of households were relocated through this direct employment program (Bureau of Indian Affairs, 1971). Today, there are more Indians living in urban areas than on reservations (U.S. Bureau of the Census, 1980d).

The statistics for income, education, mental health, and crime among urban Indians present a bleak picture. Urban Indians are the poorest, least educated, most highly unemployed (Chadwick and Strauss, 1975), and have the highest crime rate related to drunkenness (Fogleman, 1972). Living against such ecological stresses and daily survival threats, the life of an Indian family is certain to deteriorate rapidly. The children of these families are being raised with fewer contacts with traditional life. Their peers are often non-Indian, and they increasingly grow up to marry non-Indians, diluting further their Indian heritage (Price, 1981).

Despite a multitude of adversities, American Indian families have a long history of durability and persistence in survival. A research group in the San Francisco Bay Area (Native American Research Group, 1979) has shown that many Indian families living in the cities are adjusting to urban life fairly well. Their openness to learning the technological world and their persistent adherence to their own native culture contribute to their success.

Family Help-Seeking Patterns and Behaviors

The American Indian culture emphasizes harmony with nature, endurance of suffering, respect and noninterference toward others, a strong belief that man is inherently good and that he should be respected for his decisions, and so on. Such traits make a family in difficulty very reluctant to seek help. Their fear and mistrust toward non-Indians caused by past oppression and discrimination make it almost impossible for a non-Indian family therapist to gain entry into the family system. In a survey of health needs among American Indians in Minneapolis, 90% of the respondents indicated that they preferred American Indian workers as caretakers (De Geyndt, 1973). While an American Indian family experiences several stages in its attempt to assist its members, different families may have different service needs and help-seeking patterns. Judging by family life-style patterns, contemporary American Indian families can be classified into three types (Red Horse, 1980b). (1) The *traditional family* overtly adheres to culturally defined styles of living. The parent, and grandparents speak the native language. The family practices tribal religion, customs and mores and has an extended family network. (2) The *nontraditional* or *bicultural family* appears to have adopted many aspects of nontraditional styles of living. Although the parents or grandparents are bilingual, English constitutes conversational language at home. The family adopts the Anglo belief system and actively takes part in social activities with groups and individuals from the dominant culture. The structure of the family basically is extended and lies with kin from reservations and across states. (3) The *pantraditional family* overtly struggles to redefine and reconfirm previously lost cultural life-styles. Both English and and the native language are spoken in the pantraditional family. They practice a modified tribal belief system and struggle to maintain their traditional extended family network as well as cultural activities.

As would be expected, traditional families generally would not seek help or receive help from a family therapist. In their attempt to recapture and redefine cultural life-styles, pantraditional families also are not receptive to the idea of family therapy. The bicultural families are the ones most receptive to family therapy for they have adopted the dominant culture and its mores.

The different family life-style patterns among the American Indians do not imply an ongoing erosion of cultural values. Studies suggest, however, that American Indian core values are retained and remain as a constant, regardless of family life-style patterns (Giordano, 1974, p. 207). The extended family networks maintained by all three family life-style patterns are one good example reflecting the American Indian family's resistance to cultural assimilation. Lewis (1984), in an attempt to schematize American Indian's help-seeking patterns, further confirms the extended network behavior characteristic of American Indian families. When a family needs help, the extended family network is the first source to be contacted. Second, a religious leader may be consulted to resolve problems plaguing the family. Third, if the problem is unresolved, then the family will contact the tribal community elders. Last, when all these fail, the family *may* seek help from the mainstream family and health care system.

Often, when the family has contact with the therapist, the family is not psychologically or emotionally ready for help. Some families see a therapist only when ordered to do so by a court. Such contacts usually result in failure of service delivery, and they further reinforce the American Indian family's distrust of family source providers.

Applying Culturally Sensitive Family Theories, Models, and Approaches

Family Communication Theory

The family communication theory pertaining to the daily interactions among family members has a great deal of relevance and applicability in therapy with American Indian families. The following discussion focuses on the contribution of the family communication theory and is organized into two sections. The first section describes the principles of family behavior from the perspective of family communication theory. The second section describes practice principles derived from the communication theory. The discussion of the contributions of family communication theory must take into account the cultural values and family structure of American Indian families discussed previously. There are several cultural and political factors affecting members of an American Indian family in regard to their ability to communicate openly and effectively with others. These factors include

(1) The diversity of tribal languages, and the English language spoken by the younger generation at home, make effective communication among family members extremely difficult.

(2) As a child, the American Indian learns through observation and participation. He or she is not taught or encouraged to verbalize needs, wants, feelings, and intentions, because others' needs should always take precedence over one's own.

(3) As an American Indian child was respected and afforded the opportunity to be and to make her own decision at an early age, she seldom received concrete feedback (especially negative) and definitive guidelines from others. She was thus left with a great deal of uncertainty and anxiety, but few skills in problem-solving situations involving family members.

(4) American Indian extended family ties and multiple-households allow individual family members a great deal of latitude to interact vertically and horizontally with family members of different generations, ages, and sexes. When the extended family household is forced to shift to a nuclear household, as in the case of urban living, family members are not prepared to interact immediately and solve problems with only a limited number of family members.

(5) As an American Indian family is struggling to survive and to meet such basic needs as housing, food, and health care, members do not always have energy left to provide affectional needs and to repair emotional bondage with each other.

The above factors take on a great deal of significance as family therapists begin to apply communication principles of family behavior to understanding the American Indian family.

Communication principles of family behavior as they relate to understanding American Indian families. This discussion of the major principles of communication relies primarily on the work of members of the Mental Research Institute in Palo Alto (Bateson, 1972; Watzlawick, Beavin, and Jackson, 1967; Watzlawick, 1976; Jackson, 1967).

The American Indian's use of silence can evoke the single biggest misconception and frustration experienced by those who provide family service to them. It is true that sometimes silence is used as a safe response to defend against outsiders who are considered intruders. However, silence is also a customary practice among American Indians, especially during the beginning phase of a social contact. They feel no need to jump into conversation that may be offensive to the other person. There is something about time and silence among American Indians that creates a oneness of spirit that must take place before a meaningful conversation or relationship can occur. Further, American Indians also prefer other modes of communication over verbal interaction. Their historical accomplishments in arts and music are good examples of their readiness to relate and to communicate.

Second, the American Indian's respect for each individual and their use of indirectness to convey such respect in communication places the concept of metacommunication (Haley, 1963) in a different perspective. To Haley, every relationship contains within it an implicit power struggle over who defines the nature of that relationship. American Indian's interaction with others is collateral in nature, and the use of covert power to manipulate a social relationship is foreign to them. American Indian's use of indirect communication requires a great deal of sensitivity and reciprocity from other people. When indirect communication is not properly received and reciprocated, there is a threat to that relationship.

A third principle of communication relates to what Bateson referred to as the "punctuation" of communicational sequences, as exemplified in a couple relationship in an urban setting. The husband punctuates the sequence of communication thus: "I have to maintain my status as a hunter to provide for my wife." The wife, on the other hand, defines the relationship differently: "I must provide for my family since I am the only one in the family who is employable." Such a relationship can easily lead to an impasse in the couple relationship, resulting in alcoholism as a means of escape from reality.

Finally, the digital (verbal) and analogic (nonverbal) components of communication are sure to present difficulties among American Indian family members who may speak different native languages, be at different levels of acculturation, and experience extreme economic and health stress. Incongruence of communication taking the form of inappropriateness, invalidation, or paradox can exist among family members. Family members' adherence to cultural traits such as respect for individuality and noninterference and their lack of effective feedback may leave the invalidated paradoxical message unresolved.

American Indian families' diverse language background and their deemphasis upon verbal interaction as a relational means place other communication concepts such as syntactics (the grammatical properties), semantics (meaning of communication), and pragmatics (behavioral effects of communication), in a greater degree of complexity. Their use of silence to convey respect and their view that time is unimportant in problem solving can render clear and effective communication difficult if not impossible.

The principle of schismogenesis (Bateson, 1958), which states that cumulative interaction between individuals tends to result in progressive change and that whatever the balance is in a relationship it tends to become exaggerated over time, is also applicable in understanding the marital relationship of an American Indian couple. The effects of migration and the family life cycle force the couple to renegotiate their relationship constantly. This occurs at a time when the family support system is weak and the demands for meeting basic family needs such as food and housing are great. Traditionally, American Indian couples had a more egalitarian relationship than the dominant society due to the Indians' observance and respect for individuality. Their need for economic survival in a hostile environment has forced their relationship to shift more from a symmetrical (similar) to complementary (dominant/submissive) relationship. This shift often complicates the couple relationship.

Satir's classification (Satir, Stachowiak, and Taschman, 1975) of family behavior for a family member under stress has a great deal of relevance in understanding American Indian families. American Indian cultural value, such as harmony with nature, noninterference, and being-in-becoming can cause a family member to assume role behaviors such as placator (super-agreeable) or irrelevant person. However, the role of a placator can cause an individual to feel like a "nonperson." The same holds true for the irrelevant person who employs distraction as defense against unmet needs. Such distractions can take the form of physical illness or alcoholism.

The principles of behavior derived from the communication theory can contribute significantly to understanding the dynamics and interaction of an American Indian family. The following discussion aims to explicate the matter in which these principles can be applied to actual work with an American Indian family.

*Communication practice principles as they relate to work with an
American Indian family.* American Indian family interaction does not
take into account a rigid prescribed vertical and hierarchical role
structure determined by age, sex, generation, and birth order of family
members. This coupled with tribal diversity and respect for individuality
can contribute to a family member's confusion, indecision, and lack of
direction. Such an egalitarian communicative style perhaps traditionally
was functional among close-knit extended families but it becomes
vulnerable when it is practiced within a hostile environment and in an
urban setting of dominant culture.

The role of a family therapist traditionally and inherently has been
authoritarian in nature. This role may not fit well with an American
Indian family. It explains in part why American Indian families prefer
American Indian workers and why they seek help from mainstream
societal agencies only as a last resort. The challenge on the part of the
therapist, when working with American Indians, is to "join" the family
and to be accepted by them.

The communication theory is very useful in assessing the family
system and interactive pattern, yet a therapist's role in engaging the
family in renegotiation and redefinition of the power relationship is not
an easy task. The concept of power is too controlling, interfering,
noncollateral, disrespectful, and foreign to the American Indian.
Nevertheless, authority relationship and leadership are traits that
should be taught, especially for child rearing. The therapist may need to
align the authority or relationship concept with a collateral, mutually
respected, and responsible term, thus making it easier for family
members to relate and to utilize the applicability of this communication
concept. For example, instead of telling the family member exactly what
to do, the therapist can suggest different alternatives to improve
relationships with other family members.

The role of the therapist, as defined by Haley, is that of a
"metagovernor" of the family system, thus requiring intense active
participation and at times manipulation. The therapist's active leadership role prior to his acceptance by an Indian family may easily be
interpreted by the family as an unwelcome intrusion. Yet, at the
beginning phase of therapy, the therapist's active leadership role in
assisting the family to meet its basic needs can serve as a needed relief to
the family. It can also help build a good relationship between the
therapist and the family.

Haley's therapeutic tactics such as the paradoxical messages (double
bind) and prescribing the symptom (encouraging the usually dysfunc-

tional behavior) may be perplexing and disrespectful to most American Indian families. The technique of relabeling/reframing (by emphasizing the positive) will be more in congruence with the American Indian cultural emphasis on respect and individuality. While a communication therapist's emphasis on relieving concrete problems or suffering may be welcomed by the American Indian family, a rigid adherence to time-limited behavioral change may be offensive to the family's traditional time orientation.

Virginia Satir et al.'s (1975) cognitive approach, to "teach" family members to recognize family roles so that the rules and the interactional patterns may be changed for the sake of benefitting the family, has great appeal. Again, such cognitive understanding should not be attempted until a trusting relationship is developed between the therapist and family. Understanding and changing interactional patterns require the therapist to adopt the extended family ties and multiple-household framework. Satir's sculpting technique may also be appealing to American Indian families who learn by observation and participation. Her emphasis on "good feelings" within the family and among family members is consistent with the American Indian teaching of harmony, collaterality, and the general "goodness" of man. Her utilization of family history, which she calls the "family life chronology" (Satir, 1967), should help the family reminisce and value its past. This is an invaluable tool for understanding the extended family system dynamics influenced by intergenerational migration and acculturation. The skills essential in congruent communication also have applicability in work with American Indian families. Other than avoiding eye contact, as a way to show respect, American Indians basically are very observing individuals. These observational skills can be channeled and utilized for family communication. American Indians traditionally were not taught or encouraged to identify and express their needs, nor were they taught how to identify and express their feelings. Skills essential to effective feedback should be taught to American Indian families who need constant renegotiation of expectations of roles within the family.

It is generally true that effective family functioning depends on open, full, honest expressions among all family members. A therapist working with Indian families should be cognizant of the fact that some tribes (Wintemute and Messer, 1982, p. 5) prescribe that a son-in-law not talk to or have eye contact with his mother-in-law. On the other hand, open expression of positive and respectful verbal and nonverbal communication among older family members is expected and accepted. Hence this points out the flexible and differential use or potential misuse of conjoint family therapy.

To communicate effectively with an American Indian family, a therapist needs to modify his pragmatics that denote the behavioral effects of the communicative exchange. A therapist should limit his verbosity, slow down his speech, and lower his voice. At times, a therapist should not speak unless he is asked to. He can communicate by paying attention to family members' needs and by respecting them as "worthy," "good" individuals. He can communicate effectively by not being overly dependent upon the verbal mode of interaction; instead, the client's artistic ability, musical talents, or other natural assets can be utilized to facilitate communication.

Family Structure Theory

A theoretical discussion of family structure theory and its comparison with the family communication theory have been presented in the first chapter and in Chapter 2. The discussion of family structure theory here centers on behavioral principles and family practice principles. The first section examines behavioral principles of family structure theory. The second section presents family practice principles of structure family theory as they relate to assessment and therapy with American Indian families.

Behavioral principles of family structure theory as they relate to understanding American Indian families. The family structure theory strongly adheres to the system outlook and was primarily developed and advanced by Minuchin (1974) and Bowen (1976). Rather than observe the basic elements in a family transaction, the structuralists are interested in how the family is organized or structured. While stressing the importance of individuality, the American Indian family is deeply immersed in a family system that extends beyond kin to nonkin (as in namesakes) and beyond the nuclear parameter to include multiple households. The central concept in Bowen's theory is differentiation as it relates to the interpersonal, intrapersonal, and intergenerational process. Bowen's concept of a differentiated person in intrapersonal terms appears to apply to American Indian's idealization of a well-adjusted person who knows when and how to use his "head" as well as how to express his emotions. In the sphere of interpersonal activities, this same person is able to maintain a solid, nonnegotiable self in relationship within and outside the family and to take comfortable "I" positions. He does not forsake intellectual and emotional integrity to obtain approval, love, peace, or togetherness. In the sphere of family relationships, differentiation refers to the family's ability to accept change and difference from its members. The respect that the American Indian culture bestows upon each family member should make Bowen's theory compatible. The actualization of the differentiation concept may be difficult for an American Indian family whenever children do not grow up in their own family with support and teaching from the traditional extended family. William Byler cites that 25% to 35% of American Indian children are raised outside their natural family network (Byler, 1977, p. 1).

It is generally true that the process of "multigenerational transmission" is linked to the family of the past, but the level of differentiation in an individual may not be closely determined by the differential level of one's parents, by sex, or by sibling position as advocated by Bowen. The rationale behind such uncertainty is that the typical American Indian child experiences a broader sphere of interaction with extended family members in many households as compared to an Anglo child's limited interaction with only nuclear family members. Thus in the assessment of an American Indian family relationship, greater attention should be devoted to the extended family relationship and framework.

Similarly, Bowen's concept of "family projection process" in which parental emotions help to shape and define what the child becomes, even though these definitions have little to do with the original realities of the child, may not be applicable to traditional American Indian families where child rearing is not the primary responsibility of the biological parents but a common, shared duty of the extended family. A close relationship between a child and grandparents may have more to do with the family projection process than the relationship between the child and her biological parents.

The triangle, or three-person, system that Bowen considers the basic building block of all emotional systems also has a different meaning when applied to a traditional American Indian family. In a multiple-household extended family, the parental spouse system is seldom as solid and intense as it is in a single nuclear household system. If the spousal system is under stress, usually such individuals as cousins, aunts, or uncles become the vulnerable other person in the triangle. The close grandparent-grandchild relationship may run the risk of triangulation at times of stress; again, the grandparent spousal system in a traditional American Indian family is not as intense as it is in the Anglo grandparent system.

Bowen's concept of "emotional cutoff" has significant application in work with American Indian families. According to Bowen, everyone has some degree of unresolved emotional attachment to the previous generation. The "cutoff" consists of denial and isolation of the problem while living close to the parents or by physically running away as in the case of migration, or a combination of the two. As a rule, the more a nuclear family maintains emotional contact with the previous generations, the calmer, more orderly, and less problematic their lives will be. Conversely, the greater the degree of cutoff, the more the nuclear family becomes a sort of emotional pressure cooker. This concept indicates the important significance of the extended family system of American Indians.

Family structure theory focusing on the family system's structural (contextual) dynamics, especially the creation, maintenance, and modification of boundaries, which are rules defining who participates and how (Minuchin, 1974, p. 53), is useful in work with American Indian families. In an extended family system with multiple households, the subsystem boundaries between spouse, grandparents, parent-child, and siblings seldom are solid or rigid. Contrarily, many of these subsystem formations and boundaries are dangerously amorphous or diffuse. These subsystems were functional historically because of cultural value reinforcements. As times changed and as American Indian families migrated to urban areas, the original extended family ties broke down. This, coupled with racial discrimination, financial problems, and poor health care, made it difficult for individuals in the subsystems to maintain their boundaries.

The family system boundary concept has application to American Indian parents who grew up in boarding schools or away from home. The absence of spouse, grandparents, and sibling subsystem interactive models in the boarding schools may have deprived the parents of functional knowledge and parenting skills they need as adults and parents to their own children.

The family's ability to maintain subsystem boundaries is further handicapped by the fact that both parents, and sometimes older siblings, have to work outside the home. Long working hours and different working schedules can create interactional problems and difficulty within a subsystem and between subsystems. For example, if the father works a night shift and the mother works days, both will have little time to interact with each other and to maintain and solidify their spousal subsystem. Meanwhile, the father and the children may have too much interaction and older siblings may assume the mother's role in the family (boundary rupture). Some tribal customs that treat mother and daughter alike could make the spousal and parent-child subsystem more difficult to maintain (Brown and Shaughnessy, 1982, p. 30). A ruptured system boundary requires that family members use a great deal of sensitivity, effort, and energy to repair it. Raising the issue of boundary conflicts and subsequent repair can disrupt harmony within the family and was usually discouraged by the traditional culture. Finally, boundary modification and repair require sufficient interpersonal communication skills, which members of many families do not possess.

Family structure practice principles and work with American Indian families. Bowen's emphasis on differentiation of self (from the family "culture mass") as the primary goal of therapy has important implications and applications in work with American Indian families. Extended family ties are extremely important to an American Indian family. To some extent, a family framework can be used as a guide for assessment, for formulating therapy goals, and for therapy itself. Bowen's concept of "self-differentiation" should not be misconstrued as individualism or narcissism; instead, it coincides with the American Indian concept of individuality. Individualism requires that uniqueness be deviation from the normal. Individuality allows uniqueness to become the refinement of life and it requires a philosophy that can give understanding and meaning to the world. Hence, a differentiated person is not a self-centered person, but an individual who knows and values her past, including ethnic heritage and family background. A self-differentiated person is not only responsible for herself but also responsible for others, especially family members and relatives. Yet, sometimes there exist components of one's family background and structure that are dysfunctional and thus create or perpetuate disharmony within the entire family system. This is the "culture mass" Bowen refers to when a family needs to disengage or engage differently in order to ameliorate present family problems.

Family group interaction characteristic of American Indian culture should be conducive to conjoint (with every family member present) family therapy. However, the format and structure of conjoint family therapy with the therapist in charge may be too rigid and, therefore, unnatural to the American Indian way of interaction. Instead, the therapist may need to capitalize upon the ceremonial feasts (Red Horse, 1980b) as a means to facilitate family interaction. Again, due to the unnaturalness of the formal family therapy format, some family members may not feel comfortable and may remain unavailable for conjoint therapy. Bowen's technique of focusing upon one individual, usually the more differentiated or respected member in the family, should be useful. In most cases, this individual will be a grandparent of either sex depending upon the tribal practice that the family inherits. While the therapist works with an individual, the goal is to modify the structure of the emotional system of the family through that individual's change and effort.

Bowen's detached but interested, rational, calm, low-key approach to problem solving again corresponds closely to the American Indian cultural emphasis on moderation, patience, and self-discipline. His efforts in taking careful family history (multigenerational transmission records) reflects his sensitivity and respect to the cultural nurturance system, migration process, intergenerational perspective, and the need for individualizing each family.

Minuchin's differential applications of "joining techniques" during the beginning phase of therapy reflects his sensitivity to individual family differences and the wisdom that structural change in a family usually requires time and patience. His maintenance technique, whereby the therapist is organized by the basic rules that regulate the transactional process in a specific family system, goes a long way in helping to establish mutual respect and trust with the family. By employing the maintenance technique, a therapist may discover that the family problem is mainly a biased interpretation on the part of the therapist who operates under the Anglo middle-class nuclear family framework.

While Minuchin's joining and maintenance techniques are compatible with the American Indian family values and structure, his "disequilibration techniques" or family restructuring techniques generally do not share the same degree of congruence and effectiveness with this specific ethnic group. These techniques, including enactment and boundary-marking, escalating stress (by emphasizing differences), physical movement, utilizing the symptom (by exaggerating it), and manipulating mood (by escalating the emotional intensity), are much too abstract, challenging, emotional confrontational, and, therefore, antithetical to American Indian culture. These techniques, with modification, however, may work with bicultural American Indian families.

The preceding discussion on applying culturally sensitive family theories aims to provide a framework in which to understand and serve American Indian families. The communication and structure theories can be differentially applied in therapy with these families. Part 2 of this chapter explains how to integrate and apply these theories in actual work with American Indian families.

PART 2: CULTURALLY RELEVANT TECHNIQUES AND SKILLS IN THERAPY PHASES

Beginning Phase of Therapy

The beginning phase of treatment in work with an American Indian client is of paramount importance. The reason for the initial phase of treatment being so very significant is attributable to several factors. American Indian culture emphasizes self-determination and respects individuality. A family therapist will be consulted only if all other help-seeking attempts have failed. Further, American Indians' unfamiliarity with family therapy and their lack of knowledge as to what a family therapist can do make the first contact phase extremely precarious. In an attempt to capitalize on the situation to make the family's first visit profitable, a family therapist should be cognizant of the American Indians' central cultural themes and the theoretical concepts from communication and structure theories. These can serve as a guide to interacting with the family. Four specific skills and techniques are essential in work with an American Indian family in the beginning therapy phase. These skills and techniques include (1) engaging the client/family, (2) cultural transitional mapping and data collection, (3) mutual goal setting, and (4) selecting a focus/system for therapy.

Relationship Skills and Techniques in Engaging the Client/Family

How to engage an American Indian family for therapy begins with understanding why the contact takes place. Generally, rapport with a family should not be too difficult to establish if the initial contact to see the therapist is made by the family, especially by the head of the household, often the grandparent. Such a family usually is bicultural and has some knowledge and appreciation of family therapy. However, more typically, family-therapist contact occurs during a family crisis or when a member of the family runs into difficulty with such mainstream societal agencies as public schools, courts, public health, or human service institutions. The family's mistrust level will be particularly high during the first contact with the therapist.

Knowing the anxiety level of the family, the therapist also needs to be reminded that American Indian families do not wish others to meddle in their private affairs. Furthermore, they have no prior knowledge of what family therapy is and what a family therapist can do. The most familiar role the family can place the therapist in is that of a medicine man who usually performs the service in a short time with little mental involvement and participation from the family members. Therefore, during the initial contact with the family, a therapist needs to be active and directive so that she can be accepted with a "quota of leadership" (Minuchin, 1974) similar to that of a medicine man.

Being sensitive is respected; being uncertain, insecure, artificial, and insincere are unacceptable to an American Indian family. Although they may avoid eye contact as a means to convey mistrust or respect, American Indian clients are very observing. They have been long-time victims of oppression and exploitation from the past and do not want to be gullible or taken advantage of again.

If the contact has been initiated by the therapist, she needs to explain calmly and openly to the family who she is, what her role is with the agency, and the reason for the interview. The therapist's straightfor-wardness may be a breath of fresh air for the family and they may be relieved to find hope for solving their long suffering with problems.

A therapist's open, caring, and congruent communication with the family should also be simple, precise, slow, and calm. Her attention and concern for other extended members of the household will help the family feel that they are in good company with a stranger. There may be periods of silence, especially when the therapist introduces disturbing information. A therapist should allow herself and the family time to gather their thoughts and emotions before pressing on to a new topic. Due to other daily living stress factors, family members' testing out period with the therapist, and the family's uncertainty as to how to resolve the family problem, the contact phase (Haley, 1976) of therapy with an American Indian family may take longer than with the dominant culture family. It is important that the therapist respects the time differential and not overtly or covertly pressure the family for activity. Should the therapist fail to stay with "where the client is," the family may adopt a passive-aggressive approach and agree with everything suggested by the therapist, but do nothing afterward.

To minimize the unnaturalness of the initial therapist-family contact,

Minuchin's maintenance technique is helpful. This "requires the therapist to be organized by the basic rules that regulate the transactional process in a specific family system" (1974, p. 175). To do this, a therapist needs to be attentive, talk less, observe more, and listen actively. All these are American Indian communicative pragmatics.

As a means to sustain the family for longer-term therapy, the therapist needs to promote the sense that she is available at all times. Thus therapist-family contact should not be limited to weekly one-hour sessions in the office. Some sessions can be conducted at the family home and the sessions' duration may range from 20 minutes to two to three hours. Consistent with the American Indian cultural characteristic of giveaway, a family may give the therapist a gift at the end of a session as an appreciation of friendship and collaterality. The therapist should receive it without worrying about potential client manipulation. The family does not expect the reciprocity of gift exchange for they interpret the therapist's warm and helpful visit as a gift to them.

Skills and Techniques in Cultural Transitional Mapping and Data Collection

Despite American Indian families' continual efforts to resist acculturation, each family member is influenced to a certain degree by dominant cultural views. All family problems to an extent can be attributed to the family and the family members' coping mechanism with the external world controlled by the dominant culture. Therefore, it is vitally important in the course of the first therapy stage that the therapist establish which phase of the process of acculturation the family is currently experiencing and how they have dealt with the vicissitudes of previous phases (Sluzki, 1979, p. 389). Viewing the outside world with distrust and hostility, an Indian family may maintain no meaningful contact with mainstream societal agencies such as a health care agency. Such data need to be collected for future therapy purposes. In addition, family data such as tribal identity and heritage, language spoken, physical health history, and migration process are helpful in assessment. Considering the importance of extended family ties, a therapist needs to assess the strength or potential dilution of the present household boundary and support system. A sociocultural map should also include the transitional position of the multigenerational family. Bowen's concepts of differentiation, triangulation, and emotional cutoff can also be assessed by such cultural mapping. The technique of cultural mapping is very similar to the technique of constructing a genogram (Pendagast and Sherman, 1977). In taking a genogram, a therapist inquires systematically into family patterns among aunts, uncles, siblings, cousins, grandparents, and so on, in an attempt to gather information about patterns of closeness, distance, and conflict. While a genogram generally assists in understanding multigeneraltional patterns and influences, that is, the history of the presenting family's difficulties, it also provides the therapist and the family some insights in how the family wishes the problem to be resolved (Wachtel, 1982). The projective nature of this technique makes it culturally relevant and compatible in work with American Indian families who wish to resolve their family problem in accordance with traditional cultural values.

However, in constructing a genogram, the therapist needs to phrase highly structured questions such as "How did your grandparents get along?" or "Who did your mother go to when she got mad at your father (triangulation)?" carefully and, if possible, spontaneously. To be less formal and structured but more flexible and creative, the therapist should not take notes during the interview. The family should be encouraged to share background information with pride and not simply as a means to disentangle present family problems.

To collect information on structural and communicative interaction, a therapist needs to visit the family at home and to attend ceremonies where extended family members and multiple household members gather. The creative use of family photographs, Indian crafts, poetry, and music (Ho and Settles, 1984) can go a long way toward collecting invaluable data regarding individual and family functioning. The technique of cultural mapping will be illustrated in detail in Part 3, Case Illustrations, in this chapter.

Skills and Techniques in Mutual Goal Setting

The problems and disturbances that an American Indian family faces are not different from those of other families. They include an enmeshment and lack of generational boundaries, well-meant but misdirected efforts to force working relationships, misunderstandings of self and others, reenactment of the results of cutoff relationships, effects associated with unfinished grief work, and the need to cope without being overwhelmed by anxiety (Attneave, 1982, p. 61). Minuchin's (1974, p. 60) adaptation categories of family stress also are pertinent to American Indian families. These stresses include (1) stressful contact of one member or of the whole family with extrafamiliar forces, such as work or migration; (2) transitional points in the family including death or birth of a new baby; and (3) idiosyncratic problems such as a physical or mental handicap on the part of a family member.

Otto Pollak's (1964) concept of "uncompleted family" is applicable here as the therapist examines the problems faced by current American Indian families whose deficit lies not with "loss" but with "unattainment." Many clients' family problems are caused by the family's inability to provide basic needs such as food, shelter, and proper health care. Therefore, in the process of mutual goal setting, a therapist needs to be cognizant of the family's fundamental struggle for survival to satisfy their basic human needs. A family therapist will do an American Indian family disservice if she is overly concerned with psychodynamic structure but is negligent of the family's basic needs. As the primary goal is met, more basic family systemic problems may emerge. The therapist's sensitive, effective, and speedy delivery of concrete services will contribute to a trusting relationship with the family and in family reorganization therapy dictated by the need and desire of the individual family.

The process of mutual goal formulation should take into consideration American Indians' cultural trait of interdependence. Group decision takes precedence over individual choice. Therefore, whenever possible, a therapist needs to involve all family members, even extended family members, in selecting a therapy goal. Sometimes the process of involving all relevant family members can be so therapeutic that further intervention by the therapist is unnecessary.

Phillip, a 15-year-old probationer, was brought to the attention of a court-related worker when she received a complaint that Phillip was running around from house to house visiting female friends without parental supervision. When the worker inquired about Phillip's family background, she discovered that he had several aunts and cousins. When the worker called all Phillip's aunts and cousins together for a family conference, she discovered that all his cousins were young females. The worker later learned that Phillip's behavior was very natural in the extended family system.

As can be expected, group consensus in goal-setting is time-consuming, but an American Indian family has a flexible time orientation. The family can wait patiently for a group decision and will experience no urgency in completing certain tasks required of each family member for change. Hence, the time-limited and goal-directed mentality of the therapist may need moderation when working with an American Indian family.

For a therapeutic goal to have a chance for completion, it has to be realistic, comprehensible, and defined in concrete terms (Edwards and Edwards, 1984). Further, it has to be within the capacity of the client or the family.

Skills and Techniques in Selecting a Focus/System Unit for Therapy

The American Indian family nurturance system consists of extended family ties. The presenting family problem may involve an individual member of a subsystem such as a spouse. Extended family relationships should always be kept in focus, especially during the assessment period. In work with a more traditional American Indian couple who are physically and emotionally neglecting their child, a family therapist's suggestion to see the couple as the targeted therapy focus, with the goal of repairing the spousal subsystem, may be confusing and offensive to the couple. This would totally neglect the dynamic function of extended family ties. If the grandparents of the child are contacted, they could either temporarily assume the child-rearing role, or they could remind the child's parents of their respective roles. If the grandparents' marriage is matrilineal, the system unit to be selected for therapy should be the grandmother, because she is the most respected member of the extended family. Hence selecting a focus or system unit for therapy depends on the nature of the problem, the common and specific structure of the extended family, the acculturational level of the family, and the motivation and capacity of the subsystem unit selected. For instance, in the above family situation, should the grandmother refuse to work with the therapist or not speak English and no interpreter is available, the therapist may need to consult with other respected family members, perhaps a great-aunt can assume the role of the grandmother. On the other hand, if the couple is bicultural and wish to improve their marital relationship as a means to provide better care for their child, couple therapy may be in order.

Realistically, there are situations when the therapist will have access to only one family member, preferably the one who is most acculturated, self-differentiated, and respected. Bowen's family therapy theory that focuses on self-differentiation can be most helpful. Again, in applying the concept of differentiation, the family sphere of differentiation needs to be the starting point. Family undifferentiation can either manifest itself in enmeshment or isolation (Minuchin, 1974) as in the case of emotional cutoff. Once the emotional cutoff is dealt with, the client can begin working on interpersonal and intrapersonal differentiation. Regardless of which family member is seen and what the unit of focus of therapy may be, the therapist's beginning efforts must be directed toward resolving the external stress or meeting the basic unmet needs of the family.

Problem-Solving Phase of Therapy

In view of American Indian families' holistic, interdependent view of the world and their close interpersonal relationships, their interpretation of family problems and how these problems should be solved are important factors. The specific approach and direction that an American Indian family adopts for problem solving are guided naturally by their traditional value system and current capacities. Communication and structure practice principles, no doubt, have a great deal to offer a family therapist who is called upon to assist Indian families. However, the degree of a therapist's effectiveness will depend on the differential application of these practice principles and how compatible they are with American Indian cultural orientation. Five skills and techniques of particular relevance in the problem-solving phase of therapy include (1) social, moral, organic reframing/relabeling; (2) mobilizing and restructuring the extended family network; (3) promoting interdependence as family restructuring technique; (4) employing role model, educator role, and advocate role; (5) restructuring taboos for problem solving, and (6) collaborative work with medicine person, paraprofessional, and therapist helper.

Skills and Techniques in Social, Moral, and Organic Reframing/Relabeling

For an American Indian family, relationships with each other, especially with relatives, are of utmost importance. It will be totally unacceptable to them if the therapist leads them to believe that their behavior is the cause of the family's problem. Haley's and Minuchin's reframing/relabeling technique, which capitalizes on the pragmatics of American Indian culture by emphasizing the positive aspects of behavior and redefining negative behavior as positive, should have great appeal to motivating and sustaining the family's interest for help. By focusing on the ecosystem cultural transition conception of family problems, the therapist conveys to the family sensitivity and empathy. With reduced anxiety, the family can devote their energy to rearranging transactions and to problem solving within the family. During the course of marital conflict, the therapist can relabel the problem "socially" by pointing out that the migration process and urban living are difficult for American Indians who are used to strong extended family ties. In the case of psychosomatic illness resulting from unresolved interpersonal relationships, the therapist can "morally" reframe the illness to put it beyond everybody's control. Should the client adopt a passive-resistive stance, the therapist can reframe it by praising him or her for not wanting to rush into a decision affecting the welfare of other family members. The meaning or interpretation resulting from reframing may not be exact, but the important metacommunication conveyed by this technique is that all family members, including the therapist, respect and value relationships with each other and the right for individual decisions.

Mobilizing and Reconstructing the
Extended Family Network

One of the factors plaguing the American Indian family is the lack of extended family support due to the fact the family has migrated out of their native environment where mutual inter- and intrafamily support was strong. This couples with the different acculturation rates on the part of family members to make consensus decision making or problem solving within the family extremely difficult. If parents' defend against contamination by the dominant culture, an American Indian family can easily become "enmeshed" by totally retreating from the community at large. This has been a contributing factor to many of the violent and child abuse cases within American Indian families (Lewis, 1984). The skill and technique used to mobilize the extended family network should be consistent with the American Indians' nurturance system, whereby family interaction is not rigidified by a closed system.

Although a "good" student in the past, Debbie, the teenage daughter of the Tiger family, has been missing school recently. When the parents were informed of this, they displayed no surprise, but expressed cooperation with the school official in getting Debbie back to school regularly. The school social worker, who served as family therapist, happened to live in the same neighborhood as the Tigers, and she volunteered to transport Debbie back and forth to school. Through this consistent relationship, the therapist became a trusted friend of the Tiger family. To express the family's gratitude and friendship, Mrs. Tiger provided the therapist with a regular supply of home-grown vegetables. Through this informal exchange, the therapist learned that the Tigers were totally shut off from the community, which Mr. Tiger labeled as "crazy' and "not to be trusted." Mr. Tiger did not have a regular job. On his days off, "he managed to get drunk," according to Mrs. Tiger. Although Mrs. Tiger was willing to get some therapy for their family problems, Mr. Tiger insisted that he would not have any of "that stuff" (therapy). After learning that the Tigers are religious individuals who attended church regularly, the therapist referred the Tigers to a minister for consultation. The minister, although a non-Indian, was highly respected by the Indians in the community. The minister later introduced the Tigers to other Indians who also attended the same church but belonged to different tribes. Through such extended interaction with other Indians, Mrs. Tiger became more relaxed and paid more attention to Debbie, who managed to attend school regularly without the family therapist's assistance.

Hence a therapist's skill in mobilizing a social support network hinges upon her familiarity with and respect for the American Indians' need for safety and social belonging. Additionally, the therapist needs to familiarize herself with available community resources, both informal as well as formal, and to make proper referrals as needed. Proper referral, as indicated by the above case example, requires a trusting relationship between the therapist and the family, the correct referral source, and the right timing.

Promoting Interdependence as Family Restructuring Technique

Traditionally, American Indian family members grew up in a secure, comfortable environment, whereby each individual know the proper form of interactive behavior. Because of changing times, the negative influences of public boarding schools, and the pressing demands of urban living, some American Indian families are caught in a bind within their families, as well as outside of the family. In addition to their lack of early role models, and inadequate coping skills in a hostile environment, family members still retain such traditional practices as noninterference, leaving others alone, and allowing individuals to make their own decisions. Many Indian families endure suffering as a way of life. A therapist can assist these families by encouraging them to reminisce about the interdependent qualities of traditional Indian living.

American Indians are not selfish or self-centered individuals; they are considerate and pay attention to others' needs, especially to the needs of other family members. Disillusionment stemming from contemporary life and other basic survival demands to provide for the family can leave parents with no energy and resources. They need an impetus and at times a role model. A family therapist who respects Indian culture can provide this and assist the families in interdependent living.

To implement effectively the technique of interdependence promotion, the therapist needs to serve as a role model. In that, she needs to spend time, however slow the process may be, to involve everybody in the (extended) family in problem assessment and solution. The therapist's knowledge and skills in group work practice, including group structure, group membership, leadership, decision making, and dynamic communication, will be valuable in promoting interdependence within the family.

Employing Role Models, Educator Roles, and Advocate Roles

Many American Indians grew up and were educated in boarding schools and out-of-home placements. In some tribes, there is a long history of intermarriage. Thus many American Indians lack definitive parental role models. The child-rearing influence of the dominant culture and the different acculturation rates of family members compound the problem. Parents are confused as to how to conduct a household efficiently and to educate their children in a bicultural world. A therapist should serve as a consistent role model for these parents.

At times, the therapist may need to function as the parents' parent who is nurturing but firm, supportive but challenging. Because American Indians often learn best by observation and participation, the therapist should talk less and do more. When it is called for, the therapist needs to "take" the parent, along with the child (or children), for health care and to pay utility bills before the service is terminated. Some parents have no prior experience in dealing with community agencies or resources external to the family (King, 1967).

As the therapist assumes the "transitory" parental role and teacher role, her interaction with the family can be guided by both American

Indian culture values and the communication and structure theories. She should explain to the family that some new skills she is advocating may conflict with their indigenous cultural traits, but that these skills are essential for survival in the social and economic world of the dominant culture. The therapist should explain that the survival of the family is at stake and that their adaptation in a dominant society does not entail forsaking Indian culture, as recent studies have indicated (Native American Research Group, 1979).

In the family's attempt to remobilize or restructure its extended family ties, it may also need skills essential for functioning as a nuclear family. Members may need help in strengthening the subsystem boundaries, especially the spouse subsystem boundary. Without the benefit of traditional extended family ties, parents may require instruction in how to assume the executive role of a household. They may need to integrate some components of child-rearing practices so their children can succeed in public schools.

Guided by the principles of communication behavior and practice principles, a therapist can teach a family through role modeling the skills essential for open and congruent communication. Family members should also learn how to make "I" statements, feeling statements, and intention statements. They need to learn effective feedback skills and problem-solving skills (Miller, Nunnally, and Wackman, 1975).

Because many American Indian families are the victims of societal lags and intentional or unintentional indifference by agencies and institutions essential to their survival and well-being, the therapist may have to serve as an advocate for the family. The role of an advocate is not an unbiased one. The therapist should collaborate with the family, as well as with other families experiencing similar problems. The success derived from advocacy can boost family morale where in the past they had experienced only hopelessness and defeat.

Restructuring Cultural Taboos for Problem Solving

Each culture has prohibitions prescribing the proper conduct and functioning of its members. When these prohibitions are violated, an individual and his family may suffer consequences, sometimes life-threatening ones. The more traditional an Indian family is, the more closely it will adhere to cultural taboos. Obviously, each cultural taboo has served a vital function for a particular tribe at a specific time. As times change, however, and as the family moves to urban areas, traditional taboos can become dysfunctional and cause the family problems.

Mr. Dancewell belonged to a tribe that required the husband to move into his wife's household. The wife, in this particular tribe, had primary responsibility of child rearing. The husband's responsibility was to raise his sister's children, especially the male children.

Mr. Dancewell moved with his parents to a large city when he was 15. When he was 20, he married his present wife who was from a different tribe. His wife was impressed with Mr. Dancewell's interest and concern for young children, especially his sister's children. After Mr. and Mrs. Dancewell had a child of their own, Mrs. Dancewell was disappointed with the apathy her husband showed toward the new baby. She rationalized her husband's apathy by saying he did not relate to infants. She later discovered that Mr. Dancewell's behavior did not change as the child grew older, and this began to create problems in the marriage. After consulting with an elder from his own tribe, Mr. Dancewell realized that his previously learned taboo of shared parental responsibility for his child applied only for marriages within the same tribe. Because his wife was from a different tribe, the prohibition did not apply.

The above example occurs more frequently than most family therapists realize. When it happens, it should not be categorically labeled as just another client resistance. It should be carefully examined and respected. Often the therapist may need to explore and to seek help from tribal leaders, including the elders and the medicine man. Such timely consultation and collaboration with indigenous healers is consistent with the ecosystemic principles of equifinality, meaning that a number of different interventions may, owing to the complexity of systems, produce similar effects or outcome.

Collaborative Work with a Medicine Person, Paraprofessional, and Therapist Helper

A medicine person, shaman, or spiritual leader plays a vital role in the lives of many American Indian families, especially those who tenaciously hold on to their rich tradition. Even for bicultural families, the need for a medicine person and spiritual leader is still there, especially when a family member experiences grief that connects with early childhood experiences (Hanson, 1981). A family therapist should not hesitate to consult with a spiritual leader when the need arises. The leader should always be treated with professional integrity and respect. The strategic collaboration with a medicine person or spiritual leader points out once again the important need for the therapist to treat the family in a holistic fashion.

American Indian culture is diverse, and many families may resist certain aspects of the dominant culture, particularly a health care provider or family therapist. It is sometimes necessary to help the family without direct face-to-face involvement. When this is necessary, a therapist helper or link therapist (Landau, 1981) can be used. Such a person may be able to help the family resolve its problems according to its own customs. Ideally, the therapist helper is an elder or grandparent who is highly respected by the extended family. When such a person is unavailable, an other family member who sees the value of family therapy can assume the role of therapist helper. In some instances, the therapist helper does not need to be a member of the extended family but could be a highly trusted and respected individual. Once the therapist-helper is selected, she needs to have coaching sessions with the therapist to derive an assessment and therapy plan for the family. The therapist needs to be open and to learn from the helper the family's strengths and problems, and which direction to proceed in accordance with specific tribal beliefs and family behavior. The therapist provides the helper with professional knowledge regarding family structure, intergenerational perspective, and communication dynamics and skills essential to resolving family problems. Planned intermittent supervisory sessions between the therapist and the helper are needed to monitor and stabilize change in the family. Because this technique aims at problem solving that is short term (four to eight sessions) in nature, it differs with Bowen's "coach approach" directed at multigenerational family systemic change. This usually requires a longer duration and a more intensive training and supervision for the "coach."

Evaluation and Termination Phase
of Therapy

Family therapy with American Indians is a continuous process that starts slowly and also ends slowly. The usual therapeutic mentality of time-limited therapy with clear-cut successful outcome may not be applicable in work with this group. Rosen's and Proctor's (1978) model for specifying and evaluating therapy outcome is relevant in work with

American Indian families. In evaluating therapy progress with American Indian families, three types of outcome goals are to be expected. First are the *intermediate* outcomes that contribute to or create a climate for continued therapy. Some families will only allow the therapist to help them with some basic needs problems. When this is accomplished, therapy terminates. The therapist should not be discouraged that the family decides not to work on their relationship problems for this may happen later.

Second are the *instrumental* outcomes. When achieved, these are assumed to lead to the achievement of the ultimate outcomes without further therapy. This is particularly true with American Indian families whose basic needs are so inadequate or "unattained." However, once these needs are met, they could go on with the task of repairing relational bonds within the family. Third are the *ultimate outcomes*, which constitute the reasons for which therapy was undertaken. Examples of these outcome goals include a child's adjustment problem in school or at home, marital relationship, alcoholism, and physical illnesses that are causes by family relationship disturbances.

American Indians may not verbally express the progress they make in therapy. Being "present"-oriented, they may not wish to recall the painful past that brought them in for therapy. Neither will they wish to anticipate future problems they feel do not have relevance to the present situation. In the absence of verbal feedback, the therapist may need to maximize her observational skills in evaluating the family's progress. She will need to ascertain whether further therapy is required. A therapist should participate in and be a part of the family's activities, including home visits, participation in seasonal ceremonies, and other rituals. Whenever the family can maintain an open system within the outside the family, renew relationships with relatives, and deal effectively with societal agencies and resources, termination is in order. The intense interactive subsystem relationship characteristic of a nuclear family in a dominant society should not be used as a yardstick in evaluating an American Indian family. Instead, the inclusive extended family framework should always be kept in mind in the evaluation of a family's functioning.

Some family members are so psychologically isolated and emotionally deprived that the relationship with the therapist may represent the first stable nurturing relationship they have ever experienced. They may interpret termination as a major loss in their lives. A therapist needs to be comfortable with this type of dependence and not view such behavior as deceptive manipulation. The termination process should take into consideration the American Indian client's concept of time and space in a relationship. Because the relationship has taken a long time to build, it will also take a long time to end. Some families may never want to end a good relationship. They learn to respect and love the therapist as a member of their family, and they may wish to maintain contact with the therapist even after the successful achievement of therapy goals. A therapist should learn to treasure such a natural relationship and not allow her "professionalism" to spoil a genuine human sharing.

The preceding discussion should be helpful in understanding American Indian families and applying family structure and communication theoretical perspectives and emic-based practice principles. Part 3 of this chapter will present a case example to explicate and delineate how these family theoretical perspectives and emic-based practice principles can be integrated in actual work with an American Indian family.

PART 3: CASE ILLUSTRATION

The Redthunder family was referred to me by a school counselor who claimed that 13-year-old Ron Redthunder was "beside himself." According to the counselor, Ron had been a quiet, "well-behaved" student and a good athlete. Over the past three months, Ron had "changed." He now attended school irregularly with dirty clothes, exhibited destructive behavior in class, and refused to speak to anybody.

Convey interest in client.	When Ron showed up in my office, I immediately told him that I *had wanted to come by his school* to visit with him but changed my mind for I did not *want his classmates* to think that he was in trouble.
Convey sensitivity and respect for client as an individual.	Ron glanced at me and said nothing. He
Create comfortable environment for client.	then glanced at some *Indian art and craftwork* in my office. These had been given to me by my former clients. I asked him to feel
Convey Indian time orientation.	free *to take time* to look at them. Ron was also interested in the wall poster with
To shift power position and to help client feel relaxed.	pictures of Navajo Indians. I *asked Ron to explain to me* what these symbols on the

Client showed beginning trust.

picture meant. Ron smiled and said that he wished he knew.

To establish family ties.

Then, hesitantly, Ron asked if I was Indian. I replied smilingly, "No, but *I feel we are cousins* for history tells us that thousands of years ago, "Indians migrated from China." Ron was very interested in my explanation and my ethnic background.

Client showed sign of trust.

He *volunteered* that he had once heard a similar story from his grandmother who died three months ago. I responded that I was sorry to learn about the death of his grandmother. Ron commented, "It [*death* of grandmother] *hit my mother* real hard." I responded that his mother and grandmother must have been *very close emotionally*. Ron replied sadly with his eyes down, "yes!"

Sharing family secret.

Constructing a partial genogram.

Respect client's time orientation and premature self-disclosure.

I did not wish to *rush* Ron at our first meeting, so I expressed pleasure at meeting him and talking with him. I briefly explained the agency (Transcultural Family Center) function and my role as a therapist.

Entering into the client's space.

Because I was *interested in meeting his family*, with his permission, we arranged our next meeting at his home. As he parted, he quipped, "Do you know Karate?" I quipped back, "*Yes, I do know 'hi-Karate.'*" We both laughed.

Use of humor.

Flexibility with time.

Joining technique.

Cultural mapping.

Matrilineal family background, multiple household.
Growing up with traditional values.

My next visit with Ron and his mother, Mrs. Redthunder (R.) took place at their home and *lasted four hours*. The first hour *Mrs. R. explained to me how to grow vegetables*. We visited the home vegetable garden. As Mrs. R became comfortable with me, she began to talk about *her family background*. She and her husband (Mr. R.) met in Phoenix, Arizona, 15 years ago when both worked for a meat company. Mrs. R., a *Hopi* Indian from New Mexico, grew up *on a reservation* with both parents, one brother, two sisters, and one male counsin. She *recalled many good times while growing up*. Five years ago, her mother's health began to deteriorate. Mrs.

Security of extended family ties.

R. invited her to live with the family. "I needed my mother as much as she needed me," Mrs. R. stated.

Mrs. R. volunteered that her mother's recent death was by no means a surprise, but it did immobilize her to the point she *could not eat, sleep, or do her regular house* *chores.* She felt that all her energy had "gone out" on her and that her financial inability to return her mother's body to the reservation for burial was something "that I *couldn't live with.*" "All this doesn't help my high blood pressure and dental problems," Mrs. R. continued.

Depression caused by grief and disconnection.

Cultural taboo.

Allow client to gather her spirits without interruption.

After *a long pause* (about two minutes), Mrs. R. volunteered that if it was not for her son, Ron, she could never have continued to live. I inquired to what extent Ron had comforted and assisted her. "*He* *[Ron] is the only person I talk to,*" replied Mrs. R.

Mother-son enmeshment, cause for Ron's school problem.

In my next visit with the family, I had an opportunity to talk with Mr. R. He is a 41-year-old Pueblo Indian who grew up in Los Angeles. His parents had died when he was young, and he had limited *knowledge* *of his tribal background.*

Less traditional, more acculturated.

Mr. R. is a truck driver, on the road three weeks out of a month. He often expressed mixed feelings about the road and complained, "I feel a *total stranger at home.*" Mr. R. elaborated that his wife would not involve him in the care of their son, and that the *marital relationship* had deteriorated. "My *being gone* so much of the time *didn't help,*" volunteered Mr. R.

Isolation partly caused by Hopi tribal practice, excluding husband from child rearing.
Weak spouse subsystem partly caused by triangulation.
Circular repercussion.

The family's transitional cultural map is described in Figure 3.1.

Systemic diagnosis.

Structurally, it is apparent that the family relationship triangulated with mother-son, excluding the father. This phenomenon was created partly due to cross-tribal child-rearing practices, the death of Mrs. R.'s mother, the husband's job, a general lack of extended family support, and the closed

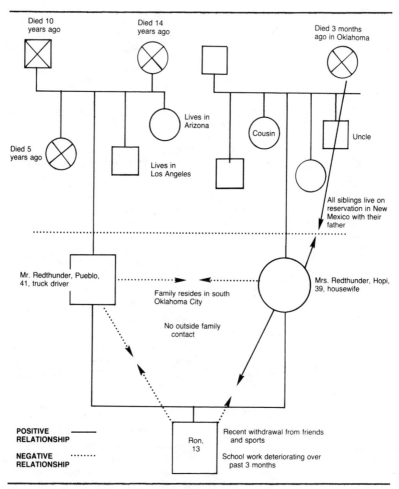

Figure 3.1 Family Cultural Transitional Map and Genogram

system that the family had with the community at large. The enmeshment between the mother and son temporarily crippled the normal development of the acculturated adolescent son whose need to individuate triggered his depression, which was manifested in problems at school.

As the first step to therapy, I took Mrs. R. *to a free health and dental clinic* (the family was in a poor financial situation). Once the

Concrete service to meet basic needs; technique of joining.

working relationship was secured, I involved the family in restructuring therapy through repairing the spousal relationship. This was hampered by Mr. R.'s consistent absence from the family because of his job. When Mr. R. was available for couple interaction, Mrs. R. showed great difficulty in relinquishing her power role (a trait she had inherited from the Hopi tradition). When the couple bogged down and was frustrated with their instructed ways of interaction, they vented, "*Our folks did not*

Expected resistance due to cultural residues.

Promoting interdependency technique.

talk to each other this way." I was empathic with their concerns but *challenged them to build an interdependent* relationship and work for the well-being of the family.

Aware of the influence of extended family ties, I *introduced the family to a Pan-American Indian organization.* There Mrs. R. met a distant cousin of her mothers. Two months later, Mrs. R.'s cousin helped her *secure a part-time job* at the same place where she worked. They later managed to take a trip back to the Hopi reservation. Mrs. R. had an opportunity to participate in a burial ceremony and to *grieve over her own mother's death.*

Restructure extended family ties.

Create an open system external to family.

A traditional grief process.

The Redthunder's *couple relationship* progressed to a point where Mr. R. was willing to spend more time at home. He began to develop and enjoy a *new relationship with his son.* Ron no longer *had difficulties at school.*

Improved spouse relational subsystem.

Restructure father-son relationship.

Problem solving through systemic change.

Over a six-month period, I had 14 contacts with the family. Most meetings took place in the family home. Some contacts lasted only 20 minutes; others lasted one to four hours. At the beginning phase of therapy, I *gave the family my home telephone number* to let them know I was always available. Since the therapy terminated, the family has continued to invite me to ceremonial feasts. Occasionally, they still supply me with home-grown vegetables.

Therapist as family member.

Good relationship never ends.

Giveaway practice.

PART 4: CULTURALLY RELEVANT TECHNIQUES AND SKILLS FOR SPECIFIC THERAPY MODALITIES

Marital Therapy

Historically, when American Indian families resided with their clan and extended family members, there was less marital discord due to clear role expectations and a strong familiar support system. As times change, American Indian families, like families of the dominant society and other ethnic groups, are subjected to rapid political and social change and ever-increasing demands within and outside the family. American Indian families gradually are forced to shift from inclusive extended family ties to an exclusive nuclear family system. They seldom are prepared for this change. Consequently, the divorce rate among American Indian couples has skyrocketed and other social indicators reflect family dysfunction in the contemporary world (Byler, 1977). When a couple experiences marital discord, other unresolved problems often appear, including alcoholism, suicide, and unemployment. Marital discord can also be reflected in parent-child conflicts, with the child bearing the parental marital symptoms (Satir, 1967). Obviously, marital therapy constitutes one of the most important therapeutic modalities for the prevention of family breakdown and erosion. The following guidelines are suggested while providing marital therapy to an American Indian couple.

Assessing when Marital Therapy Is Indicated

The primary focus of marital therapy is on the dyadic interpersonal relationship between husband and wife. The importance of this relationship centers on a nuclear family system framework with the implication that the family has only its limited nuclear family members to interact with and to meet their needs. However, such is not the case within the American Indian extended family system. Individual members grew up traditionally in an extended family clan system and children tend to maintain such a system when they grow up, marry, have children and grandchildren. This system provides them with security, hope, and the necessary means to meet their needs and for problem solving, including marital problems. Hence it is vital that a marital therapist keep this emic cultural framework in perspective when recommending marital therapy for problem solving for an Indian couple. If a therapist neglects this framework, she may find it impossible to mobilize the couple for problem solving.

Incorporating the Extended Family System in Marital Therapy

By using the extended family system framework, a therapist can assess marital problems according to the relational transaction the couple has with extended family members. Minuchin's system boundaries concept can be extremely helpful in assessing the degree of enmeshment or disengagement experienced by the couple. Couple enmeshment can take the form of excessive interaction between the couple excluding other subsystems such as children and other relatives. However, couple enmeshment within American Indian families may take place between one partner with his or her family of origin, such as grandparent, father, mother, aunt, uncle, cousin, and so on. Bowen's intergenerational perspective can be used to assist the enmeshed partner to redefine and restructure a new relational boundary.

Couple disengagement occurs most frequently among urban American Indian families who are burdened by different working hours, the rapid pace of urban life, and total isolation from the extended family and from the community at large. Often the solution to couple disengagement is mobilization and restructuring of extended family ties whereby the couple can regain a support system. To do less, the therapist may tend to exacerbate further the couple relationship and cause a breakdown of the marriage. At times, the general unavailability of extended family ties and the high percentage of intermarriage among urban American Indians may leave couple therapy as the best viable alternative for resolving marital problems. Couple therapy can often be used to teach problem-solving skills, family developmental task skills, child-rearing skills, financial management, and sexual adjustment.

Assessing the Couple's Readiness for Couple Therapy

Couple therapy for problem solving with the family is a totally new concept to most American Indian couples. In the past, couple conflicts were resolved within the extended family system or clan with the elders prescribing proper directions. Because self-disclosure is uncommon among most Indians, disclosure of unpleasant marital secrets to a stranger may become totally unbearable. However, situations do develop whereby a family therapist is called in for assistance. Such situations normally develop when the couple's child experiences behavioral problems at school or in the community, when a family member becomes seriously ill, or when a family member faces legal problems resulting from drunk driving, and so on.

As American Indians become increasingly acculturated and involved in intermarriage, more are seeking marital therapy to help resolve their problems. The therapist should first assess how ready each and both partners are for marital therapy. Factors involved in assessing the couple's readiness include (1) motivation (what brings them in for therapy), (2) each partner's level of acculturation, (3) their ability to interact verbally in conjoint therapy, (4) traditional tribal practices relating to husband/wife relationship, and (5) their realistic expectations of the role of the therapist. Generally, the couple is ready and can be benefited by couple therapy if they seek it and are committed to work toward improving their situation. The more acculturated the husband and wife are, the less resistive they are in therapy.

Marital therapy will be valuable only if the couple can interact with each other and with the therapist. This can be difficult to assess initially because American Indians are less prone to verbalize. Each partner may belong to a different tribe, each prescribing different sex-role relationships with children, in-laws, and relatives. The use of a genogram to sort out these differences at the beginning of a marital therapy session can help the couple understand and resolve their problems. The couple needs to understand that the therapist is not a medicine person who will solve their problem for them. The role of the therapist and the respective roles of the couple in therapy should be specified and agreed upon before actual therapy is initiated.

Teaching the Couple Communication Skills

American Indian couples, like married couples of other races, wish to live in a harmonious relationship with each other. The nuclear family system created by the process of migration and cultural change forces them to interact intimately for daily problem solving. Often the couple is ill-prepared. In addition, if the husband and/or wife grew up in boarding schools or away from home, they were deprived of a functional couple interactive model. Specially, the couple needs to learn that conflict is an inherent part of an intimate couple relationship. The couple should learn how to detect "pinch point" in a relationship before it develops into a "crunch" or "out of hand" situation. They need assertiveness training in relating their feelings and intentions to each other. Instead of assuming an irrelevant (Satir, 1967) role or a blamer role, each partner should learn to communicate openly and congruently in a "I count me, I count you" style. The couple needs to learn effective communication feedback skills and techniques so each can be listened to without disruption and distortion. To resolve a difficult problem in which both partners have a deep emotional investment, a structure for effective sharing is needed. In such a structure, a mutually agreeable time, a place, and energy are reserved for problem solving. The couple needs to realize that although other basic needs of daily living, such as cooking, washing, and child rearing, are important and should take precedence, effective couple relationship at times can be as important or more important than taking care of those daily chores. If the couple's conflict remains unresolved, it drains their energies and effectiveness in performing the necessary daily chores. At times, one partner or the other can become physically ill and incapacitated because of continued unresolved marital strife. American Indians respect others and value egalitarian interdependent relationships. Marital therapy can provide the missing link for their realization of a harmonious relationship.

Using Cotherapists as Interactive Models

Consistent with American Indians' learning style of observation and active participation, a cotherapist model can be ideal in marital therapy with American Indian couples (Norlin and Ho, 1977). Preferably, the composition of the cotherapist team should be male/female. The leadership style of the cotherapist team should be guided according to the tribal customs on the part of the husband and wife. For example, if the wife came from a matrilineal tribe, the female cotherapist may need to be more assertive at least at the onset of the therapy session. Leadership style on the part of a cotherapist team changes according to the needs presented by the couple in therapy. The cotherapist team approach provides an American Indian couple with many advantages, including (1) an effective interactive model for the couple to emulate, (2) a therapy process that resembles a natural extended family system interaction, and (3) a secure learning environment for the couple to observe another couple (therapist team) disagreeing. It also serves as an educative and experiential tool to teach the couple how to express warm and supportive feelings.

Divorce Therapy

The divorce rate among American Indians ranks very high. This is to be expected as many political and social factors are working against married couples. These factors include the breakdown of extended family ties, highest rate of unemployment, unmet physical and economic needs, poor physical and mental health, highest rate of alcoholism and attempted suicides, and intermarriage. American Indians' traditional respect for individuality, a person's right to make his or her own decisions, and their strong belief in noninterference make divorce a socially acceptable behavior, and there is no negative stigma attached. Further, the unconditional acceptance of a divorcée by the extended family and the practice of multiple households facilitate post divorce adjustment and greatly reduces the burden that a divorcée normally experiences. Even though divorce is fairly common among American Indians, some divorcées have difficulties and need therapy. The following recommendations are provided to ensure such clients receive services responsive to their needs.

Exploring Divorce Experiences and Consequences

Some Indians experiencing divorce harbor guilt feelings. Such guilt feelings may occur when a person thinks he has behaved irresponsibly and that his doing so adversely affects his children. Early experiences in boarding schools and Christian religious teachings may also arouse guilt feelings. If a person lacked a warm, secure home environment to grow up in as a child, he may project that his primary mission in life is to provide for his children a stable home environment. Such unreal intergenerational transmission is sure to produce disappointment and can make a person feel unfulfilled and extremely depressed. A couple's depressive symptoms, in turn, can affect their normal functioning.

Traditionally, when an individual experienced divorce, she had the blessings and the support of her extended family, who usually lived nearby. Because of migration and other factors related to job opportunity, the divorcée may be far away physically and emotionally from her original extended family. The vacuum created by divorce can throw the divorcée into a state of total frustration and desperation. This crisis can be compounded by the fact that the divorcée has no prior knowledge or experience in utilizing community health and social services. The role of the therapist is to assess the client's needs and act quickly to help the client resolve them.

Providing the Client with Extended Family and Social Support

Divorce can be especially traumatic if the decision to end the marriage is not mutual and if the divorced partner (usually a female) has no employable skills. Further, the divorcée may be left with several children to support. The therapist's first task is to assess structurally the extent of the divorcée's extended family support system. Should the divorcée's extended family system be unavailable due to geographical distance or emotional cutoff, the next best possible extended family system for the divorcée may be the Pan-American Indian Organization or an Indian church group. The divorcée also needs to be informed of public health and social agencies that can provide temporary relief for herself and the family.

Whenever the divorcée is temporarily incapacitated by the divorce, the therapist needs to "assume th executive role" of the family. This involves finding a means to meet the family's basic needs and to provide the divorce with concrete and emotional support. Concrete support may include transporting her to a health clinic and helping her food shop. Some clients, during this critical stage, become very emotional and highly dependent. The therapist should anticipate and be comfortable with the client's dependency, while at the same time helping her to become interdependent and work with other support groups.

Postdivorce Adjustment and Building New Relationships

Once the critical stage of divorce is stabilized and the family's basic needs are being met, the therapist's next task is to engage the client to assess her emotional feelings about the previous spouse. Some clients find it difficult to acknowledge the finality of the divorce. The former spouse, after all, remains her children's father. The therapist's role is to sensitize the client to the possible negative effects this emotional tie may

how to go about getting what she needs. These characteristics should not be misconstrued as competitiveness and aggression, which are antithetical to American Indian culture. Instead, they are essential qualities to live responsibly with oneself and with others.

Therapy with a Reconstituted Family

Because of American Indians' past and present experience in living in multiple households, the reconstituted family phenomenon should present less of a problem to them than it does for the dominant culture families whose past references are limited to the single-household nuclear family. Yet, an Indian family's composition, their past relationships, and loyalties with previous marriages make life in a reconstituted family a potentially conflictual one. The following recommendations are suggested in providing family therapy for a reconstituted family involving American Indian families.

Focusing on Parental Coalition

Many American Indians remarry because of their love and affection for what is best for their children. American Indians are not used to living on their own, nor do they choose to live by themselves. When an opportunity arrives to share households with another single parent or family, they choose to do so for the sake of the whole family. Problems arise when the children encounter conflicts with their stepparent or stepbrothers or sisters. If children are no longer happy, as originally expected by the parents, the couple may want to end the marriage.

Minuchin's structural theory has a great deal of appeal in terms of helping an American Indian couple solidify their marital relationship. This is the primary step to ensuring the good functioning of the constituted family. A mutually supportive couple relationship influences the success of the parents' relationship with the children (Duberman, 1975). American Indian parents are not accustomed to focusing on themselves, nor do they have prior experience in forming close spousal relationships. Solidification of the spousal subsystem boundary does not come easy for them. A therapist can motivate the couple to work on their relationship as a means to ensure their children's happiness in the reconstituted family.

A couple in a reconstituted family may carry with them unrealistic expectations from previous marriages. Such expectations usually are distorted and fantasy-based. These can be detrimental to the present marriage and should be discouraged.

Clear Role Definition and Expectations of
Family Members

Mutual expectations of the reconstituted couple need clarification. Other family members, including siblings, cousins, aunts, or uncles who live in the same household, also need a clear understanding of their roles and functions in the reconstituted family. American Indians grow up in groups and are familiar with group discussion for problem solving. It is vital that each family member's role be clearly spelled out and understood so that unnecessary misunderstandings are avoided and potential conflicts have a base for satisfactory resolution.

Expectation often must be carefully negotiated. Tribal differences, varied backgrounds of reconstituted families, and past experiences with previous spouses and family all complicate the negotiation process. The therapist can challenge family members and remind them that interdependent living is characteristic of American Indian culture. Any newly reconstituted family should learn negotiation and problem-solving skills that require assertive effort and readjustment of traditional time orientation. They need to learn that constant negotiation among family members is integral to family well-being, including the reconstituted family.

Involving Extended Family Members

The well-being of a reconstituted family depends on the family's relationship with its extended family members. This is particularly true with American Indian families, whose strong influence is deeply felt by every family member from the moment of birth. If the interface between the reconstituted family and the extended family is strenuous, the former will run the risk of being enmeshed. The emotional cutoff from extended family members is so costly that it is bound to have a negative effect on the reconstituted family and all its members. The therapist should assess the degree of influence that the extended family exerts on the reconstituted family. If the influence is strong, the therapist may need to involve an extended family member(s) in therapy sessions. The therapist should never assume that the interface between the reconstituted family and the extended family naturally constitutes an "enmeshment." In American Indian culture, such relationships generally characterize strength and should be respected and capitalized on in family therapy, particularly with reconstituted families.

PART V: CONCLUSION

This chapter has focused on the holistic view and emic approach in work with American Indian families during different phases of family therapy. Despite their rich tradition and cultural heritage, American Indian families historically have been victimized by rapid social changes and insensitive acculturation legislation and political processes. Today, they are like immigrants in their own native land. To survive, they are forced to adopt economic and political skills of the dominant culture, while at the same time tenaciously and courageously trying to preserve their own culture.

The strength of the American Indian family lies with its strong extended family ties and multiple household systems. Within this interdependent framework, a family finds its place and derives its worth. This same traditional system provides a family with problem-solving strengths. A family therapist can serve American Indian families only if she recognizes the strength of the extended family system and respects the individual and his traditional culture.

4

Family Therapy with Hispanic Americans

PART 1: PRETHERAPY PHASE CONSIDERATIONS

The Hispanic American Family Structure

Hispanic Americans constitute the second largest minority group in the United States and the fastest growing ethnic group in the country (Russell and Satterwhite, 1978). Current census figures show the Hispanic population to number 12 million (U.S. Bureau of the Census, 1980a). The census breakdown of Hispanic groups reports: Mexican American, 7.2 million; Puerto Rican, 1.8 million; and Spanish, 3 million. The latter category includes persons of Central or South American, Cuban, and "other" Spanish origins. These estimates are probably very conservative. Spanish-surnamed Americans have been typically undercounted due to inaccurate census procedures, such as failure to provide enough bilingual interviewers (Hernandez, Estrada, and Alvirez, 1973).

Hispanic Americans are also known as Chicanos, Latinos, Mexicanos, Hispanos, Spanish-speaking Americans, Spanish Americans, and Spanish-surnamed Americans. Although the Mexican American, the Puerto Rican, the Cuban, and other Spanish-speaking minorities in the United States share a Hispanic cultural background, there are important differences among them. In Puerto Rico, the indigenous Indians were virtually eradicated by the Spaniards, who replaced them with African slaves (Fitzpatrick, 1981). Today's Puerto Rican culture reflects that blend. In Mexico, native Indian populations had achieved a high degree of civilization but still were highly subjugated by the Spaniards. Mexican culture became a blend of the Indian and the Spanish (Padilla and Ruiz, 1973). The Cuban culture is a blending of

Spanish and African cultures (Bustamante and Santa Cruz, 1975; Ortiz, 1973), and its unique historical connection to powerful nations such as Spain, the United States, and the Soviet Union further distinguishes Cubans from other Latin countries.

The majority of Hispanic Americans live at a low socioeconomic level. They are also severely underrepresented in higher levels of education and in occupational and professional jobs (U.S. Bureau of the Census, 1980c). Research has shown that Hispanics "suffer the full impact of the 'culture poverty' . . . low income, unemployment, underemployment, undereducation, poor housing, prejudice, discrimination, and cultural/linguistic barriers" (President's Commission on Mental Health, 1978, p. 905). Despite the severe economic stresses and the adverse political/social acculturation process, Hispanics usually do not seek mental health services, not even family therapy (Casas and Keefe, 1980; Acosta, 1977). Factors contributing to their not seeking and receiving proper services include institutional barriers, language difficulty, poor finances, and a reluctance to bring shame to the family. The family is viewed as the primary source of support for its members (Bernal and Flores-Ortiz, 1982). Because the family plays a very vital role in the lives of this large ethnic group, the following discussion aims to present an overview of the cultural values and the family structure of Hispanic Americans.

Cultural Values in Relation to Family Structure

The heritage of Hispanic Americans is rich and diverse. However, some commonalities do exist, such as shared lineage with both Spanish and local indigenous Indian groups. Certain unifying cultural concepts also distinguish them from the dominant society. These cultural concepts form the foundation for the Hispanic-American family structure and relationships. These cultural concepts include familism, personalism, hierarchy, spiritualism, and fatalism. Each of these is described below.

Familism. The Hispanic American has a very deep awareness of and pride in his membership in the family. The importance of family membership and belonging cuts across caste lines and socioeconomic conditions. An individual's self-confidence, worth, security, and identity are determined by his relationship to other family members. The importance of family is evident in the Hispanic's use of family names

(Fitzpatrick, 1981). The man generally uses both his father's and mother's name together with his given name, for example, Jose Garcia Rivera. Garcia is his father's family name and Rivera is his mother's family name. If the man is to be addressed by only one name, the father's family name is used. This reflects the patriarchal pattern of the Hispanic family.

Because the family is of great importance to the individual, each member has a deep sense of family obligation. The needs of the family collectively may supersede individual needs. The family is the strongest area of life activities. It is a closely knit group in which all members enjoy status and esteem (Ulibarri, 1970, p. 31). During good times or during crisis, the family's name and family members' welfare always come first. It is this sense of family obligation that should be capitalized on during therapy.

Personalism. Along with the concept of familism, a Hispanic defines his self-worth in terms of those inner qualities that give him self-respect and earn him the respect of others. He feels an inner dignity (*dignidad*); and expects others to show respect (*respeto*) for that "dignidad." This concept of personalism probably emanated from the caste system that exists in most Latin American countries. The rich and the poor are *fixed* in their socioeconomic status, with limited opportunities for mobility.

White middle-class Americans stress individualism and actually value the individual in terms of his ability to compete for higher social and economic status. The Hispanic culture values those inner qualities that constitute the uniqueness of the person and his goodness in himself. A Hispanic who believes that every individual has some sense of personal dignity will be sensitive about showing proper respect to others and demanding it for himself. This expectation is intensified when a Hispanic first encounters a non-Hispanic and interprets the latter's insensitivity as personal insult or disdain. Contrarily, if personalism is reciprocated in a social or professional interaction, trust is developed and so is obligation. Hence a Hispanic family may seek and perhaps benefit from family therapy not because of agency affiliation or the professional reputation of the therapist, but simply because of the therapist's skill and ability to convey *personalism* when dealing with the family.

Closely related to the concept of personalism is the quality *machismo*, literally, maleness. Machismo is referred to as a quality of personal magnetism that impresses and influences others. It is a style of personal daring by which one faces challenge, danger, and threats with calmness and self-possession. A man's display of machismo can become a stumbling block to the family therapy progress. Conversely, machismo is a quality that can also be challenged and promoted during the course of family therapy (Bernal and Flores-Ortiz, 1982).

Sense of hierarchy. Historically, the Hispanics lived in a world of two class systems: high and low. Members rarely conceived the possibility of moving out of the class into which they were born. Social class position was as fixed and natural as the parts of their bodies. The Hispanic sense of hierarchy is further manifested in the leadership structure of the family where the father occupies the role of superior authority and the mother's role is to follow. In addition to gender hierarchy, there is also generational hierarchy in which parents expect to be obeyed when they advise their children. Younger children are expected to obey older children who serve as role models. The Hispanic has a distinct concept of personal worth from an individual's position in the social structure. The concept of hierarchy has great therapeutic implications for family therapy and in the dynamics of family communication and the problem-solving process.

Spiritualism. Hispanics celebrate life. They emphasize spiritual values and are willing to sacrifice material satisfaction for spiritual goals. Catholicism is the predominant religion for Hispanic Americans (Grebler, Moore, and Guzman, 1973). Their Roman Catholic ways of worship, however, differ from other ethnic groups, such as the Irish. Hispanics believe they can make direct contact with God and the supernatural without the assistance of intervention of clergy. A significant part of the Hispanic population, especially the Puerto Ricans, believes in spiritualism. They believe the visible world is surrounded by an invisible world inhabited by good and evil spirits who influence human behavior (Delgado, 1978). Thus spirits can either protect or harm, and prevent or cause illness. In order to be protected by good spirits, an individual is expected to produce good and charitable deeds in a secular world.

Folklore that combines the heritage of Spanish Catholic medical and religious practices with African and Indian belief systems is common among Hispanics. For example, the practice of *santeria*, which combines Catholicism with Yorubans, an African belief, and the practice of *espiritismo* (exorcising evil spirits) are prevalent throughout Latino communities (Gonzales-Wippler, 1975; Morales-Dorta, 1976). Hence with certain families, mobilizing the support systems available through these folk traditions can augment family therapy, and the combination should have powerful therapeutic effects.

Fatalism. Hispanics value the spirit and soul as much more important than the body and worldly materialism. A Hispanic person tends to think in terms of transcendent qualities such as justice, loyalty, or love. He is not preoccupied with mastering the world. He has a keen sense of destiny (partly related to fundamental fears of the sacred) and a sense of divine providence governing the world. The popular song, "Que sera' sera' " (Whatever will be, will be) and "Si Dios quiere" (If God wills it), reflect the Hispanic's expression of fatalism. This fatalism may in part explain why Hispanics refuse, or are reluctant, to engage in family therapy. The fatalistic attitude can serve as a functional quality leading to the acceptance of many tragic and unfortunate events as inevitable. Furthermore, it softens the sense of despair or personal failure that is the common by-product of the middle-class American value system.

These common cultural Hispanic values of familism, personalism, hierarchy, spiritualism, and fatalism significantly influence Hispanic family organization and structure. A discussion of how these values affect subunits and overall family interaction follows.

Traditional Family Structure and Extended Family Ties

The Hispanic nuclear family is embedded in an extended family network that includes such relatives as grandparents, uncles, aunts, and cousins (Madsen, 1964). The extended family often includes lifelong friends also, and kin created through a Catholic baptismal custom. The child by this process acquires a godmother (*madrina*) and godfather (*Padrino*) who directly share responsibility for the child's welfare and thus form coparent bonds with the child's parents. The function of godparents is to provide security, guidance, and love for the godchild. They may be chosen from among members of the extended family or from outside the family. Reasons for selecting a particular godparent may include proximity, friendship, wealth, and social or political status. The two most important types of godparents are those selected at baptism and marriage. The godparents of baptism assume responsibility for the child if birth parents become unable to fulfill their duties. Godparents of marriage contribute to the expenses of the wedding and may function as mediators between the couple in case of quarrels or separations (Abad, Ramos, and Boyce, 1974).

During times of crisis, transferring children from one nuclear family to another within the extended family system is a common practice among Hispanics. Unless the practice is regarded as a problem by the family, a therapist working with the family should not criticize or attempt to alter such arrangements.

Interdependence, both intergenerational and lateral, characterizes the Hispanic extended family supportive network. Alvirez et al. (1981) use "familism" to describe this system of extended kinship ties and its interdependence beyond the nuclear family. These family connections and the frequency of contact among members tend to be greater than those of Anglo Americans (Padilla, Carlos, and Keefe, 1976).

Mate Selection and
Husband/Wife Relationship

Traditionally, intermingling and dating among young Hispanics was much more restricted. A young man interested in a young woman was expected to speak to the parents of the girl, particularly the father, to declare his intentions. Therefore, a serious courtship could never even begin if the families disapproved. When a marriage materialized, Hispanics usually practiced patrilocal residence, whereby a young bride lived with her husband's family. The traditional ideal prescribed that the daughter-in-law have the same obligations as a daughter and, therefore, perform many domestic chores under the supervision of her mother-in-law.

The hierarchical role of male dominance and female submission rooted in Spanish customs defines the husband and wife relationship. The husband assumes the instrumental role of provider and protector of the family and the wife the expressive role of homemaker and caretaker. The Hispanic man is expected to be dignified, hardworking, macho. *Machismo* (maleness, virility) to the Hispanic man is a desirable combination of virtue, courage, romanticism, and fearlessness (Abad, Ramos, and Boyce, 1974). Because it is the wife's responsibility to care for the home and to keep the family together, the husband is not expected to assume household tasks or help care for the children. This role arrangement results in wives assuming power behind the scenes, while overtly supporting their husband's authority (Stevens, 1973). Because it is the existence of children that validates and cements the marriage, motherly love (*el amor de madre*) is a much greater force than wifely love.

The outward compliance with the cultural ideal of male dominance and female submission may be more social fiction than an actuality. In reality, Hispanic families may include husbands who are domineering and patriarchal (Penalosa, 1968), who are submissive and dependent on their wives for major decisions, or who follow a more egalitarian power struggle (Hawkes and Taylor, 1975). Also, as Hispanic Americans move up the socioeconomic ladder to more middle-class levels, assimilation of Anglo life-style occurs, and husband-wife sex-role delineations become less strict.

Parent-Child Relationship

The parental functions of Hispanics follow the cultural prescriptions for the husband-wife relationship. The Hispanic father disciplines and controls, while the mother provides nurturance and support. Consistent with the Hispanic hierarchical cultural orientation, the status of the parents is high and that of children low. Parents engender the respeto (respect) of children through complementary transactions. Most parents would not expect or want to be friends with their children.

The role of the mother is idealized and equated with self-denial and abnegation. While the father generally is not involved in the caretaking of the child, he protects the mother and demands that children obey her. He usually is relaxed and playful with younger children and more stern and strict with older children, especially daughters (Fitzpatrick, 1981, p. 209). The father's disciplinary role reduces his direct involvement with the children while it reinforces the mother's centrality in the family. Such a coalition between mother and children is fairly typical among Hispanic families and should not be labeled as "pathological triangulation" in need of change or therapy.

Although Hispanic families today usually reside in single households (Mindel, 1980), extended family members, such as grandparents, uncles, aunts, and godparents, perform many parental functions. They provide nurturance, support, guidance, and controlling influence for the children. Child-rearing practices that reflect Hispanic American parental attitudes have been described using the dimensions of cooperation versus competition and achievement aspirations. While Anglo American children show greater competitiveness and achievement aspirations, Hispanic American children show greater cooperation (Kagan and Buriel, 1977).

Sibling Relationship

The sibling relationship within a Hispanic family is characterized by a large size, vertical hierarchical structure, and male sex-role dominance.

Relationships between cousins are often close, especially between *primo hermanos* (first cousins), and may resemble a sibling relationship. Due to parental encouragement to form solidification within the family, it is common for Hispanic children to have few peers or friends other than their siblings and cousins.

Early in life, siblings are assigned real responsibilities necessary for the functioning of the household (Murillo, 1971, p. 104). They are expected to get along with each other, with the older taking care of the younger and the brothers protecting the sisters. Hispanic parents typically accord authority to older siblings and delegate supervisory and caretaking functions to them. This subordinates the younger children to the older children and makes all of them responsible for household chores.

Cross-sex sibling companionship is curtailed at adolescence and is replaced by complementary functions such as girls doing household chores and boys chaperoning and protecting girls. Female siblings learn their proper role early in life. A girl is afforded less freedom than her brothers. She begins to play the role of mother and homemaker by caring for younger brothers and sisters and by helping with the housework. Because children are taught respect, cooperation, and control of aggression (Rothenberg, 1964) at an early age, there is little sibling rivalry. Even during adulthood, emotional support, guidance, and practical help among siblings is usual. Male dominance and sibling order remain the compelling factors in adult-sibling relationships and interactions.

Intermarriage

Hispanic Americans have a long history of intermarriage, and this trend seems to be continuing. According to the 1980 census, in New York state, 34% of second-generation Puerto Rican men and 32% of second-generation Puerto Rican women married and living with their spouses are married to non-Puerto Ricans. Nationally, this is higher: 68% of second-generation Puerto Rican men and 65% of the women married and living with their spouses were married to non-Puerto Ricans. In Albuquerque, Los Angeles, and San Antonio, the latest available figures indicate as many as one in three Mexican Americans marry an Anglo (Alvirez et al., 1981).

Upward mobility for Hispanics is positively associated with inter-marriage (Grebler et al., 1970). Third-generation Hispanics exhibit higher rates of intermarriage than do those of the second generation (Alvirez et al., 1981). Spanish-surnamed females tend to marry outside of the ethnicity more frequently than do Spanish-surnamed males. They do so to gain social class standing and possibly a more egalitarian marriage. Marital conflict can arise when Anglo females tend not to be as husband- and family-oriented as Hispanic males expect them to be. Greater stability is, therefore, predicted for the Anglo male/ Hispanic female type of intermarriage as compared to the Hispanic male/ Anglo female marriage (Muguia and Cazares, 1982). Regardless, there is a higher potential in any intermarriage for instability and divorce (Ho, 1984). In view of the diverse cultural background and family patterns of Hispanics and the dominant culture, these intermarried couples are expected to have a high rate of conflict.

Divorce and Remarriage

The majority of Hispanic families remain two-parent families throughout their lifetimes, despite a higher unemployment rate, poorer health, lower socioeconomic conditions, and stresses inherent in immigration and acculturation. National statistics and research data have consistently supported the fact that the divorce rate among Hispanics is lower than that for Anglo populations (Frisbie, Bean, and Eberstein, 1978; Alvirez et al., 1981). The one exception to this is common-law marriages in urban cities where the single-parent household is not uncommon among Hispanics (Fitzpatrick, 1981, p. 197).

The low divorce rate of Hispanics may be closely related to their cultural values of familism, where self-worth is dependent upon one's belonging and one's obligation to the family. The Hispanic's vertical family structure with male dominance conflicts with the egalitarian concept of the dominant society, but it clearly explicates the role definition in marriages. Spousal relationships are reinforced by cultural traditions and by extended family ties. The Hispanic female's realistic expectations of the wife's role may help to reduce frustration and disappointment generally associated with romantic love as cherished in the egalitarian relationships of the dominant culture.

The fact that the predominant religion of the Hispanics is Catholicism, which has a strong prohibition against divorce, also contributes to the low rate among Hispanics. Marriage is very much a two-family affair, and a marriage can not be dissolved easily without the sanction of both families. When divorce does occur, the parent granted custody of the children usually has the moral and the practical support of the extended family.

Immigration and Acculturation

Immigration and acculturation can cause tremendous stress for any family. Members are faced with learning a new language and new social and political ways of life. Feelings of isolation and despair are common among new immigrants. To ascertain the impact of immigration and political and cultural adjustment of a Hispanic family, the therapist should start out by identifying their original birthplace(s). Not all Hispanics are immigrants. For example, many Mexican Americans who reside in the southwestern United States were born in the United States. Due to a political agreement between the United States and Mexico and Puerto Rico, immigrants usually enjoy freedom of travel back and forth to visit relatives. Such visits reduce the emotional cutoff normally associated with relocation and immigration. On the other hand, Cuban immigrants until just recently were not allowed to visit their relatives in Cuba.

The timing of migration is another factor affecting the adjustment rate of Hispanics (Casal et al., 1979). For example, the Cuban migration of the 1960s was overrepresented by Whites, disproportionately composed of the upper and middle classes, and heavily aided by major federal (U.S.) programs. Conversely, the 1980 influx of Cuban immigrants was found to consist of 40% non-Whites who were poorly educated and sociopolitical dissidents (Spencer et al., 1981). The new arrivals are destined to encounter more severe immigration and adjustment problems than the 1960 group of immigrants.

Migration usually produces a transitional crisis in the family with predictable stages (Sluzki, 1979). Membership change within the family during migration necessitates family restructuring of roles and functions and transactions. The traditional hierarchical role structure may run into conflict when the husband/father becomes unemployed. The acculturation rate of the children can threaten authoritarian parents who may have to depend on their children to translate for them when dealing with community agencies, immigration authorities, and health care services. The faster rate of acculturation for young Hispanics (Szapocznik et al., 1978) has increased stresses and conflicts in many families. Lack of support outside the family system and fears of crime, drug addition, and more acceptable sexual mores often cause parents to be strict and overprotective with adolescents, especially daughters (Badillo-Ghali, 1977). Children often rebel against their parent's rigid discipline and reject traditional customs that they consider inferior to American mores.

Hispanic women appear to require more time to acculturate than men. This may be due to the passive-submissive role of women in their traditional culture (Szapocznik et al., 1978). If women must work outside of the home to help support the family, they frequently suffer role confusion and conflict. The wife's employable status and earning power may be essential for the economic survival of the family, but it threatens the superiority role of the husband/father. The wife's long working hours outside the home can affect her satisfaction and self-image of a "good" mother. Poor economic conditions, and the frustration and stress inherent in the acculturation process result in various mental health problems for Hispanics (Ruiz, 1977).

Help-Seeking Patterns

Studies indicate that Hispanics do not consider mental health services a solution to their emotional and family problems (Padilla et al., 1976; Casas and Keefe, 1978). Acosta et al. (1982, p. 64) gave the following reasons for Hispanic's underutilization of health and mental health services: (1) language barrier, (2) cultural and social class difference between therapist and patients, (3) insufficient number of mental health facilities, (4) overuse or misuse of physicians for psychological problems, (5) reluctance to recognize the urgency for help, and (6) lack of awareness of the existence of mental health clinics.

Hispanic Americans consider the family their primary source of support. It is difficult for a husband/father who is the head of the family to admit that he is not fulfilling his leadership role of providing for the family. Before outside help is solicited, godparents or compadres usually are consulted. If the family problem involves marital discord, the compadre of marriages may function as mediator for the couple (Falicov, 1982). In a Puerto Rican family, the padrino also is used to mediate intrafamily conflict and as an advocate for the family (Fitzpatrick, 1981). The padrino is an individual, in a higher position of the family structure, who has a personal relationship with the family for whom he provides material needs and emotional guidance.

Because Catholicism plays a vital role in the life of Hispanic Americans, in times of stress and illness, priests, folk healers, and religious leaders can be strong family resources. It is not unusual for a Hispanic American family to equate the role of the family therapist with that of a priest and to expect some immediate help from the therapist. At other times, the Hispanic American client may see the family therapist as a physician to whom he traditionally seeks help for emotional and psychological problems (Padilla et al., 1976).

Mexican Americans attribute family conflicts and financial difficulty as two main causes for their emotional problems (Moll et al., 1976). Among this group, family therapy is fairly well accepted as a methodology for family problem solving, as well as for individual symptoms. Further, the therapist is respected as an individual who possesses authoritative knowledge about human interaction.

In terms of family service needs, Hispanic families can be categorized into three types (Padilla et al., 1976; Casas and Keefe, 1978): (1) newly arrived immigrant families, (2) immigrant-American families, and (3) immigrant-descent families. Newly arrived immigrant families need information, referral, advocacy, and such concrete services as English-language instruction. Due to cultural and language barriers, they seldom seek personal or family therapy. Immigrant-American families are characterized by cultural conflict between foreign-born parents and American-born children. They need help in resolving generational conflicts, communication problems, role clarification, and renegotiation. Native or immigrant-descent families usually are acculturated, speak both languages at home, and can seek help from mainstream social sources, including private practice family therapists.

Applying Culturally Sensitive Family Theories, Models, and Approaches

Behavioral principles of the family communication theory and family structure theory are discussed in this section. Practice principles derived from these theories will be reviewed also. The family communication theory and the family structure theory are useful to a therapist as she or he prepares to work with Hispanic American clients.

Family Communication Theory

The following discussion of the major principles of communication is based primarily on the work of the Mental Research Institute in Palo Alto (Bateson, 1972; Watzlawick, Beavin, and Jackson, 1967; Jackson,

1967, 1968) and the work of Miller, Nunnally, and Wackman (1975). Several factors delineated by Watzlawick et al. are helpful in understanding the pragmatics of communication with Hispanic American families.

Because all behavior is communication of one kind or another, it is impossible not to communicate. A Hispanic American's style of communication is often governed by traditional hierarchical structure. He tends to be formal, indirect, and guarded in public, especially when dealing with a therapist who is considered an authority figure (Falicov, 1982, p. 149). If there are profound differences in style and in motivation, a Hispanic may endure the first encounter with a therapist without displaying signs of displeasure, but he may not return for the next scheduled session. To ensure that a therapeutic communication continue, the therapist should solicit feedback from a Hispanic client. The therapist should state clearly that the client will not be contacted again if he fails to meet the next appointment. The concept of metacommunication, defined as information containing a command, is highly relevant to Hispanic American families. According to Haley (1963), every relationship contains within it an implicit power struggle over who defines the nature of that relationship. The traditional hierarchical structure of the Hispanic American family experienced limited power struggles, because each family member knew his or her position and status in relation to other family members. The infusion of dominant cultural influences on individualism, the process of immigration, and family life cycle adjustment have greatly altered the traditionally prescribed vertical and hierarchical role structure determined by age, sex, generation, and birth order of family members. One of the preliminary challenges for the therapist may be to help the family rework its metacommunication process for problem-solving purposes.

A third principle of communication relates to the "punctuation" of communicational sequences (Bateson, 1972), as exemplified in father-daughter conflict. The immigrant father punctuates the sequence of communication thus: "To be a responsible macho father, I have to make my American-born daughter mind me." The teenage daughter, on the other hand, defines the relationship differently: "I am an American teenager now and a separate individual; I must differentiate myself from my overcontrolling father who tries to suffocate me." The punctuation of the communicational sequences dictate the style each family member adopts. It is the complementary of punctuation that ensures harmonious living within a family.

Finally, the concept of digital (verbal) and analogic (nonverbal) communication has important implication in therapy with Hispanic American families. Although most are bilingual, some traditional families are more comfortable with the native Spanish language when dealing with crises or problem-solving issues. Clients who speak English with difficulty may have the added demands of decoding and encoding (Pitta, Marcos, and Alpert, 1978). Language difficulty causes problems in deciding the extent to which there is congruence between the message and the way it is delivered. Incongruence may take the form of inappropriateness, invalidation, or paradox. The different acculturation rates of family members can also complicate the digital and analogic communication. An important role of the therapist is to assist family members to validate information sent and received.

If a Hispanic American client is reluctant to speak English in therapy, it may be related to such communication concepts as syntactics (the grammatical properties), semantics (meaning of communication), and pragmatics (behavorial effects of the communication). These concepts become complicated as different family members' acculturation rates vary. They are responsible for much of the miscommunication in daily living and in the problem-solving process.

The principle of schismogenesis (Bateson, 1958) states that cumulative interaction between individuals tends to result in progressive change. The cultural transitional process and the strong influence of the egalitarian couple relationship of the dominant culture have greatly affected the traditional complementary (dominant/submissive) relationship of the Hispanic couple. While the Hispanic husband struggles to maintain a complementary transaction, the wife may try to negotiate a symmetrical (equal) relationship. The principle of schismogenesis is helpful in understanding the marital relationship of a Hispanic American couple as well as other aspects of a family emotional system, such as triangulation and scapegoating.

Satir's classification of family behavior for a family member under stress (Satir, Stachowiak, and Taschman, 1975) helps to explain a Hispanic father's behavior during stressful periods. It is not uncommon for a father to assume the blamer role, find fault in others as a means to reassure his machismo, and accuse others as a way to resurrect his power in the family. The in-between (husband and children) position occupied by the Hispanic mother often places her in a placator role of agreeing, pleasing, and apologizing. In addition to these two dysfunctional roles, other family roles such as "super-reasonable" and "irrelevant" hinder open communication among family members. The therapist should help family members abandon these roles and adopt genuine and congruent ways of relating to one another.

The principles of behavior derived from the communication theory have contributed significantly to understanding the dynamics and interaction of the Hispanic American family. The following discussion focuses on the manners in which these principles can be applied in actual therapy with a Hispanic American family.

Communication Practice Principles

Hispanic American family interaction revolves around a prescribed vertical and hierarchical role structure determined by age, sex, and professional authority. Because of the authoritative role of the therapist, family members often find it impolite or inappropriate to disagree during a therapy session. It is important that the therapist actively encourage the family to express their positive and negative reactions to the therapy goal and process. The hierarchical role structure places the father in a spokesman role, and his machismo cannot be openly challenged, especially by his own children. It is advisable that beginning family therapy sessions be divided between the spouse subsystem and sibling subsystem. Further, to respect the authoritarian parental position, parents should be interviewed first and the siblings second. When the parents are ready to be interviewed with their children (assuming the therapist is bilingual), Spanish can be used to communicate with the parents and English can be used with the children. An interchange of languages is useful for delineating blurred generational boundaries (Falicov, 1982, p. 158).

To maintain a complementary relationship with the Hispanic family, especially the father, the therapist's communicative style should be less direct, less confrontational, and more businesslike. The therapist's use of humor, allusions, and diminutives may soften the directness and are often more effective forms of communication consistent with the Hispanic cultural transactional styles (Falicov, 1982, p. 149).

The communication theory is helpful when assisting the family in problem solving, renegotiation, and redefinition of power relationships. Hispanics find the concept of power idiosyncratic, threatening, competitive, disrespectful, Western, and, therefore, foreign. Although the role of the therapist, as defined by Haley, is that of a "metagovernor of the family system," a therapist's activity should be guided by the pragmatics of Hispanic cultural values. For example, the therapist should use the polite form of the pronoun "you" (*usted*) with adults to indicate respect. Children can be addressed in the familiar form (*tu*) (Bernal and Flores-Ortiz, 1982, p. 358). Haley's therapeutic tactics, such as prescribing the symptom (encouraging the usual dysfunctional behavior), may be confusing and disrespectful to Hispanic American families. However, Haley's paradoxical messages (double bind) are often effective in work with an authoritarian father who rigidly reinforces what is expected of him culturally. By joining the father's resistance, a therapist can help him explore alternate ways to fulfill his obligatory parental role. Haley's therapeutic technique of paradoxical intervention will be presented in detail in the case presentation section of this chapter.

Haley's technique of relabeling/reframing (by emphasizing the positive) is consistent with the Hispanic American culture's emphasis on respect and interdependence. The relabeling technique also can help the family shift from the disease model to an interpersonal perspective that Hispanic culture views as significant.

Virginia Satir's communication theory (1967) can be used to help Hispanic family members recognize the dysfunctional roles they sometimes assume. She also challenges family members to be compassionate toward each other and to help each other to feel good and "respected." Familism is very important, and Hispanics are taught to sacrifice self-interest for bettering other family members and the family as a whole. Satir's theory focusing on the "feeling good" component of each individual and the entire family should greatly appeal to Hispanic American clients.

Interacting harmoniously during times of transition and crisis requires communicative skills, including effective styles. Miller, Nunnally, and Wackman (1975) focused on skills and techniques that relate to each other in a "I count you, I count me" manner. This can be used effectively for problem solving with Hispanics. Traditionally, Hispanics are taught to be cooperative, and "other-centered" in interpersonal relationships. An exchange of real feelings and intentions among all individuals, at the early stage of therapy, therefore, may not be conducive to problem solving. Miller's work on "alive and awareness" provides an alternative.

Family Structure Theory

This discussion of family structure theory centers on work developed and advanced by Bowen (1978) and Minuchin (1974). Reviewed here are behavorial principles and practice principles of structure family theory as they relate to assessment and therapy with Hispanic American families.

Bowen was trained as a psychoanalyst. He based his theory on a clinical study of schizophrenia at the Menninger Clinic in the early 1950s and at the National Institute for Mental Health in the early 1960s. Specifically, Bowen was impressed with the "emotional stuck togetherness" and the intensely transactional nature of the nuclear family system (Bowen, 1978, p. 207). Bowen did not specify the ethnic composition of the "sick" families under study, so one must assume his family sample represents Anglo middle-class American families. Bowen bases his concept of "differentiation of self" on this intense emotional "stuck togetherness" characteristic of a nuclear family. The concept may not have the same degree of relevance to Hispanic families whose strong sense of familism extends beyond the nuclear family to include extended family members (*compadres*). Because of the inclusive relationship with extended family members, interaction within the nuclear family is seldom so close and intense.

The Hispanic husband and wife interaction is not usually based on romanticism as is common in egalitarian relationships where there is more emotional stuck togetherness. Because the spousal system boundary is never that close, it may not be so susceptible to the process of triangulation, a three-person system that Bowen considers the building block of all emotional systems in and outside of the family. The central nurturing role of the Hispanic mother and the disciplinarian role of the father may create an alliance between mother and child that will exclude the father. Such a structure coalition is well accepted within the Hispanic family structure, as opposed to Anglo family culture, which views this situation negatively. Further, the Hispanic wife's sense of familism, hierarchy, and family obligation discourages her from subverting her husband's relationship with her or sabotaging her child's relationship with his father. Under normal circumstances, a Hispanic usually conducts him- or herself according to what is best for the whole family even if it requires self-sacrifices. However, during moments of crisis triggered by acculturation, triangulation may develop.

While the cultural practice of familism with extended family members makes the nuclear emotional system less intense and triangulation less likely, it may weaken the "family projection process" and the "multigenerational transmission process" described by Bowen's theory. Bowen defines the concept of emotional cutoff as unresolved emotional attachment to parents (1978, p. 382). It is prevalent among newly arrived Hispanic immigrants, particularly the 1980 wave of Cuban refugees. The immigrants' inability to return for home visits further compounds their adjustment problems and feelings of isolation.

Minuchin looks at the structure of the Hispanic American family system. It is characterized by its clear hierarchical role structure as determined by age, sex, generation, and birth order of family members. The authority distribution within the family is clearly defined: the father acts as head of the household; the mother acts as mediator between the children and their father; and older children, especially males, exert authority over younger siblings. The dominant culture family structure places husband and wife in an equal relationship with different levels of authority over their children (Minuchin, 1974, p. 52).

A therapist working with a Hispanic family should not assume that the spouse boundary is diffuse just because the spousal system of the Hispanic family is structured differently (hierarchical instead of egalitarian). It is also important to keep in mind that while the Hispanic father acts as spokesman for the entire family, in actuality the mother may be the true power behind the surface family structure (Garcia-Preto, 1982).

The Hispanic American family generally is large, and parents are usually burdened with meeting the economic survival needs of the family. It is not unusual, therefore, for the older sibling to have the responsibility of caring for younger children and assisting with other household duties normally performed by adults. A therapist should avoid interpreting this as boundary diffusion and should not label an older child as "parental child" (Minuchin, 1974, p. 53). This complementary accommodation between spouses and between parents and children characterizes the strength of the Hispanic American family structure.

Immigration, acculturation, and the family life cycle transition sometimes undermine the Hispanic father's authoritarian position. The children's acculturation rate is usually faster than the parents'. The parents may have to rely on their children as interpreters, given that children often learn English faster than their parents. The Hispanic father may be unable to find a job in the United States. If the mother does find a job outside the home, she may seek a more egalitarian relationship with her husband. She may also be torn between performing her traditional wife and mother role and working to support the family economically. The entire situation can create a state of enmeshment characterized by the diffusion of intergenerational boundaries (Minuchin, 1974, p. 54).

Minuchin's concept of different sources of stress reflecting the family system and its structure is relevant to work with Hispanic American families. His emphasis on the "stressful contact of the whole family with extrafamilial forces" (Minuchin, 1974, p. 63) sets him apart from other theorists whose major concerns are confined to the extended family or the nuclear family system. By focusing upon the extrafamilial forces, Minuchin is sensitive to the political, social, and cross-cultural processes of poverty and discrimination that many Hispanic American families face after arriving in the United States. Minuchin advocates that family therapists assume the role of an ombudsman. They can then assist the family in reorganizing various social institutions and structures for its own benefit.

Structure Practice Principles

"Differentiation of self" is a universal process, varying only in quantity and quality among different cultures. For example, Anglo Americans may believe sending an adolescent to work outside the home encourages the adolescent's differentiation of self. The same behavior should not be expected of a Hispanic adolescent whose parents need him to assist with daily house chores. Furthermore, his ethnicity and lack of fluency in English may prevent his finding and keeping a job. Hence different cultures define and facilitate the process of "differentiation of self" differently. It is the responsibility of each therapist to learn about the specifics of the Hispanic American culture and to assist the client to differentiate accordingly.

Bowen's focus on increasing differentiation by obtaining, organizing, and understanding the family's history makes sense in terms of accurate assessment of individual and family needs. The process, however, may be antithetical to the Hispanic American's "present" orientation. Newly arrived Hispanic Americans may be reluctant to invest energy, time, and financial resources to find out what is wrong with their parents, relatives, and ancestors. The research process toward differentiation may be a more viable therapeutic tool with acculturated middle-class Hispanic American families.

Bowen's premise that parental relationship dictates the entire nuclear family's emotional system is logical. His preference for singling out the couple relationship as a therapeutic target (Bowen, 1978, p. 175) may alienate the parents. The mother often feels more challenged to perform as a good mother than as a wife. Bowen's most recent emphasis on concentrating on the individual in family therapy can be applicable in dealing with an authoritative, rigid Hispanic father who does not tolerate family members challenging him. In defending this one-to-one therapeutic technique, Bowen writes: "From my orientation, a theoretical system that 'thinks' in terms of family and works toward improving the family system is family psychotherapy" (Bowen 1978, p. 157). The one-to-one therapeutic modality may be the only workable resolution for many Hispanic American families. This is the preferred modality when interaction is rigidified by traditional role structure and the family as a whole is not amendable to family therapy because of mistrust, inadequate resources, or language barriers.

Bowen's definition of the role of a therapist is that of a culture-broker (Bowen, 1978, p. 540). This is consistent with the emic approach to work with Hispanic Americans. His heavy reliance on the client to be active and to do the research, assessment, and differentiation process may not be congruent with the Hispanic American's perception of the therapist as an expert. Hence the therapist's role as teacher, researcher, strategist, supporter, or cheerleader should be conducted with a greater degree of activity, especially at the onset of therapy with Hispanic clients.

Minuchin's differential applications of "joining techniques" are especially helpful during the engagement phase of therapy with a Hispanic American family (Bernal and Flores-Ortiz, 1982). The strategic use of the "maintenance" technique enables the therapist to organize by the basic rules that regulate the transactional process in a Hispanic American family system. By following the transactional process of a specific family, the therapist can capitalize on the "personalism" quality essential for establishing a working relationship with the family. In work with a three-generation Hispanic American family presenting a rigid hierarchical structure, the therapist may find it advisable to address the grandfather first. Adherence to the family transactional process may indeed perpetuate the pathogenic structure of the family. Such a transitional joining technique is essential if the therapist is to have any impact on the family. Once personalism is cultivated and trust is developed, the therapist can use his or her role as "padrino" to unstructure and restructure the family.

The technique of tracking is helpful for the therapist to examine the content of family interaction and to analyze family structure. The therapist should keep in mind that Hispanic American family structure differs from that of the dominant culture, and the degree of intensity within each subsystem varies as compared to the dominant culture. For instance, while the Hispanic spouse subsystem is not as strong and intense as that of the dominant culture, the Hispanic sibling subsystem and the extended family subsystem are much stronger and more involved. Minuchin's system boundary-making and restructuring techniques are helpful, provided they are adapted to the Hispanic family structured framework.

In applying Minuchin's disequilibration (of boundary) technique, the therapist can use different modalities including interviewing the parental subsystem separately, using Spanish to communicate with the parents, and using English when speaking to the children.

While Minuchin's "joining techniques" are generally sensitive to the Hispanic American family structure, his family restructuring techniques such as escalating stress (by emphasizing differences), utilizing the symptom (by exaggerating it), and manipulating mood (by escalating the emotional intensity) are highly confrontational. They should not be used prior to developing a trusting relationship. The strategic application of these techniques will be illustrated in the case illustration part (3) of this chapter.

The preceding discussions aim at presenting a clear picture of the cultural values and family structure of the Hispanic American family structure. The communication and structure family therapy theories are reviewed along with their application in therapy with Hispanic clients. Attention will now be directed to culturally relevant techniques and skills in three phases of treatment: beginning, problem solving, and termination-evaluation.

PART 2: CULTURALLY RELEVANT TECHNIQUES AND SKILLS IN THERAPY PHASES

Beginning Phase

The engagement phase of therapy is a critical period for Hispanic American clients. Therapists must recognize its importance and be cognizant of the traditional help-seeking patterns of this group. Such patterns include the Hispanic American client's underutilization of therapy, high dropout rate, language barrier, lack of financial resources, and unfamiliarity with family therapy as a viable therapeutic modality for family problem solving.

The following discussion attempts to apply and integrate the cultural knowledge of Hispanic Americans and communication and family structure theories used during the beginning phase of family therapy. Specifically, four major skills and techniques are considered essential in therapy with a Hispanic American family in the beginning therapy phase. These skills and techniques include (1) engaging the client/family, (2) cultural transitional mapping and data collection, (3) mutual goal setting, and (4) selecting a focus/sytem for therapy.

Engaging the Client/Family

There exists a long history of discrimination against Hispanic Americans. Such clients find it difficult to trust a family therapist who is perceived as representative of the majority system. The level of mistrust is compounded by the fact that some Hispanics do not have the proper documents to reside in this country. It is important that the therapist defines her role early with the client and disassociates herself from any immigration connection. To develop an element of trust, a therapist can help the client feel comfortable by displaying in her office objects, pictures, or symbols of the Hispanic culture. Because the social interaction of the Hispanic American is governed by hierarchical role structure, the therapist needs to address the father first. To convey a sense of respect, the therapist is advised to use the polite form of the pronoun "you" (usted) with adults. A tone of acceptance that avoids confrontation is especially essential during this period.

The language factor is most important during the engagement phase with a family who is unable to speak English (Gonzalez, 1978). It can be humiliating especially for older Hispanics who try to speak English but are unable to be understood. Using children as translators immediately reverses the authority structure of the family, and it may further alienate the parental subsystem, especially the father. When there are no Spanish-speaking therapists available, it is advisable to use Hispanic adults as interpreters. However, Abad and Boyce (1979) found that the use of translators produced distortions that result in limitations and frustrations for both therapist and client. On the other hand, a study by Kline et al. (1980) indicated the use of translators did not have an adverse effect. Rather, Spanish-speaking patients felt greatly understood and were positive about their treatment experiences.

Hispanic families often expect the therapist to act as a medical doctor. The therapist can capitalize on this "pragmatic communication" to be active, polite, and willing to give advice. The family may have experienced past discrimination. The therapist is advised, therefore, to acknowledge the family's as a means to "join" the family emotional process. In addition, she needs to create good feelings (Satir, 1967) within the family by praising their efforts to confront the difficult problems of daily living.

The application of relationship skills in the process of joining take into consideration the differences between each Hispanic American subgroup. For instance, in engaging Cuban families in therapy, attention needs to be devoted to empathizing with the family's defensive element myths about returning to Cuba (Bernal and Flores-Ortiz, 1982, p. 360). A third-generation Puerto Rican family, however, may be more concerned with "respect" and "disrespect." To maintain the Hispanic American family's "present" and "doing" orientation, a therapist should provide the family with personal observation, positive feedback, and concrete suggestions. The therapist's acknowledgment of the important contributions made by various family members can revitalize the familism cherished by the family. Her "relabeling" of the family difficulties as family transactional issues provides the family with hope and concrete solutions to their problems.

Transitional Mapping and
Data Collection

The therapist should demonstrate personal interest in the family to be consistent with the Hispanic American orientation of personalism. This can be accomplished by first determining the cultural background of the family and inquiring about it. This shifts the focus of the therapy session away from the "problem" of the "identified patient," and it provides the family an opportunity to educate the therapist who plays the role of a cultural broker. As the therapist assumes the role of a researcher, Minuchin's "tracking technique" (1974) is helpful. It allows the therapist to follow the subjects discussed by family members like a "needle follows the record groove" (Minuchin, 1974, p. 176).

Once the preliminary problem has been identified, the therapist proceeds to obtain information essential to understanding the family system and its context. The frameworks of Boszormenyi-Nagy and Krasner (1980) are helpful in ascertaining the family's connectedness with their birthplace, culture, or roots:

> Having roots and legacies in common is a nonsubstitutive bond among people that not only outlasts physical and geographical separations from family of origin, but also influences the degree to which offspring can be free to commit themselves to relationships outside of the original ties, including marriage and parenthood of their own [p. 768].

To ascertain the migration phase of the family, the therapist needs to inquire how long the family has lived in the United States. Families, as well as individuals within the family, acculturate at different rates. This can cause added stress and problems with each other in family transactions (Szapocznik et al., 1978). The therapist can assess the degree of connectedness to the culture of origin by asking the reason behind the family's immigration. The therapist should also inquire who initiated the move, and what connection the family already had in the United States; other questions pertaining to the political, social, and family pressure preceding the move; and which family members remain in the home land. These questions can generate important information for ascertaining the invisible obligations (Boszormenyi-Nagy and Krasner, 1980). An assessment of a Hispanic American family's connectedness to its culture is critical for it leads to "identifying cultural and relational resources; understanding of loyalty conflicts; obtaining a broader contextual view; and developing legacy-based therapeutic strategies" (Bernal and Flores-Ortiz, 1982, p. 363).

Considering the importance of extended family ties, a therapist needs to assess the strength or potential dysfunctioning of the present household boundary and support system. The technique of cultural mapping and genogram is helpful in assessing the multigenerational patterns and influences. It also provides some insight as to how different Hispanic groups wish to resolve their family problems in accordance with traditional values.

Mutual Goal Setting

The basic problem inherent in the process of mutual goal setting stems from different perceptions of the therapist and the family. Again, the therapist's knowledge and receptivity toward Hispanic culture is valuable not only in the problem identification process, but also later at the implementation stage. Many of the problems experienced by Hispanic American families, especially newly arrived families and families of lower socioeconomic class, are basically social and involve learning to cope with environmental stresses. The therapist's responsiveness to the family's request for immediate, concrete services and to act occasionally as the family's advocate helps to open up other problems plaguing the family (Mizio, 1979).

Falicov (1982, p. 154) further divides therapeutic goals with Hispanic American families into three categories: (1) therapeutic goal related to situational stress, (2) therapeutic goal related to dysfunctional patterns of cultural transition, and (3) therapeutic goal related to transcultural dysfunctional patterns. Situational stress occurs at the interface between the family and the new environment. Problems may include social isolation, unfamiliarity with community resources, or poverty. Dysfunctional patterns of cultural transition are interactional patterns that were once adaptive to cultural transition but later became rigid in the family's functioning. An example of dysfunctional patterns is a parent-child role reversal due to different rates of acculturation. Transcultural dysfunctional patterns are basically universal and are characterized by a limited range of repetitive interactional behaviors, hierarchical imbalance with rigid coalitions, developmental impasses, and other family system boundary problems.

The process of mutual goal formulation requires that the therapist be cognizant of the conflicting value orientations many Hispanic American families face. For instance, Hispanic Americans are brought up with interdependence values that conflict sharply with the independence values held by the dominant culture including the therapist (Acosta et al., 1982). A Hispanic American client is not likely to formulate therapy goals that will benefit him- or herself only. Similarly, the significance attached to the parent-child, especially mother-child, dyad is much more important than the marital dyad in Hispanic culture. Although the child's presenting problem may be attributed to a dysfunctional marital relationship, therapy goals focusing on repairing the marital subsystem at the onset of therapy will be strongly resisted. Another therapy goal emphasizing the parents' families of origin or multigenerational transmission may also be too threatening, too time-consuming, and antithetical to the Hispanic Americans' "present" and "doing" orientations. Conversely, therapy goals focusing on the parent-child relationship challenge the wife's desire to be a good mother. Through learning how to perform dutifully in a mother-child relationship, the mother may learn how to interact differently with her husband. Until the family as a unit can experience success in the parent-child relationship, other goals involving individual family members in differentiating or facilitating the marital subsystem for boundary repair may never materialize.

Hispanic American clients exhibit a strong "present" orientation. Therapy goals need to be specific, concrete, practical, and short term (Acosta el al., 1982). They should be formulated without undermining the hierarchical structure role of the family.

Selecting a Focus/System Unit for Therapy

Understanding and respecting the Hispanic American family's cultural norms and present social context are perhaps the most important skills in defining the family's problem and selecting a focus on family subsystem unit for therapy. For example, a Hispanic American's obligation to family is so strong that it is not uncommon for a nuclear family to involve the extended family as their major locus of social activities. Such intense frequent extrafamilial contacts are uncommon according to Anglo family norms and should not be misconstrued as a symptom of enmeshment.

When situational stress involving the whole family or some individual family members occurs, a therapist needs to adhere to the hierarchical structure of the family by consulting with the father prior to implementing any therapeutic strategy. The closeness of the mother-child relationship makes it necessary to consult with the mother before intervention focusing on the child.

Occasionally, the dysfunctional family pattern may involve diffuse marital subsystem boundaries. Conjoint couple therapy is not recommended as a therapeutic modality. The husband's sense of machismo and defense may intensify in the presence of an outsider, that is, the family therapist. Similarly, the passive role structure of the wife may intensify her confusion and ambivalence toward her husband during dyadic marital therapy. Whenever marital therapy is conducted with a more acculturated Hispanic couple, Bowen's detached, calm, and intellectual approach is helpful. It is particularly useful in terms of diffusing the emotionality of the marital relationship and guiding marital interaction according to cultural norms.

As a sign of fulfilling familial obligations, Hispanic children usually refrain from openly challenging their parents in the therapist's presence. A separate session with siblings may be in order for negotiating issues they may not normally discuss in their parents' presence. Through structured sibling therapy, the diffuse boundary of sibling relationships is solidified. Such a restructuring of the sibling subsystem can, in turn, extricate an overprotected child from the parental subsystem.

Considering the importance machismo plays in the father's role as head of the family, conjoining family sessions with every family member present may be too threatening to the father. Hence Bowen's therapeutic strategy of focusing on the self-differentiation of one person (preferably, the father) may be most appropriate. With this one-to-one therapeutic modality, the father no longer needs to be concerned with his traditional obligatory authoritarian role. Instead, with the help of the therapist who listens to him empathically, the father can examine different alternatives to facilitate his role as the family head.

On the opposite end of the target-focus-continuum, therapeutic activities involving the extended family can be used to deal with developmental impasses connected to cultural transition. Such activities may include initiation rites or fiestas like weddings, baptism, and graduation. These can facilitate the smooth transition marking the traditional family life cycle.

Problem-Solving Phase

The following discussion focusing on the problem-solving phase of therapy with Hispanic American families considers the cultural norm, family structure, traditional help-seeking behavior, and capacities of this particular population. In addition, the application of communication and family structure theories has been integrated into the therapeutic process. Specifically, seven skills and techniques are of particular relevance in the problem-solving phase of therapy. They include (1) employing home visits as problem-solving tools; (2) skills and techniques in social, moral, and organic refraining/relabeling; (3) mobilizing and restructuring the social and extended family network; (4) promoting familial obligation as a family restructuring technique; (5) employing role models, educator role, and advocate role; (6) paradoxical intervention for problem solving, and (7) collaborative work with a folk healer, paraprofessional, or therapist helper.

Home Visits

Hispanic American families generally lack specific knowledge about health and mental health services. They have limited financial resources and transportation, and may be unfamiliar with family therapy as a viable resource for problem solving within the family. Home visits should be a logical therapeutic tool for reaching this particular ethnic group. In some instances, home visits may be the *only* way of initiating or maintaining a relationship with a Hispanic family (Mizio, 1979). Thomas and Carter (1971) also have stressed the significance of reaching out to the family and seeing the family in their natural environment, that is, their home. In addition to locating therapy in the home, joining the family in an emotional manner is recommended by Spiegel (1959). He advocated that therapists should become assimilated into the lineal chain of influence (which bears upon the pathologic deviation of family members) by making themselves known to many of the family's kin. Pittman et al. (1971) found that family therapy in the client's home gave the family members an increased opportunity to reveal their health and maintain freedom of movement when anxious.

With Hispanic American families, home visits can be used effectively by therapists to personalize their relationship with the family. The fact that the therapist spends time and effort to visit with the family helps the latter to perceive the therapist as genuine and trustworthy. The therapist's impact on the family system will automatically increase if the family is able to relate to her as they would to a compadre. The effectiveness of home visits has been proven in family therapy with multiproblem Puerto Rican families (Hardy-Fanta and MacMahon-Herrera, 1981).

Social, Moral, and Organic Reframing/Relabeling

Hispanic American families' interaction is guided by hierarchical role structure and interdependence. Haley's and Minuchin's reframing/relabeling technique can be effective with this group. By using this technique, the therapist capitalizes on the communication pragmatics of Hispanic American culture by emphasizing the positive aspects of behavior and redefining negative behavior as positive.

Rolando, a 15-year-old, was referred by his father who claimed that the boy was totally "out of control." The family migrated from Mexico City eight years ago. Rolando spoke fluent English and occasionally served as interpreter for the family. According to the father, Rolando's problem started about one year ago when he began to stay out late and to skip school frequently. The father was employed as a carpenter but was laid off intermittently. Rolando's complaint was that he was tired of having no money to spend and that he wished he was allowed to get a job. After father and son had repeatedly exchanged words of conflict, the therapist reframed Rolando's rebelliousness as a way to express his family obligation, that is, to help the family financially by getting a job. The therapist further reinforced the father by commenting that Rolando's concern and obligation for the family was learned from the father. The therapist's reframing helped both the father and son view their behavior in a more positive vein. Thus it also helped them to reestablish a more open line of communication.

During the process of relabeling, the therapist should be sensitive to complementary roles within the Hispanic American family, For example, a wife's accusatory remark to her husband, "You never come home," can be relabeled (to the husband) as "Your wife enjoys your company very much. She want to know what she can do to influence you to want to spend more time with her." A therapist's relabeling may not accurately reflect the true meaning of what was said, but the important underlying message relabeling can help to convey to the family is that all family members respect each other and that harmonious living is the primary family concern.

Social and Extended Family Network

Hispanic American families are well-known for their emphasis on familism. Studies have indicated that Hispanic Americans make use of the extended family network much more extensively than Anglos and Blacks (Mindel, 1980). A social support network is essential for newly arrived Hispanics who need a place and a way to bridge the ecological deficit, to ventilate frustration, to learn acculturated social skills, and to form friendships. In addition, the extended family or social network helps the individual or the family to reconnect with their culture of origin.

Hispanic American families feel a strong tendency toward reconnection with their culture of origin, but not all Hispanics have the same degree of access to their home country (Bernal and Flores-Ortiz, 1982, p. 364). Puerto Ricans have the best access to the cultural roots because of historical antecedents, relative proximity, cost of travel to the island, and legal status. Conversely, because of political pressures and an economic blockade, Cuban Americans are the most disconnected group from their country of origin. Despite the close proximity to the frontier, Mexican Americans have not had access to their native roots because of immigration impositions.

In an effort to mobilize social networks, the therapist's role may become that of a "social intermediary" or "matchmaker." Minuchin (1974, p. 63) has described specific strategies geared toward the alleviation of environmental stress and the cultural adaptation process. One immediate resource for communal activities is the parish or parochial school. Some priests, if sensitive to the problems of acculturation, can offer significant spiritual support, especially when dealing with physical illness, old age, and death (Falicov, 1982, p. 154).

Familial Obligation

The process of acculturation has not diminished the Hispanic American's need to be valued by others, especially by family members. A person's worth is dependent upon the quality nature of his or her relationship with other family members. A Hispanic father may feel multiple threats to his integrity. As a result, he is more likely to show reluctance especially at the engagement phase of therapy. A therapist should examine the positive cultural meanings of a Hispanic father's machismo. Such factors can include loyalty, fairness, responsibility, and family centrality. These qualities can bridge, rather than bar, the way to engaging a Hispanic American father in family therapy (Ramirez, 1979). Thus a therapist needs to reconsider the negative stereotype of machismo and appeal to the father on the basis of his importance to the well-being of his family.

Roberto, the second son of Mr. Ruiz, a Puerto Rican, has been in trouble with the school authority because of a disciplinary problem. The school principal's efforts to meet with Mr. Ruiz failed when Mr. Ruiz would not respond to the principal's request for a conference. The school principal informed Roberto that he would remain suspended until his father came in for a conference. The Ruiz family did not respond for a week. The school social worker wrote to inform Mr. Ruiz of her desire to meet with him at his home regarding Roberto. In the letter, the worker mentioned that Mr. Ruiz might be very busy and have difficulty scheduling an appointment. She said that she needed his guidance in how best to work with his son. The worker also proposed a time and date for the home visit.

When the home visit actually occurred, Mr. Ruiz was apologetic about the inconvenience his family problem might have caused the worker. In addition, Mr. Ruiz was hospitable and expressed great appreciation for the worker's visit. He vowed that he would do whatever was needed to help his son.

Promoting familial obligation as a means of resolving family problems can also be used in other situations. A Hispanic American wife publicly assumes the supportive role to her husband, but privately or covertly she may undermine his authority, especially in regard to child-rearing practices. To be consistent with Hispanic communication pragmatics, the therapist should not encourage the wife to express openly her hostility toward her husband. Instead, the therapist needs to encourage the wife to suggest openly and publicly to her husband other alternatives in child rearing. The public support that the husband is receiving from his wife can reinforce his powerful role as patriarch, and, at the same time, he may become more receptive to new ways of child rearing.

More than anything else, a Hispanic American wishes to get along with others (interdependence), especially family members. The therapist's task is to promote this essential quality and capitalize on its strengths.

Role Models, Educator Role, and Advocate Role

The process of migration and acculturation often creates confusion and disorganization for individual members as well as for the whole family. While experiencing loss due to transcultural migration, a Hispanic family has to be concerned at the same time with "unattainment" (Pollak, 1964), which can threaten the basic survival of the family. The therapist's role as cultural translator, mediator, and model (Anda, 1984; Minuchin, 1974) is vital to help the family form an open system with available community resources. The newly established network based on mutual aid can provide needed economic, emotional, and educational assistance to families in cultural transition.

A Hispanic American family's dysfunctional patterns often relate directly to a lack of proper role modeling. Traditional role-modeling might have been functional in the past, but it becomes dysfunctional as family members experience different cultural norms and life cycles. This frequently occurs at a time when the support system is weak. Hence the therapist must first assume a translator/mediator role and assess which part(s) of the family system need translating or mediating. The therapist's next step is to assume the educator role in explaining the nature of their family problem and ways family members can interact differently to help solve the problem. In keeping with the Hispanic American's "present" orientation, the therapist should explain clearly and exactly what is expected of each family member (Acosta et al., 1982, p. 74).

Being sensitive to the Hispanic American culture does not preclude the therapist attempting to produce change in areas that restrict the family's ability to alter their circumstances or solve their problems. A therapist's task is not to change the Hispanic American patterns of family interaction, but to alter those specific patterns that are dysfunctional within the family (Miller, 1959). For example, a Hispanic American couple experiencing acculturation but desiring harmonious family living may need to learn an egalitarian model of male-female relationship. The power of alignment that characterized the family is challenged by presenting a model of transaction in which the husband pays attention to what the wife has to say, in which there is give and take, and in which each partner has a voice in decision making. Particularly helpful according to Satir (1967) and Miller, Nunnally, and Wackman (1975) are family communication skills that include mutual reinforcement, methods of constructive disagreement, the use of feedback, brainstorming, decision-making options, and so on.

Many Hispanic American families, especially those who are in the lower social economic class and those who do not possess legal immigration documents, are the victims of societal lags and intentional or unintentional indifference by agencies. The therapist at times may need to assume an advocate role for the family. Because these families do not wish to draw public attention to themselves, it is important that the therapist's biased advocate role on their behalf not subject them to further agency humiliation or discrimination.

Paradoxical Intervention

The Hispanic American family's definitive role structure can be rigidified by the acculturation process. They then are reluctant to modify their pattern of interaction. Frequently, in encountering these families, their implicit message is "change our problem, but don't change us or anything else." From a systemic view, these families are not really resisting as much as trying to preserve traits they feel are essential to maintaining the family itself.

A families' persistence in maintaining the old pattern of behaviors may be so entrenched that usual therapeutic techniques are ineffective. Haley's (1976) paradoxical intervention is an appropriate technique for such "resistant" or "stuck" families. The paradoxical intervention has been termed "therapeutic paradox" of the "counterparadox" or "therapeutic double bind." It assumes that an identified problem serves an essential function in the maintenance of the family system, and that a hypothesis is developed accordingly to explain its relationship. This hypothesis is explained to the family in positive terms describing how the identified problem (behavior) may be helping the family. The family and the symptom-bearer are cautioned against any change. This leaves the family with their own paradoxical situation.

In responding to the family's paradox with a counterparadox, the therapist has respected the family's efforts to preserve its coherence. Thus Minuchin's joining principle is being applied. The family then can respond to the therapeutic double bind in one of the following alternatives: (1) accept their problem as inevitable and unsolvable, (2) accept the possibility of change, or (3) reject the therapist's hypothesis. Most families will adopt the third alternative if they still perceive the therapist as untrustworthy. Therefore, it is absolutely essential that the therapist establish trust with the family before the technique is used. Strategic application of this technique will be described in the case illustration (Part 3) in this chapter.

Collaborative Work with a Folk Healer, Paraprofessional, or Therapist Helper

Folk healing practices among Hispanic Americans have been labeled as "dangerous prognostic signs and as evidence of reliance on primitive defense mechanisms, which if they persisted were ultimately destructive to the integrative functions of the ego" (Douglas, 1974). For example, the phenomenon of "espiritismo" has been diagnosed as hallucinatory or psychotic thought processes (Purdy et al., 1970). However, many Hispanic American clinicians have refuted such claims and concluded that folk practitioners are appropriate within their respective cultural contexts (Douglas, 1974; Garrison, 1977). For example, "espiritismo" has been found to provide integrative and identity factors to migrant minorities in their acculturation process (Douglas, 1974). It helped to discharge tension and anxieties generated in social life as well as providing face-to-face contact and interpersonal intimacy (Rogler and Hollingshead, 1965). The practice of "santeria" helps to delineate the explanation of the irrational, problem-solving skills, and regress "in the service of the ego" (De La Cancela, 1978). And finally, "curanderismo" has been identified as providing a Catholic therapeutic method of confession and reassurance (Kiev, 1968). De La Cancela (1978) has identified some similarities between Western psychotherapy and folk

healing. Such similarities include the admission of unacceptable im-
pulses and emotions and their displacement to culturally acceptable
outlets, practitioners' acceptance and tolerance of deviance and the use
of introspection and identification as therapeutic process, and the
amount of training required of a practitioner. In view of the functional
similarities between folk healers and family therapists, the necessity and
wisdom in the integration of these two practices is obvious. The actual
collaborative work between the family therapist and the spiritualist will
be illustrated by a case example in Part 3 of this chapter.

The rigid role structure of some Hispanic American families may
render them unreceptive to family therapy or unresponsive to conjoint
family therapy where all family members are present for problem
solving. In acute cases, the therapist may need to adopt the therapist-
helper concept (Landau, 1981). Through this approach, the therapist
can avoid face-to-face direct contact or confrontation with the family.
The chosen therapist-helper, an extended family member (pedrino) or a
nuclear family member, can act as a therapeutic agent through the
guidance and supervision of the therapist. Such a therapist-helper could
possibly reduce outside intrusion, eliminate language barriers, and
alleviate transportation, cultural, and financial difficulties. This approach can ensure that the change direction goes according to the need
and cultural norm of the family.

Evaluation and Termination Phase

In view of the Hispanic American client's value on serendipity,
chance, and spontaneity in interpersonal relationships, any rigid
scheduling or objective criteria for evaluating the therapeutic outcome
will meet with resistance. Therefore, it is important that a therapist
respect what the family has to say about the progress or improvement of
their situation. One example would be the family's emphasis on the
welfare of the child. A therapist can evaluate the strength of the spousal
subsystem by inquiring about the new transformation of the parent-
child subsystem. By listening to each parent describe his or her
interaction with the child, the therapist can obtain a clearer picture as to
how the parents interact.

The assessment of family therapy progress should also be guided by
the therapy goal. If the therapeutic goal relates to situational stress, the
therapist's evaluation should be directed to the interface between the
family and the new environment only. Any evaluation of intrafamilial

functioning is inappropriate except to establish a new contract involving a different therapeutic goal. In assessing therapeutic goals relating to dysfunctional patterns of cultural transition or transcultural dysfunctional patterns, a therapist needs to be cognizant of the unique cultural perspectives of the Hispanic American culture. Hispanic culture views family structure, differentiation of self, emotional cutoff, and so on differently than Anglo culture. Unless the family interactive pattern is detrimental to the growth and development of family members, any suggestion for its repair may run the risk of misjudgment in evaluation.

Hispanic Americans usually display strong feelings of obligation, interdependence, and fatalism. Because of this, a family tends to deemphasize the extent of its family problem. The family usually is so considerate of the therapist's time and effort that they prefer not to burden the therapist but to terminate therapy prematurely. It is important that the therapist use home visits or be a part of the family's social environment in order to evaluate firsthand how well the family is progressing.

Generally, therapeutic goals will relate to situational stress and will be short term. Accomplishment of therapeutic goals is assessed according to whether the family is able to obtain concrete services, including community resources, essential financial help, and health care services. Therapeutic goals related to transcultural dysfunctional patterns usually involve role conflict or role reversal between parent-child or husband-wife. Accomplishment of these therapeutic goals is measured in terms of compatibility of roles and reduced situational stress. For instance, securing gainful employment for the Hispanic husband may reverse the role conflict he felt when he was unemployed. Therapeutic goals related to transcultural dysfunctional patterns involving intergenerational transmission or idiosyncratic problems (Minuchin, 1974, p. 65) may require longer-term therapy.

The Hispanic American client's value of interpersonal relationships and family ties makes the process of termination foreign to them. The enabling role that the therapist plays in the therapeutic process will win the therapist trust, in that the family truly trusts and accepts the therapist as a member of its extended family. Termination, on the other hand, can be a big loss especially to some families who are culturally and emotionally cutoff. Therefore, it is important that a therapist be comfortable with this element of human relationships and not feel threatened by the family's interdependent behavior as deceptive manipulation.

The preceding discussion should be helpful in understanding Hispanic American families and applying family structure and communication theories and emic-based principles. Part 3 of this chapter offers a case example to explicate and delineate how these family theoretical perspectives and emic-based practice principles can be integrated in actual therapy with a Hispanic American family.

PART 3: CASE ILLUSTRATION

Mrs. Herrera, a 46-year-old Puerto Rican widow, was referred to us (Transcultural Family Study Center) by the community mental health center. She was hospitalized there for three days because an "unexplainable" seizure she suffered. Mrs. Herrera refused to be hospitalized any longer, but did agree to seek help from our center. According to Mrs. Herrera, her 15-year-old daughter, Graciela, was "driving her crazy."

The family's cultural transitional map and genogram is described in Figure 4.1.

During my first meeting with her, Mrs. Herrera was very inquisitive about my ethnic background and asked if I spoke

Convey respect to client's culture.

Spanish. *"I wish I could,"* I replied spontaneously. Mrs. Herrera volunteered that she used to frequent one Chinese restaurant in Puerto Rico and knew several Chinese waiters who spoke Spanish. I told Mrs.

Use personalism to establish common ties.

Herrera that *my maternal grandfather used to work* in a Chinese restaurant in Panama and learned to speak Spanish there. Mrs. Herrera asked if I had immigrated from Panama. I told her that I came *from Hong*

To establish common ground (immigrant experience with the client).

Kong when I was 19 years old. Mrs. Herrera volunteered that she had come from Puerto Rico 25 years ago *with her* husband and a 2-year-old daughter, Fanta,

Migration background.

who now lives in New York City. Her second daughter, Graciela, was born in New York City, where they have close extended family ties. The family moved to

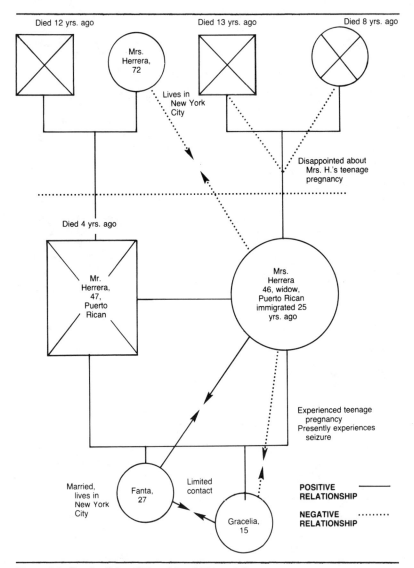

Died 12 yrs. ago

Mrs. Herrera, 72

Lives in New York City

Died 13 yrs. ago

Died 8 yrs. ago

Disappointed about Mrs. H.'s teenage pregnancy

Died 4 yrs. ago

Mr. Herrera, 47, Puerto Rican

Mrs. Herrera 46, widow, Puerto Rican immigrated 25 yrs. ago

Experienced teenage pregnancy
Presently experiences seizure

Married, lives in New York City

Fanta, 27

Limited contact

Gracelia, 15

POSITIVE RELATIONSHIP ———

NEGATIVE RELATIONSHIP ·········

Figure 4.1 Family Cultural Transitional Map and Genogram

Oklahoma City six years ago when the oil business was booming. Mr. Herrera suffered a head injury at work and died two years after the accident.

Problem identification.

Presenting problem.

Loyalty and security to employment.

Intergenerational emotional system.

Specification of problem single-parent nuclear emotional system; failed to fulfill familial obligation.

Joining the client.

Multigenerational emotional transmission.

According to Mrs. Herrera, her husband "was not much of a husband" for he got drunk and "chased after women all the time." Due to her husband's job-related death, Mrs. Herrera receives a pension from the company for which he had worked. I responded to Mrs. Herrera's family background information with great interest and empathy and I *inquired how she managed the family after her husband's death.*

Mrs. Herrera sighed, *"This explains what I am here* to see you about." Mrs. Herrera continued that right after her husband's death four years ago, her first daughter, Fanta, returned to New York City to marry her old boyfriend, leaving Mrs. Herrera to take care of Graciela by herself. Mrs. Herrera has thought about returning to New York City but her present job as an office clerk has prevented her making a major career move. "I am no college graduate, and I *like my present job real well.* Besides I *cannot stand my mother-in-law,* who lives in New York City," continued Mrs. Herrera.

Then Mrs. Herrera proceeded to inform me that lately she had some vigorous hyperkinetic trance that had caused her to miss work and led her to hospitalization. "That clinic and the medication did me no good," complained Mrs. Herrera. *When asked to elaborate on her trance,* Mrs. Herrera broke down crying. She reflected that perhaps the trance was related to *her difficulties with Graciela who would not mind her.* Mrs. Herrera recalled that the last two seizures happened right after Graciela walked out on her during an argument. I *empathized by saying that* she felt she had no control of the situation. Mrs. Herrera agreed and elaborated that when she was Graciela's age, she also *had great difficulty with her father* who would not allow her to have boyfriends. "I wished I had listened to my father. Instead I got myself pregnant and had to have an abortion," continued

Familial obligation.

Encourage the client to grieve.

The necessity for and value of home visits.

Joining the family.

Joining and establishing rapport with Graciela and cultural mapping.

Cultural mapping.

Need to be in touch with family of origin.
Social isolation.

Lack of cultural and religious contact.

Reestablish cultural and religious ties.

Client shows sign of acceptance.

Therapist's use of accommodation technique.

Mrs. Herrera. "Before my husband died, he asked me to promise him that I would *take good care of Graciela,*" Mrs. Herrera cried again. "You feel you have failed your husband," I empathized. Mrs. Herrera nodded and *cried louder.* Before the session ended, I asked if she could bring Graciela with her for the next session. Mrs. Herrera replied that Graciela told her that she would never come to "no agency to see no shrink." I arranged a date to visit with *her and Graciela at their home.* Mrs. Herrara thanked me for listening to her problem.

At the home visit, Mrs. Herrera had arranged for Graciela to meet me. The Herreras lived in a predominately White neighborhood. They decorated their home neatly. I *was inquisitive about the wall posters* showing scenery of Puerto Rico, I asked Graciela if she had been to Puerto Rico. She replied only once the year before her father died. *I asked if she could show me pictures of her father* and other relatives who live in Puerto Rico and in the states. Graciela was cooperative and relieved that I did not focus immediately on her relationship with her mother. *While going over the family photo albums* and listening to both Mrs. Herrera and Graciela, I commented how *much they must miss their relatives.* Mrs. Herrera sighed, and said, "We have nothing to do with anybody anymore!" Mrs. Herrera continued that lately they *had not been to Mass* and that they just did not feel comfortable in attending the White Catholic Church. I asked *if they knew of a Hispanic Catholic Church* nearby. Mrs. Herrera replied that she did but she never inquired more about it. I told her that I knew the pastor of that church. With their permission, I would ask the pastor to visit with them. Mrs. Herrera nodded and said, "Of course."

I then directed my attention to Graciela who at this time was preparing herself a sandwich. She *asked me if I wanted one,* and I said, "yes." Meanwhile, *I encouraged*

Show interest and assess Graciela's social functioning.

Graciela to share with me things that interested her, including her daily activities.

After listening to Graciela's description of her school and social activities, I *complimented her for being a good student* academically for being popular among her peers. Graciela was quite apologetic about the problems she might have caused her mother, but insisted that "*I must live my own life.*" Mrs. Herrera interrupted by saying, "As *long as you are my daughter* and live with me in the same house, you ought to let me know when and where you are going." Graciela capitalized on the situation to point out to me, "You see, this is what I have to put up with all the time." She left hurriedly and walked toward the kitchen.

Recognizing client's strengths.

Sign of acculturation and individualism.

Family life cycle adjustment.

Reframing from negative to positive.

I commented *that I could see how each of them showed caring* toward each other differently. Before I left, we *exchanged appreciation for the time spent with* each other. We also agreed on the time of my next visit. I reminded them a *Catholic priest might* be visiting with them. Mrs. Herrera was concerned that the next time she had a seizure, she might be "put in hospital for good," I comforted her by letting her know that I would *consult with my Hispanic colleague* who was also a folk healer and that he might be of assistance to her in regard to her seizure. Before my next visit with the Herreras, the Hispanic priest visited the family. Mrs. Herrera was thrilled to inform me that *Graciela went to Mass with her for the first time in six months.* Mrs. Herrera was also glad to share with me her visit with the folk healer I had recommended. Mrs. Herrera informed me that the folk healer explained to her that her seizure was a *form of "despojo"*—a cleansing of her spirit. Her seizure served the function of letting her know that something was wrong in her life. A malevolent spirit, imposing itself for whatever purpose, was the cause, and a despojo was part of the cure.

Personalism.

Collaborative work with priest.

Collaborative work with folk healer.

Sign of improved relationship.

Puerto Rican spiritualism.

Collaborative work with folk healer.

When I consulted with the folk healer, he confirmed what Mrs. Herrera had already told me. The folk healer also informed me that he intended to treat Mrs. Herrera with traditional rituals involving the despojo, with herbal remedies and baths, and perhaps exorcisms. The folk healer also confirmed that Mrs. Herrera's difficulty with her daughter definitely was related to the evil spirit that was plaguing her. When I asked Mrs. Herrera about her relationship with her daughter, Mrs. Herrera *warned*

A sign of Mrs. Herrera's emotional "stuckness."

that Graciela was her primary responsibility and that no *counselor from the school or the mental health clinic was* going to tell her that she should leave her daughter

Implying to worker that he should not interfere.

alone. Mrs. Herrera's behavior was a product of her culture, her own teenage pregnancy experience, her injunction from her deceased husband, life cycle adjustment to a teenage daughter, and her emotional enmeshment with Graciela who represented the only person with whom she interacted in her immediate environment.

Joining with the client's resistance or emotional "stuckness."

I *empathized by* stating that I could understand and appreciate her position and that *Graciela should feel fortunate to have* a *mother who really cared about* her. Mrs.

Reinforcing cultural norm and reframing.

Herrera asked if I had any suggestion in regard to her dealing with Graciela. I *encouraged Mrs. Herrera to keep close* tabs on Graciela's whereabouts and to

Paradoxical intervention.

telephone Graciela occasionally at a previously arranged time. Graciela rejected my proposal immediately, but Mrs. Herrera compromised by stating, "If I could keep track of you, then I would be willing to let you go out with your friends more often." After a short pause for consideration, Graciela agreed. As a reward, I suggested that once a week both of them spend one fun evening together outside of the house.

An elaborate system was arranged for Mrs. Herrera to keep track of Graciela. For instance, on Saturday evening, Mrs. Herrera was to call Graciela at 10 p.m., 12 midnight, and 1 a.m., Sunday morning,

The task was arranged intentionally so it had little chance for success.

Repair of parent/child subsystem.

Result of paradoxical intervention.

Removal of presenting problem.

Family "closed" system became an "open" system.

Reconstruct extended family and support system.

Therapist became a compadre to the family.

before Graciela returned home. Because the purpose of the telephone calls was to ensure Graciela's safety, the call was intended to be brief. However, it was Mrs. *Herrera's responsibility to call on time.* After the first week, Mrs. Herrera was successful in fulfilling her end of the agreement. At the end of the second week, Mrs. Herrera complained that she got tired especially on Saturday evenings doing nothing but waiting to call Graciela. She volunteered that her weekly *outing with Graciela had been enjoyable* and that her overall *relationship with Graciela seemed to have* improved. Mrs. Herrera asked if it was "okay" if she discontinued calling Graciela on her night out. I replied, "Who is going to take care of Graciela?" "She [Graciela] is a big girl now, *and besides I trust her,"* replied Mrs. Herrera.

As Mrs. Herrera's relationship with her daughter improved, the seizures stopped. The family had *increased its involvement* with church. Through church activities, Mrs. Herrera made friends with several *Hispanic single parents.* "When Graciela had a night out with her friends, I gave myself a night out with my friends, too," quipped Mrs. Herrera.

I had seen the family a total of 13 times, which covered a time span of four months. Six sessions were held conjointly with both Mrs. Herrera and Graciela. Five sessions were held with Mrs. Herrera alone, and two sessions were spent individually with Graciela. Two months after the termination, Mrs. Herrera twice referred two Hispanic American families to our agency for service. She made these families *promise to say "hi" to me* when they saw me.

PART 4: CULTURALLY RELEVANT TECHNIQUES AND SKILLS FOR SPECIFIC THERAPY MODALITIES

Marital Therapy

The traditional Hispanic American cultural values of familism, personalism, and hierarchy, and Catholicism may be responsible for the low Hispanic divorce rate. Unfortunately, married couple conflicts remain an integral factor in the overall functioning of a family. Such conflicts are further exacerbated by the immigration and acculturation process. Traditional Hispanic health-seeking behavior inhibits couples generally seeking help for their problems, especially those family problems that center on sensitive marital relationships. Only the middle class and more acculturated couples may seek marital therapy for their family problems (Falicov, 1982). The couple's unfamiliarity and reluctance to improve their marital relationship may result in a host of other family problems involving alcohol, drug abuse, psychosomatic illnesses, and children acting out. Because of the couple's conscientious role as parents, they may be more receptive to seeking therapy for their child. The therapist should not prematurely and openly confront the couple about the real nature of their couple relationship or the cause of their child's problem. Instead, the therapist needs to adopt Minuchin's joining technique and use the parent-child focus as an indirect means to resolve the couple's conflicts. The following specific guidelines are suggested while providing marital therapy to a Hispanic American couple.

Incorporating the Extended Family System

The traditional closeness in a parent-child relationship can be a source of marital conflict. Minuchin's system boundaries concept relating to enmeshment and disengagement is helpful in assessing and restructuring the spousal relationship. Because of the hierarchical role structure of the Hispanic American couple relationship, the therapist should not use the egalitarian relationship framework as a guide or standard for couple performance. The important focus here is to rectify the problem area for which the family came and is willing to cooperate. What constitutes an appropriate level of self-differentiation or couple subsystem differentiation is cultural-specific and highly idiosyncratic. "Respeto"for the individual and couple's dignity is vital especially in the assessment stage of couple therapy.

If the husband refuses to cooperate because of "machismo," the therapist again can mobilize extended family member(s) to help. Padrino, a godparent by marriage, is often an ideal person with whom the therapist can work collaboratively to improve the couple's conflict. Working collaboratively with the padrino, in addition to sometimes being the only way to get the couple to cooperate, offers the following advantages: (1) It enables the couple to resolve conflict in a culturally relevant and natural fashion; (2) it reduces cultural and language barriers; (3) it mobilizes the natural source of the problem-solving approach; and (4) it reinforces the client's extended family system ties. The specifics of working with the padrino who serves as a therapist-helper is described in Landau's (1981) work with immigrants.

Strategic Use of Individual Interview

The Hispanic American husband sometimes has difficulty openly admitting that marital conflicts exist. His wife is usually reluctant to challenge openly her authoritarian husband in the therapist's presence. Under such circumstances, individual interviews can be used as a tool to bridge the gap. The individual interview is particularly beneficial at the beginning phase of therapy. First, it promotes the development of rapport or personalism. The one-to-one interview contact facilitates the development in each spouse of the secure feeling that the therapist "understands and is concerned about me, not just my marriage." Such feelings of "respeto" are particularly important whenever the individuals experience massive negative internalized introjection during the early stage of personal development (Kernberg, 1975). A therapeutic context facilitated by the one-to-one interview fosters trust and diminishes cognitive distortion detrimental to problem solving. Second, the individual interview provides an opportunity for the disclosure of intimate information that spouses are often reluctant to disclose in a conjoint couple interview. Examples of such information include extramarital affairs, incest, or thoughts of divorce. Such information is vital to the understanding of the couple's problem, as well as to their motivations and capacities for resolving marital conflicts.

To rectify the confidentiality, secrets, and triangulation issues prevalent in marital therapy, the therapist should inform the couple at the beginning of the individual interview that confidentiality will be maintained. The therapist may also suggest disclosure of some specific information considered essential to resolving the couple's conflict. Again, disclosure of particular information should be mutually agreed upon between the individual and the therapist, with the individual client assuming the disclosing role. In view of the Hispanic culture's emphasis on familism and familial obligations, spouses usually are cooperative and do whatever is necessary to resolve their conflicts.

Teaching Communication and Problem-Solving Skills

Despite the couple's willingness to improve their relationship and to resolve conflicts, most Hispanic American couples are conditioned by a traditional cultural upbringing that prescribes how a couple should interact. As the nature of a couple's relationship shifts from hierarchical to egalitarian, the traditional mode of couple interaction, especially for sensitive problem-solving issues, may no longer be functional. Hence the couple needs to learn new ways of relating to each other on both the cognitive and affective levels. On the cognitive level, the couple is advised to specify their expectations of each other and of their marriage. They need to learn when and how to use "I" statements (Satir, Stachowiak, and Taschman, 1975) to relate to each other in a self-differentiated way. They need to learn communicative feedback techniques and a style of communication that is congruent, direct, and open (Satir, 1967).

In addition, the couple needs to be sensitized to realize that their ability to communicate openly and directly on the cognitive level is influenced by their ability to empathize with each other's feelings. To teach a spouse to communicate empathically, the therapist can request that both the husband and wife think about and then communicate (either to the therapist or to the spouse) his or her understanding of the feelings and view point of the other. Such understandings are then checked out with the other spouse and inaccuracies are corrected (Guerney, 1977). Particular attention should be given to each spouse's understanding of (1) what he or she has done or said that has aroused hurt feelings in the other, and (2) what the other wishes would have happened instead of what did happen (desired alternative behavior).

To help a Hispanic husband rectify prior learning of "machismo," the therapist can offer cognitive awareness training. By asking questions such as "When you first began to feel angry, what were you thinking?

What were you saying to yourself as your wife disagreed with you? What were your images of your partner and yourself during this time?" The husband can be helped to recognize many irrational thoughts and perceptions that he had been conditioned to have. Examples, such as "If I let her push me around like this, I'm not a man," or "she is exactly the same as my mother," help a husband/wife bring into conscious awareness many irrational thoughts and feelings that are dysfunctional in their relating to each other as a couple.

Divorce Therapy

The divorce rate among the Hispanic American population is relatively low in comparison to the Anglo population (Falicov, 1982, p. 140). As stated previously, there are several factors explaining why the divorce rate among Hispanic's is not as high as other groups. Familism and the Catholic religion both strongly discourage divorce. Hispanic couples traditionally considered marriage as a family or extended families matter and that its dissolution will provoke strong negative sanctions by extended families. Hispanics basically are pragmatic and realistic in their selection of a mate, and they seldom rate romantic love as the most important ingredient in their marriage. Harmony within the family and the welfare of the children are the primary motivators in most Hispanic marriages. However, the process of immigration and acculturation has threatened many of these traditional values. Many acculturated wives no longer wish to be "unequal" of "inferior" to their husbands. The more acculturated husbands may also find traditional married life-styles unromantic and boring. A husband's dissatisfaction with a "business"-type spouse relationship may cause him to establish a more romantic relationship outside the marriage. This can lead to marital discord and divorce.

Again, in view of the Hispanic American's unfamiliarity with family therapy, only the more acculturated and financially capable couple will seek divorce therapy. The majority of the divorce therapy clients come to the attention of the therapist during moments of crisis, such as when the husband abruptly decides to get a legal divorce, or the wife decides to divorce her husband because of physical abuse. In either instance, divorce therapy is conducted under extremely stressful circumstances. It requires quick decisions on the part of the client(s) as well as the therapist. The following recommendations are offered to ensure that such clients receive services responsive to their needs.

Exploring Divorce Experiences and Consequences

Most Hispanic Americans consider divorce as the last resort to resolve their conflicts. The therapist should be attentive and nonjudgmental in assisting the individual or couple to determine if divorce is the final alternative. If the client is heavily indoctrinated in the Catholic religion, divorce can be a traumatic and guilt-ridden experience. This, coupled with feelings of family obligations, can temporarily immobilize or distort the individual's cognitive abilities. As the therapist empathizes with the client's anxiety or uncertainty about divorce, she also needs to confront the client about the realities he or she will face as the result of a divorce. Under no circumstances should a therapist offer moral judgment. Doing so would compound the client's feeling of guilt.

The final decision for divorce entails the husband/wife shifting from a collateral to an individualistic orientation. This may cause great pain and uncertainty and it also can temporarily immobilize a person's normal functioning. For individuals who have experienced a great deal of rejection and criticism in the past, the divorce experience can reactivate such repressed negative self-images, causing the individual to feel unlovable, unworthy, and repulsive (Kohut, 1972). If the individual is a spiritualist, he or she may experience "despojo" or other emotional of physical symptoms requiring medical or folk healing attention. Hence the therapist's ability to assess the client's situation in an interpersonal, intrapersonal, and cultural content is extremely important during the early phase of divorce therapy.

Extended Family and Social Support

Once the divorce has been decided, the therapist needs to assess the client's coping skills and capacities, along with the presently available social support system. The client's extended family normally is a good support source for economic, child care, and emotional needs. These resources will not be readily available to some clients, especially those who are "newly arrived." Then the therapist's role is to link the client's needs with existing resources, taking advantage of agency resources provided by the mainstream society.

Because divorce is unacceptable in traditional Hispanic culture, some divorced clients may find their extended families unsympathetic, hostile, and unsupportive. The therapist then becomes the client's only source of emotional support. The therapist should not interpret the client's behavior as overdependency. This reliance should be regarded as an expected normal transitory behavior characteristic of an individual experiencing emotional stress and cultural transition. If a client is unable to endure excessive emotional cutoff and strongly desires contact with the extended family, the therapist can serve as a mediator between the client and his or her extended family.

The client will be involved deeply in the crisis of divorce and emotional alienation from the former spouse and possibly from the extended family. A divorced mother may require assistance in conducting her daily chores or such responsibilities as parenting. Again, the therapist can assume an active role, including transporting the children to school or clinics, and so on, in order to assist the client during this trying period.

Postdivorce Adjustment and New Relationships

Traditionally, the mother-child relationship among the Hispanics is strong. The absence of a father from the family because of divorce can easily intensify the mother-child transaction and foster enmeshment symptoms (Minuchin, 1974). To avoid this, therapy with the mother may include (1) sensitizing her to the dangers of enmeshment; (2) encouraging children to have more interaction with the extended family, peers, and other adults; (3) and encouraging the mother to capitalize on the divorce experience and to enjoy single life and friends.

The traditional hierarchical role structure of the Hispanic culture does not prepare the mother to assume a disciplinary role with her children or to assume the "executive" role essential to daily family living. The therapist needs to teach the mother's single-parenting skills and assertive skills essential in dealing with matters outside of the home and on behalf of the family. A divorced mother will probably have strong feelings of family obligation and guilt. Some divorcées experience great difficulty in letting go of the ex-spouse. Her children's conscious or unconscious fantasy or maneuvers in getting their father back into the family do not help the mother cope with divorce or the feeling of loss. The client's "unfinished business" fosters her enmeshment with her children and may retard her effort and opportunity to establish a new emotional relationship. Referring the client to a divorce support group is beneficial to a divorcée who perceives her personal loss or unhappiness as unique and helpless.

Single-Parent Therapy

Even with a low divorce rate, the number of Hispanic American single-parent households is unusually high. In a study of Puerto Rican family households in New York City, 28% of them were headed by a female (Fitzpatrick, 1981) who was the only parent in the family. The high rate of single-parent households may be partly encouraged by New York City's regulation that financially subsidizes female-headed households. Another explanation could be the fact Hispanic American families disfavor legal divorce. Whatever the reason, the fact remains that there is an increased number of Hispanic American families headed by a female who is the only parent in the family (U.S. Bureau of Census, 1980b). Generally speaking, there are great stresses and demands generated in two-parent households. When the parental or adult figures are reduced to one, the demands and stresses related to running a household become enormous. The following suggestions aim to assist these families in resolving problems characteristic of single-parent households.

Mobilizing the Support System

One of the strengths of a Hispanic American family is its strong familism and extended family ties. When the father is absent from the family, a reduction in family income usually results. In addition, the mother has to assume double roles as both nurturer and disciplinarian to the children. Meanwhile, the mother is deprived of a constant companion with whom to share problems and exchange emotional and physical needs. The therapist's intervention is to ascertain the level of need for all family members and to link the family members' needs to existing family system resources. During moments of crisis, it is not unusual for different siblings to be cared for by different relatives (Fitzpatrick, 1981). This practice is consistent with the Hispanic American orientation of familism.

Some Hispanic Americans, due to their new arrival status, geographic location away from major cities, or conflict with the extended family, need services provided by the mainstream societal agencies. They may have no knowledge of or experience with such agencies. The therapist's role is that of a mediator or advocate whose primary responsibility is to assist the client in obtaining what she needs and is entitled to for her family.

Hispanic single parents are usually willing to work outside of the home to provide for the family, but they lack employable skills. Some of them also have great difficulty reading and writing English. The therapist's role is to refer them to the Hispanic cultural center or the appropriate language or job training facilities where they can learn English and employable skills. It is important to attend to the basic needs of the single parent and her family prior to attending to the psychological and emotional transactional needs.

Restructuring the Family

The absence of the father from the spousal system and from the family as a whole requires family renegotiation and a restructuring of the family system boundary (Minuchin, 1974). The Hispanic American hierarchical role structure by age and sex can easily place the oldest male child in the family in the absent father role. Thus the intergenerational boundary between parent-child is ruptured and an enmeshment is created between mother and the oldest son. The traditional closeness of the mother-child relationship should not be misconstrued automatically as enmeshment. However, if the mother-child relationship excludes other siblings or extended family members, there is a concern as to whether the present relationship is conducive to the normal development and optimum functioning of the mother or the child.

In discerning the appropriateness or inappropriateness of a mother-child relationship, the therapist needs to consider the following factors: (1) the normal developmental needs of the child and the mother; (2) the degree to which the present mother-child relationship is meeting or not meeting the mother's needs or the child's needs; and (3) the relationship between the presenting family problem(s) and the mother-child relationship. Generally, if the present family problem is unrelated to the mother-child relationship, the therapist should not focus upon the mother-child relationship.

To assist a single parent to function effectively, the therapist is advised to assess if daily household tasks such as cooking, cleaning, children attending schools, and so on are properly taken care of. In addition, the therapist needs to assess if the mother is effective in providing emotional nurturance for her children. In some instances, the mother also is expected to deal effectively with institutions and agencies such as schools, churches, or health care clinics. It is important that the single parent is aware of different roles she plays on behalf of the children and the family. It is also important that the therapist be supportive of the mother and not be unrealistically demanding of her.

The therapist may need to perform some of the essential duties for the single parent during this crisis-filled transitional period. As the crisis period subsides, the therapist needs to assist the mother in rearranging the family structure so that the essential tasks can be accomplished more efficiently without disturbing the intergenerational boundary. For example, older siblings can be assigned new tasks, including bringing home income like the father previously had done. Similarly, younger siblings can be expected to assume more household chores previously done by older siblings. The single parent can avoid quick burn-out this way can continue with the task of becoming self-sufficient enough to raise the children by herself.

Differentiation of Self

Hispanic American females' traditional devotion to motherhood makes the adjustment to single-parenthood a bit easier. Yet, the period of "singlehood" created by divorce can reactivate repressed, unresolved emotions and conflicts. For some single parents, this period can reinforce their feelings of low self-concept and unworthiness. It is important that the therapist assess developmentally where the client is and be attentive to her unresolved needs.

Bowen's (1978) concept of differentiation of self is most applicable at this stage of therapy. The client at this time needs to assess where she has been and where she wants to go. A Hispanic American's sense of familism and strong ties to the extended family are sources of strength. A single parent also needs to be aware of the fact that she is a separate individual and has some control over how others treat her and how she acts and reacts to others. This period of "singlehood" can be capitalized on. The therapist can encourage the single mother to reflect upon her strengths and future direction. She needs to evaluate her previous marital relationship and to derive some self-understanding about the kind of person she is, as well as the kind of persons she wishes to meet. Clients from the lower socioeconomic status are overly burdened with the demands of survival. However, they also are entitled to self-understanding and normal growth development. They need knowledge about how to survive physically and materially. They need skills to help them manage their lives more intelligently and satisfactorily.

Reconstituted Family Therapy

Hispanic Americans have a strong sense of familism and obligation to family of origin. Problems abound when there is a marriage of an ex-spouse with children of a previous marriage. If members of a reconstituted family carry with them unresolved conflicts from the previous spouse, or father or mother, their transactions with current reconstituted family members tends to become entangled. The following suggestions are offered in providing family therapy for a reconstituted Hispanic American family.

Focus on Parental Coalition

Bowen (1978) emphasizes the importance of self-differentiation from family of origin. Minuchin (1974) stresses the necessity for establishing a strong spousal subsystem in family living. This is particularly important in the case of a reconstituted family with children from previous marriages. Many individuals enter a reconstituted family without ever having successfully worked through or terminated previous relationships with ex-spouses. Such unresolved feelings are stumbling blocks to building a strong coalition with the present spouse. If the present marital relationship is not firmly grounded, child-rearing practices involving children from both previous and present spouses can cause confusion and difficulty. A majority of reconstituted families were built upon the premise or fantasy that remarriage is good or essential to the normal development of their children from a previous marriage in that every child needs an adult male or female with whom to model. Children from the previous marriage will probably experience ambivalence and difficulty within the present family context. The "unspoken" contract promised by the new marriage is, therefore, broken and the new marriage may fail.

Therapy with a reconstituted family requires impressing upon the parents the necessity for a close reliance on each other. This is difficult when Hispanic American mothers are more devoted to maternal or motherly love for their children than maintaining romantic relationships with husbands they traditionally respect and defer to. A Hispanic American mother may feel that she owes loyalty to her children and nothing to her present husband who before marriage was just a friend. Therefore, it is important that the therapist emphasize to the spouses, especially the wife, that a strong marital coalition is a prerequisite to ensure the healthy and normal development of all children in a reconstituted family.

Building a strong parental coalition often is a brand new concept to spouses of reconstituted families. Many spouses come from familial backgrounds filled with marital conflicts. This, coupled with their most recent negative experiences with an ex-spouse, makes parental coalition an illusion. A strong parental coalition may require each spouse to modify traditional husband/wife roles. It may require a more egalitarian mode of interaction. The therapist, in being consistent with Hispanic American culture, needs to emphasize the welfare of the children and the overall well-being of the entire family. Within this context, the couple can work to strengthen their marital relationship.

Define Roles and Expectations

The characteristics of a well-functioning family are its clear role definition and expectations. This has great implications as it applies to reconstituted families. Because of old habits and long-time familial obligations, each family member is taught and conditioned how he or she should behave in a family context. The reluctance on the part of some family members to cooperate in a reconstituted family may result from a lack of clear direction and expectations, as well as from loyalty to one's own father, mother, or other family members. It is important that the therapist allows and encourages all family members to express their discomfort and ambivalence about the new familial composition. A consensus should then be derived specifying the roles and functions of each family member. The Hispanic American culture prescribes that children respect all adults. It is a common practice among Hispanic Americans for adults to raise children who are not their own (Garcia-Preto, 1982).

As a strategy to rectify problems with stepchildren in reconstituted families, some authors (Haley, 1976; Minuchin, 1974; Carter and McGoldrick, 1980) suggest that the stepmother take a passive role, leaving the father/stepfather to take charge of the children. This directive is in direct opposition to Hispanic American culture, which prescribes a woman's responsibility is to care for her children on a day-to-day basis. The stepmother may feel totally displaced and resentful if she is advised to take a hands-off position in dealing with the children. If the therapeutic objective is to weaken the enmeshment between mother and child, the therapist may advise strengthening the parental subsystem boundary, and/or if the father-child subsystem is strengthened, then enmeshment between a mother-child subsystem diminishes.

In interacting with stepchildren, a stepfather's "machismo" and traditional sense of hierarchy should be tempered with flexibility and humility. Most Hispanic American stepfathers expect "respeto" and deference from stepchildren, who, due to their loyalty to their biological father, may not comply. Therefore, a stepfather needs to be challenged to understand that a stepchild's total deference to his authority may be construed as disowning his or her biological father. At times, especially when the child is experiencing adolescent independence, deference to authority figures is unrealistic and may be incongruent with the child's normal development. If a "natural" stepfather-son relationship fails to materialize, the stepfather should not interpret it as a personal insult or failure on the part of the child's mother to cooperate. If the stepfather-son relationship lacks the love and affection most stepfathers romanticize, their relational transactions can still be civil. They would not then jeopardize the parental subsystem relationship or the overall functioning of the family.

Extended Family Members

When a couple desires to establish a reconstituted family, members of the extended family may not be as eager. Some extended family members may have strong ties with the divorced spouses and their children. Reluctance and unreadiness on the part of the extended family can sabotage the development and functioning of a reconstituted family. This is particularly true with Hispanic American families who value familism and extended family ties. Therefore, it is important in therapy with a reconstituted family that the therapist assess the level of enmeshment or differentiation that the divorced spouse and the children experience with relatives of the previous marriage. In addition to paying attention to the daily or weekly contact that the children maintain with relatives of the previous marriage, the therapist needs to ask each individual in the family about his or her present feelings and contact with relatives of the former marriage.

If there is "excessive" contact between the child and the relatives of a former marriage, the therapist needs to inform the parents of the potential setbacks such contacts will have on the reconstituted family. If necessary, the therapist can visit relatives or extended family members who are "overly involved" with the child. The therapist can solicit cooperation from the extended family members involved in the enmeshment. Once the extended family members are convinced that their overinvolvement may interfere with the normal development of the child in the reconstituted family, they will probably cooperate. If a child in the reconstituted family is unable to adjust, the extended family may care for the child temporarily. This is a common practice among Hispanic American families (Garcia-Preto, 1982).

PART 5: CONCLUSION

Hispanic Americans are becoming the largest non-White ethnic minority group in America. Their socioeconomic status, political discrimination, and poor physical and mental health problems must not be overlooked. Hispanic Americans have a keen sense of relating their health and mental health problems to improper interpersonal relationships and dysfunctional family transactions. They are receptive to family therapy, provided the therapist is knowledgeable and respectful of their culture, which values familism, personalism, hierarchy, fatalism, and spiritualism.

Many Hispanic Americans are gradually acculturated to the middle-class mainstream society, but a vast majority of them still are struggling with basic survival needs. They experience racial discrimination, poverty, poor physical and mental health, and substandard housing and education. These are the families with whom the therapists can expect to have frequent contacts. These families need more than feeling good about themselves and other family members; they need the basic necessities to survive. Hence the role of a therapist in working with Hispanic Americans extends beyond the psychologically oriented healer role to include other essential and functional roles. These may consist of roles as cultural broker, mediator, educator, and advocate. The therapist needs to involve and work cooperatively with priests and other spiritual and indigenous leaders who are influential in the clients' lives. Finally, the strength of the Hispanic American family lies within its familism and extended family ties. These should be employed as guiding posts for assessment and therapy considerations.

5

Family Therapy with Black Americans

PART 1: PRETHERAPY PHASE CONSIDERATIONS

The Black American Family Structure

The Black American family is more diverse than has been recognized; there is no such entity as "the Black family." The diversity that exists among Black families is a reality determined by a complicated interplay of factors. To understand the Black family, Billingsley (1968, pp. 50-51) suggests viewing it as a social system interacting with a number of other systems, and that its historical perspective be reviewed in order to comprehend its structure and function. He further explains that Black people operate with a differentiated social structure that governs their behavior, and that Black family structure should be perceived as an adaptation to a set of social-political conditions existing in the family's wider social environment. Unfortunately, until relatively recently, most studies of Black family life have focused on the lower income group, while ignoring the "stable" poor Black and the middle-class Black families. The deviation of Black families from White middle-class norms has led to the labeling of the Black family as "pathological" (Moynihan, 1965).

Blacks have emigrated to the United States from many different countries over the past four centuries. Today, the largest group of Blacks in the United States are those of African origin whose ancestors were brought directly here as slaves (Brown and Forde, 1967). Of a total of over 200 million people in the United States, approximately 26 million, or 12%, are identified as Black (U.S. Bureau of Census, 1980a). Between 1970 and 1979, the Black population grew more than twice as fast as that of the White population (14.4% increase for Blacks versus 6.3% increase for Whites). A larger proportion of Blacks than Whites continue to live in urban areas. In 1979, 90% of all Black families lived in metropolitan areas, and over 50% resided in central cities (U.S. Bureau of the Census, 1979). 52% of Black families comprised both the husband and wife, but a significantly larger percentage of Black households than White households (45% for Black, and 13% for Whites) were headed by a woman (U.S. Bureau of the Census, 1980b). The rate of unemployment among Blacks has also increased in the last decade. In 1980, Black unemployment (11.8%) was higher than it was in 1969. In 1979, 11.7% of Blacks were unemployed, compared to 5.2% for Whites (U.S. Department of Labor, 1980). There is also a wide discrepancy between Black and White median family income. In 1980, the median family income for Blacks was 12,674 and for Whites, 21,904 (U.S. Bureau of Census, 1980c). There are equally as many poor Black families currently as there were a decade ago, but the number of poor White families has decreased (U.S. Bureau of Census, 1979). Education and occupation make little impact on this racial gap in income levels. For instance, college-educated Black men earn less than college-educated White men. Black women college graduates earn less than White men with only high school diplomas (National Urban League, 1978). Despite falling far behind Whites in almost every social and economic area, Black families as a group have shown an amazing ability to survive in the face of impossible conditions (Billingsley, 1968). The following discussion aims at presenting cultural values that serve as a pillar for the survival and accomplishments of the Black families.

Cultural Values in Relation to Family Structure

The cultural values of Black families are influenced by three major sources: (1) residuals from Africa, (2) identification with mainstream America, and (3) adaptations and responses to the "victim" system that is a product of racism, poverty, and oppression (Pinderhughes, 1979). The circular feedback process of the victim system works as shown in Figure 5.1.

Pinderhughes (1976) believes the victim system is the single most important factor preventing Blacks from having a unified culture and from integrating the Black culture with that of the American mainstream. In his review of the strengths of Black families, Hill (1972)

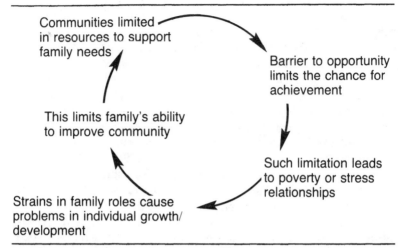

Figure 5.1 Circular Feedback Process of the Victim System

identified several cultural themes that he believes form the bases of survival for Black families. While these values are basically responses to the problem of the victim system and powerlessness (Solomon, 1976), they are also themes that underlie the diversity of Black families and communities that give them coherence. These themes include (1) strong kinship bonds among a variety of households; (2) strong work, education, and achievement orientation; (3) high level of flexibility in family roles; and (4) strong commitment to religious values and church participation. Along with these cultural themes, the (5) humanistic orientation and (6) endurance of suffering are added to form a broader base for understanding and appreciating the patterns and functioning of Black families. The following sections discuss each of these cultural themes as they relate to Black family structure and functioning.

Strong kinship bonds. Strong kinship bonds and the extended family are heavily influenced by traditional African culture, which valued collectivity above individualism (Clark, 1972, p. 13; Nobles, 1974). It is generally acknowledged that the Black kinship network is more cohesive and extensive than kinship relationships among the White population. This assumption is validated by the U.S. census data (1979) that indicate a larger proportion of Black families take relatives into their households. Strong kinship bonds can provide valuable functions and needed service to Black families. Stack (1974) has described how kinship ties and extended family problems may become an integral part of family life. Other studies have revealed that kinsmen help each other with financial aid, child care, and house chores, and other forms of mutual support (Martin and Martin, 1978; Shimkin et al., 1978). Further, strong kinship bonds enhance the emotional relationships within the extended family network and beyond. It helps the family to deal with environmental threats in such a way as to ensure the survival, security, and self-esteem of its members (Chestang, 1976).

Strong education and work achievement orientation. Parents in Black families have plenty of experience with the victim system and the harsh reality of the racist American system. Yet they still believe that the essential path to success in life is through higher education, work security, and social mobility. Parents or older siblings frequently make self-sacrifices to enable the younger members of the family to secure a good education. This "reciprocal obligation" (McAdoo, 1978) process explains why some older children drop out of school. They enter the labor force as a means to support their younger siblings' education. Studies have also indicated that a majority of low-income Black parents aspire to a college education for their children and that an overwhelming majority of Black college students come from lower-and working-class families (Hill, 1972, p. 13).

The high unemployment rate among Blacks is a direct result of the victim system, and it should not be misconstrued as Blacks lacking a work incentive or work ethic. Contrarily, Hill (1972, p. 19) cited data that indicate that 60% of the Black poor work as compared with about 50% of the White poor.

Flexibility in family roles. The widely accepted standard (of the dominant society) that the husband-father performs the instrumental (i.e., economic) functions while the wife-mother carries out the expressive (i.e., domestic and emotional) functions, does not apply to Black families. According to Billingsley (1968, p. 25), such a framework for examining the functioning of Black families is too simplistic for it fails to take into consideration of historical and political perspectives of the Blacks. Many Black husband-fathers perform expressive functions while wives-mothers perform instrumental functions. This pattern of functioning is related to the fact that, historically, the Black female had greater access to the economic opportunity structure of society than the Black male did. The fluid interchanging of roles within the Black nuclear family is assumed to have emerged out of the economic imperatives of Black life. Even older children participate in caring for younger siblings and occasionally working to augment the family income (Jackson, 1972). Because the wife-mother may assume instrumental functions, therapists should not assume that Black families are matriarchal. Contrarily, most research supports the fact that an equalitarian pattern typifies most Black Families (Scanzoni, 1975; Kunkel and Kennard, 1971).

Commitment to religious values and church participation. The Black church has served a nurturing function for Black people for many years. A committed religious orientation was a major aspect of the lives of Black people in Africa and during the era of slavery. The church plays a vital role in the escape of Blacks from the oppression of slavery. Today, in times of crisis, religion and the social services provided by the church have been supportive elements in revitalizing hope for the Black people. In addition to providing Black families with services such as senior citizen activities, child care, educational groups, parenting groups, and housing development, the church also provides latent functions such as helping to maintain family solidarity, status conference, leadership development, release of emotional tensions, social/political activity, and amusements (Staples, 1978). Because the Black church has been a much stronger force as helping resource than traditional agencies and helping practitioners, Solomon (1976, p. 327) suggests a church-focused social delivery system as an alternative structure to meeting the needs of Black families.

Humanistic orientation. In the midst of their daily struggle for survival in a racist society, Black families have not lost sight of the value and the importance of concern for each other. Solomon (1976, p. 169) has referred to this value dimension of the Black family as "more humanistic and [Blacks] have greater validity than the hollow values of middle-class American society." This humanistic attitude that forms a family pattern is, no doubt, connected to a strong religious orientation, but without the Puritan influence. The Puritan work ethic characteristic of White American values is predominately task-oriented and motivated by economic achievement to the exclusion of other values. The Black humanistic orientation stresses person-to-person relationships and their cultivation. Baraka's (1973) work in the area of Black expressive culture through music, dance, and literature is suggestive of this humanistic aspect of Black culture. The humanistic orientation of Black culture can have strong implications during various therapeutic phases. It is the working alliance or relationship that is most significant or preferred over the accomplishment of a specific task according to a specific time frame.

Endurance of suffering. In view of the adversity Black Americans face, they have developed great tolerance for conflict, stress, ambiguity, and ambivalence. Further, they have developed a "healthy cultural paranoia" (Grier and Cobbs, 1968) that make them highly suspicious of others who differ from themselves in color, life-style, and values. The Black people's reluctance to explore and understand their suffering is also related to their strong religious or spiritual orientation. Emotional difficulties may be viewed as the "wages of sin," and interpersonal conflicts are generally construed as not following the "Lord's teachings." To seek relief from a family therapist rather than through prayer may signify an absence of trust in God. The Blacks' endurance for suffering may partly explain their underutilization of social services and high dropout rate in therapy.

These common Black American cultural values of strong kinship bonds, education and work achievement orientation, flexibility in family roles, religiosity and church participation, humanistic orientation, and endurance of suffering significantly influence Black American family organization and structure. A discussion of how these values affect subunits and overall family interaction follows.

Mate Selection and Husband/Wife Relationship

Due to the excess number of Black women vis-à-vis Black men, Black women are experiencing great difficulty in finding a compatible mate. Factors contributing to the shortage of Black men include a high rate of mortality, incarceration, and intermarriage (Stewart and Scott, 1978). According to 1979 census data, it is estimated there may be as many as two million Black females without a male counterpart. This fact may also contribute to the large number of female-headed households in the Black community. When it comes to finding a mate, the middle-class woman has no advantage over the lower-class counterpart. Bayers's (1972) study showed many Black college women, especially those at Black institutions, remain single. Many college graduated Black women marry men with less education. Such marriages have a greater statistical probability of ending in divorce.

In times of high unemployment, Black women have historically worked outside the home and have often been the sole wage earners. Hence the husband-wife relationship of a Black couple has been more egalitarian then for the White American couple. Such role flexibility between male and female is also a part of socialization process within the

Black culture (Scanzoni, 1971; Jackson, 1973). Some therapists (Baga-rozzi and Wodarski, 1978) suggest that when power is shared equally between the couple, the probability of successful conflict resolution is greater than when large discrepancies exist.

Regardless of socioeconomic status, most Black males expect recognition as head of the household. However, their inability to provide for the family due to discriminating practices in the work field has greatly affected their role identity and involvement with their families. A family therapist should not misconstrue the Black fathers' inability to provide as peripheralness. Instead, creative approaches should be used to involve the fathers during family therapy (Hopkins, 1973).

Parent-Child Relationship

While a Black father's involvement with his children generally is hindered by economic restrictions, a Black mother is generally recognized for her devotion and care of her children. Many Black women consider motherhood a more important role than that of wife (Bell, 1971). The role of Black mothers is often criticized because they do not conform to middle-class modes of child rearing. Billingsley (1968, p. 28) has pointed out that child rearing or "socialization is doubly challenging for the family must teach its young members how to be human, but also how to be Black in White society."

Lewis (1975) has outlined four characteristics of child rearing within a Black family. These characteristics involve valuing personal unique-ness and include the following: (1) individual attributes often serve as the most important criteria for judging others; (2) inhibitions on the expression of one's uniqueness are regarded as undesirable or hurtful; (3) the individual is viewed as a powerful self-willed entity, taking an active role in manipulating the environment; and (4) involvement with other human beings takes precedence over involvement with inanimate objects. It is generally recognized that a Black child's self-esteem and self-image are interwoven with group identity and group esteem. Studies have concluded that regardless of the region where a Black child lives or his socioeconomic background, he or she is aware at about age seven of the social devaluation placed on his or her racial group by the dominant society (William and Morland, 1976). This information, however, should not lead to the conclusion that all Black children internalize the poor esteem of the major society. Rosenberg (1979) has found that the

level of self-esteem of Black school children does not differ a great deal
from that of White school children, and that Black children in racially
homogeneous school situations who do not experience conflicting
attitudes of the larger society had even higher images of self-worth than
White school children.

In disciplining the children, Black parents may use physical measures,
but this is done with love and care. Staples (1976) attributes the
increasingly high Black child abuse rate to reporting bias and a
reflection of the effect of poverty and racism on the Black parent-child
relationship. The frequent absence of the father or male figure has long
been considered a negative factor in the psychological and emotional
development of a Black child (Rainwater, 1966). However, Hare (1975)
and Rubin (1974) have concluded that the fatherless child does not
significantly suffer from the absence of a father. This, in part, may be
corrected by the Black child's opportunity to have male role models
among the male kinsmen in his extended family network. Staples (1976,
p. 83) offers another explanation for the relatively undamaged self-
esteem of a father-absent Black child, that of countervailing influences
such as religion, reference groups, group identification, and positive
experiences in the extended family.

Sibling Relationship

There are three important factors that characterize the sibling
relationship within the Black family. First, there is generally equal
treatment of both sexes. From infancy and early childhood, children of
both sexes are treated equally, fostering a sense of personal uniqueness
and intensity in interpersonal relations. However, sex-based differences
in socialization patterns do emerge in early adolescence. Both sexes are
encouraged to complete their education, to find work, and to accept
family responsibilities. It is important to the Black families that a girl be
self-sufficient and independent, given the one-down position of Black
woman in White American society. According to Baumrind (1972), the
parents' expectation of an adolescent girl may carry with it an explicit
objective of developing toughness and self-sufficiency. Parental expectation is not perceived by the adolescent girl as rejection but as nurturing
and caretaking (Baumrind, 1972, p. 266). Despite differences in parental
expectations for adolescent boys and girls, there are few differences
attached to preferred male and female personality types or traits. Black
adolescents are taught that such traits as nurturing and assertiveness are

desirable for any individual, regardless of sex. Such nonbiased sex roles and traits are directly related to the young Black person's ability to relate to their future spouse in an egalitarian fashion and to prepare them for flexibility in performing various family roles.

Second, there are clear responsibilities assigned to siblings on the basis of age. A young child after the age of three is frequently placed in the care of an older sibling, male or female, who may care for a group of children. The oldest child's authority over the child group is strong, and so are his or her nurturing responsibilities for the younger siblings. The expectation of an older sibling caring for younger siblings represents a functional adaptation of families in which both parents or a single parent must work. Although it is evident in some cases that maturational development of the Black adolescent has been somewhat handicapped by insurmountable responsibility in other instances, it has provided an opportunity for further growth and maturation.

Third, the firstborn, regardless of sex, receives special preparation for a leadership role in the child group. It has been an established fact that, almost universally among Black families, the firstborn child receives more mothering and stimulation in infancy than do the children who follow (Lewis, 1975).

Intermarriage

Because laws against interracial marriage were declared unconstitutional by a United States Supreme Court decision in June 1967, intermarriage between Blacks and Whites has increased rapidly. In 1960, there were 51,409 Black-White marriages; in 1970, the total number of Black-White marriages had increased to 64,789 and by 1977, the number had increased to 125,000 (Bureau of the Census, 1978). According to public opinion polls, there is a growing tolerance of Black-White marriages (Bontemps, 1975).

Although a great deal has been written about the "abnormal" social and psychological characteristics of those involved in Black-White marriages, Porterfield's (1978) research study indicates just the opposite. A majority of the respondents involved in the study indicated no sign of pathological abnormality or any crusade against prejudice. With few exceptions, the respondents' motives for intermarriage do not appear to be any different from those individuals marrying in the conventional style, that is, within one's own race.

The sex-ratio between Black-White marriage shows that out of 125,000 known Black-White marriages, 75% consisted of a Black man and a White woman (U.S. Bureau of Census, 1978). Porterfield (1982) speculates some factors may have facilitated the development of this pattern. These factors include (1) Black men rebelling against White society; (2) Black men's perception that the White woman is a status symbol; (3) Black men's perception that the White female is less domineering than the Black female; (4) physically, the White female is perceived as more attractive; and (5) availability. Furthermore, there is a considerable concern that a disproportionate number of Black men in intermarriage are members of the middle class, and the dissolution rate for such unions is higher than for intraracial marriages (Heer, 1974).

There is a discrepancy of opinion among the Black community in regard to Black-White marriages. While some view this phenomenon as one channel through which equality can be achieved, others feel that such a marital union is inconsistent with a developing sense of Black peoplehood. Traditional older Blacks and many Black females are in opposition to Black-White intermarriages. The Black women's protest is mainly related to the disproportionate number of Black males to Black females. As society continues to become more sensitive to individual freedom and personal rights, future Black-White marriages can be expected to have a more acceptable climate for success. Social scientists and family therapists can play a vital role in Black-White marriages by objectively analyzing this phenomenon so that many of the fears, myths, and misconceptions can be corrected (Ho, 1984).

Divorce and Remarriage

Despite the Blacks' intense ties to family and their flexibility in family roles, marriage has proven to be an unstable institution for them regardless of socioeconomic class. As a group, the Blacks' divorce and separation rate is double that of White. In 1975, 30% of Black women who had ever been married were separated or divorced, compared to 20% of similar White women (U.S. Bureau of the Census, 1977).

One factor that is clearly attributable to the high divorce rate among Blacks is the American racist society, especially with regard to Black males. The high unemployment rate among Black males contributes neither to their self-concept not to their performance as an equal partner in marriage. The middle-class marriage among Blacks is less negatively affected by poverty than by the shortage of Black males, especially in the higher educational brackets. Bayer (1972) reported that there are approximately 60 college-educated Black males available for marriage to every 100 Black female college graduates. Many Black college women, especially those at Black institutions, remain single. Those Black women who marry Black men with less education risk a high probability of having the marriage end in divorce.

The shortage of Black males available for marriage is forcing Black women to reconsider the traditional idea of a long-lasting monogamous marriage. While they remain committed to an exclusive male-female dyad, they are considering more radical life-styles than the traditional concept of marriage (Smith, 1978). One study has confirmed the existence of informal polygamy among Blacks (Scott, 1979). The continued shortage of Black males and the Black females' coping mechanism to this phenomenon have significant implications in marriage and family therapy. While the therapist understands the Black males' pressure to be constantly sought after for marriage, she or he should also be empathic toward the Black females' barrier in pursuing a permanent marital relationship. Furthermore, female-centered family models among Blacks should not automatically spell gloom for family members because a household and an independent nuclear family are not synonymous. As we examine closely the network of family relations that bind households together, we come to appreciate the strength and richness of Black family life with or without the constant presence of the adult male.

Impacts of Discrimination, Migration, and Cultural Adjustments

Like every other ethnic minority group, Black Americans are forced to adapt to American mainstream and victim systems. While some families exhibit unusual strength and flexibility, and tolerance for ambiguity and creativity in their relationship with the systems, other families consistently experience difficulty in value conflict and identity confusion. For example, American values of individualism, independence, autonomy, ownership of material goods, achievement, mastery, efficiency, and future planning are in direct opposition to Black American cultural values that stress collectivity, sharing, affiliation, deference to authority, spiritualism, and respect for the elderly. In an attempt to survive the oppressive victim system, some Black Americans adopt a value orientation that emphasizes cooperation to resist powerlessness; strict obedience to authority in the context of felt oppression; toughness of character and creative activities in the form of art, music, and sports. When translated behaviorally, this value orientation can lead an individual to free emotional expression, immediate gratification, manipulative relationships, and passive-aggressive, rebellious, or aggressive characteristics. While these values and behaviors have an adaptive function to powerlessness, they also can be maladaptive to a person's mental health and interpersonal relationships (Pinderhughes, 1982). Young (1969) has outlined four possible ways in which a Black family can adapt to discrimination and biculturality. A Black family can (1) attempt to meet crises as they arise; (2) physically remove themselves from any stresses caused by a racist society; (3) willfully maintain externally imposed or self-imposed segregation; or (4) remove major barriers to assimilation into the opportunity structure. Scanzoni (1971) shows that the Black middle class has opted to function by removing barriers to assimilation. However, the path to assimilation is costly and it tends to generate cultural value and familial relational conflicts.

Surprisingly, given the pace of racial integration, few Blacks have beome assimilated into the mainstream mode of behavior. Blacks still congregate in separate facilities and organizations on White university campuses. They continue socializing in the inner cities after moving to the suburbs and maintain solidarity with extended family ties and with the Black community (Staples, 1978).

Family Help-Seeking Patterns and Behaviors

Black families often hesitate to seek mental health services. In addition to their general mistrust toward mainstream institutions, Blacks rely heavily upon extended family ties and church organizations during times of crises. Such patterns of help-seeking are typical among all Black families regardless of socioeconomic class (McAdoo, 1977). Reliance on natural support systems produces fewer feeling of defeat, humiliation, and powerlessness. Martin and Martin (1978) label such practice the "mutual aid system." It operates on the twin premises that families should seek security and independence, but that where family integrity is threatened, sharing resources and exchanging services across households are crucial.

Many Blacks still view therapy as "strange" and think of it as a process for "strange or crazy people" only. Their contact with family therapy is usually precipitated by crises and happens when other sources of help have been depleted. The Blacks' underutilization of psychological help and family therapy is also related to their general mistrust of the therapist, especially the White therapist (Jackson, 1973). The Blacks' negative attitudes toward therapists may explain to some extent why Blacks have been found to drop out of therapy earlier and more frequently than Whites (Sue et al., 1974).

While Blacks do prefer Black therapists over White therapists, they also prefer competent therapists over less competent Black therapists (Sattler, 1977). Competent skills and techniques in work with Blacks must take into consideration the complexities of life, particularly family and community life, from a Black point of view. Since 1972, there is evidence that Blacks are utilizing psychological services in increasing numbers and at much higher rates than expected. Sue et al. (1974) reported that in the Seattle, Washington, area Blacks utilized facilities at a higher rate proportionate to their population.

Applying Culturally Sensitive Family Theories, Models, and Approaches

The ecological systems paradigm, comprising both the family communication theory and family structure theory, is a useful framework for conceptualizing Black family interactional processes for it transcends ethnic, racial, and socioeconomic boundaries. This system paradigm also offers specific guidelines for analyzing and restructuring family functioning. Behavioral principles of the family communication theory and family structure theory are discussed in this section, along with practice principles derived from these theories.

Family Communication Theory

The following discussion of the major principles of communication is based primarily on the work of the Mental Research Institute in Palo Alto (Bateson, 1972; Watzlawick, Beavin, and Jackson, 1967; Jackson, 1967, 1968) and the work of Miller, Nunnally, and Wackman (1975). Several factors delineated by Watzlawick et al. are helpful in understanding the pragmatics of communication with Black American families.

Because all behavior is communication of one kind or another, it is impossible not to communicate. Black Americans are often labeled by therapist as nonverbal and incapable of dealing with feelings. Clark (1972, p. 65) states that the usual Black response in a state of anxiety has either been passive or aggressive—either say nothing or become loud, threatening, and abusive. However, the Black's behavior in therapy is not the same as it is at home. Their passive or aggressive behavior in therapy is a manifestation of their frustration and displaced anger toward the therapist, especially the White therapist. Grier and Cobbs (1968) suggest that the issue of trust for some Blacks reflects "healthy cultural paranoia" or a refusal to identify with and trust persons differing from themselves in color, life-style, and value.

The concept of *metacommunication*, defined as information containing a command, is highly relevant to Black American families. Despite the fact a Black child is taught to value his or her uniqueness and that the egalitarian relationship is a cornerstone of the Black family, metacommunication occurs when a family's basic security and safety needs are threatened. While passive-aggressive behavior characteristic of metacommunication is destructive in family relationships, a therapist's task is to assist the family to identify and rework its metacommunication process to problem solving.

Another principle of communication relates to the "punctuation" of communicational sequences (Bateson, 1972), as exemplified in mother-son conflict of a single-parent family. The mother punctuates the sequence of communication thus: "To be a responsible single-parent, I have to make my teenage son obey me." The teenage son, on the other hand, defines the relations differently: "I am old enough to work to help financially support my family and my mother; I am entitled to be treated like an adult with equal rights as my mother." The punctuation of the communicational sequences help to identify the nature of the power relationship and conflict. The role of the therapist is to assist family members to arrive at complementary punctuation.

Finally, the concept of digital (verbal) and analogic (nonverbal) communication has important implications in therapy with Black American families. Some Black families, especially the lower income families, communicate mostly through paraverbal channels in the pitch, tempo, and intensity of the verbal messages and the accompanying kinesthetic modifiers (Minuchin, 1967, p. 206). Different family members, due to age and interaction with the mainstream society, may possess different degrees of digital and analogic communication. Such differences are sure to cause communication problems in deciding the extent to which there is congruence between the message and the way it is delivered. The role of the therapist is to assist the family members to validate information sent and received and to avoid incongruent, invalidated paradox.

Satir's classification of family behavior for a family member under environmental or family internal systematic stress (Satir, Stachowiak, and Taschman, 1975) helps to explain a Black father's peripheral role in the family. The victim system places the Black adult male in a most vulnerable position. His unemployment status (possibly due to racist discrimination) in turn deprives him of self-worth and resources to provide for his family. He is cast in a "placator" role or irrelevant role assuming no responsibility. The Black mother being forced to head the household sometimes assumes the role as "blamer" in the family. When her authority is challenged or threatened by her husband or teenage children, she finds herself assuming the "super-reasonable" role. The children in such a stressful home environment can become "irrelevant" as a means of repressing their need for independence. The therapist should help family members avoid assuming these maladapted roles and adopt genuine and congruent ways of relating to one another.

Family therapy is an interactive process. The principles of behavior derived from the communication theory have contributed significantly to understanding the dynamics and interaction of the Black American family. The following discussion focuses on the manners in which the principles can be applied in actual therapy with a Black American family.

Communication Practice Principles

Because of the egalitarian power orientation within a Black family, the father should not be expected to lead the discussion during therapy. The Black mother's active involvement during therapy should not imply that the family is matriarchal. If the father is unavailable for therapy, it does not necessarily mean that he is disinterested or uninvolved. The father's absence may be caused by job overload or other responsibilities impeding his meeting with the family for therapy—generally at a convenient time for the therapist. The therapist needs to be flexible with scheduling, including arranging separate sessions for the father at a time most convenient for him. Similarly, the therapist may use written correspondence to help the father keep abreast of the therapy process. In view of the Black American's egalitarian and humanistic orientation, communicative skills employed by the therapist to help the family should not oppress or exploit either party in the family (Pinderhughes, 1976).

The Black family's inactive or nonverbal participation at the onset of therapy may convey the family's discomfort or mistrust of the therapist and the therapeutic process. The Black family's mode of communication also may be a reflection of their culture, particularly characteristics such as enduring suffering. Further, the family's minimal involvement in the early stages of therapy may be related to their religious beliefs that conflict with the therapist's cultural or religious beliefs. For example, regardless of the family's practicing religion, the philosophy by which Black parents raise their children often has deep religious influences. The biblical principle "spare the rod, spoil the child" is commonly used to support physical punishment and is an acceptable mode of discipline; it should not be interpreted as child abuse. Communication theory helps the therapist to understand and to appreciate what is *not*, as well as what is being communicated.

As a member of the victim system, regardless of socioeconomic status, every Black family experiences considerable anger because of discrimination or harsh treatment by the White society. Such anger needs to be dealt with in the therapy process (Halpern, 1970). Helping family members recognize and deal with this anger can be an essential communicative process in family therapy with Black Americans.

Haley defines a therapist's role as that of a "metagovernor of the family system." The therapist's communication should be guided by the pragmatics of Black American cultural values. For example, the humanistic and egalitarian orientation of the Black family may be offended by a therapist who uses professional jargon and who assumes familiarity with adult family members before asking their permission. The therapist who assumes the privilege of addressing adults by first names may elicit unverbalized anger. The adult family members may view the therapist as disrespectful (Hines and Boyd-Franklin, 1982).

Haley's therapeutic tactics, such as prescribing the symptom (encouraging the usual dysfunctional behavior), may be confusing to Black American families who are goal-directed and prefer problem solving in concrete terms. However, Haley's paradoxical messages (double bind) are often effective in work with a Black mother who rigidly reinforces what is expected of her culturally. By joining the mother's resistance for change, a therapist can help her explore different ways to fulfill her obligatory maternal role to safeguard her child from external threats and negative influences. Haley's technique of relabeling/reframing (by emphasizing the positive or behavior that can be changed) is consistent with the Black American culture's emphasis on humanistic orientation and harmonious living reflective of Black religious beliefs. The relabeling technique also can help the family shift from the disease model to an interpersonal or environmental perspective.

Virginia Satir's communication theory (1967) informs family members of the different dysfunctional roles they may occupy in family transactions. Because family members learned to assume different dysfunctional roles, they can also learn to relinquish these roles and to assume new functional roles. This educational focus of family interaction is consistent with the Black Americans' educational achievement need. Satir's theory focusing on the "feeling good" component of each individual reaffirms the Blacks' strong kinship bonds and humanistic orientation.

Capitalizing on the Black family's capacity for egalitarian power relationships, Miller et al.'s (1975) "I count you, I count me" mutual respect and support style of communication can be most responsive in helping the family members in problem solving. Through this style of communication, family members learn that they have control in interacting with others. Such control of power is integral in genuine interpersonal relationships, especially for some Blacks who are led to believe that they are essentially powerless.

Family Structure Theory

This discussion of family structure theory focuses on work developed and advanced by Bowen (1978) and Minuchin (1974). Reviewed here are behavioral principles and practice principles of structure family theory as they relate to assessment and therapy with Black American families.

The societal projection process, identified by Bowen (1978) is relevant as it applies to the powerless position of Black American families. This process creates societal scapegoats with which the Black clearly has been identified.

In the societal projection process, one group (the White society and the benefactors) maintains the illusion of competence at the expense of "unfortunates" by "helpfulness and benevolence." The benefactors assume the blamer role, accusing the unfortunate as inferior and underserving. Such a societal projection process, like the family projection process, creates and maintains homeostasis for a social system. In this manner, Bowen's societal projection process is similar to the formulation of the victim systems of racism and oppression.

In response to the internal threats created by a racist society, a Black family may protect themselves by maintaining rigid boundaries. The father's inconsistent involvement with the family due to job overload or unemployment can be highly susceptible to the process of triangulation, a three-person system that Bowen considers the building block of all emotional systems in and outside of the family. Given the reality that most Black families are embedded in a complex kinship network of blood and unrelated persons, the process of triangulation may not have the same meaning and intensity as for a traditional nuclear family.

As members of the victim system, some Black parents are determined to create a more favorable environment or future for their children. They expect their children to earn greater rewards from the opportunity structure than they themselves were able to achieve. Many Black middle-class parents actually warn their children of the consequences of associating with people who might interfere with their social and economic achievement (Scanzoni, 1971). Such intensity of purpose is relevant to Bowen's concepts of "family projection process" and the "multigenerational transmission process." These processes are responsible for many couple difficulties and parent-child conflicts.

As a means to cope with economic deprivation and demands, and also to escape from strong parental control and introjection, many Black families move away from their extended families and close friends. They then experience "emotion cutoff," defined by Bowen as unresolved emotional attachment to parents (Bowen, 1978, p. 382).

Minuchin views the structure of the Black American family as characterized by strong family ties, egalitarian relationships, and flexible family roles. Under normal conditions, such a structure can produce cohesion conducive to the developmental growth of all family members. Minuchin points out, however, that "the stressful contact of the whole family with extrafamilial forces" (1974, p. 63) can produce role confusion and power conflict within a family. By focusing upon the extrafamilial forces, Minuchin is sensitive to the political, economic, social, and cross-cultural processes of poverty and discrimination faced by many Black American families.

Black parents usually are burdened with meeting the economic survival needs of the family. Older siblings are assigned the responsibility of caring for younger children and assisting with other household duties. This structure should not be misconstrued as boundary diffusion, and thus Minuchin's (1974, p. 53) "parental-child" concept may not be applicable in this situation. This unique complementary accommodation between spouses and between parents and children characterizes a unique strength of the Black American family structure. However, as Minuchin cautions, such a family structure can be vulnerable if the parental delegation of authority is not explicit and the child lacks the power to carry out the responsibilities he or she attempts to assume. Moreover, if the parents abdicate their responsibilities, the child may be forced to become the main source of guidance, control, and decision making at a time when developmentally he or she is unprepared to handle these roles.

Structure Practice Principles

Bowen's societal projection process suggests that the therapist be open to exploring the impact of the social, political, socioeconomic, and broader environmental conditions of the families. Those environmental conditions or systems most likely to impinge on Black families include welfare, the courts, schools, Medicaid, food stamps, public housing, and so on. These systems are the integral components of the daily functioning of many Black families. The therapist must be knowledgeable about social service systems and other help-providing agencies and be willing to work collaboratively with various service providers on behalf of the family.

Bowen's concept relating to "differentiation of self" may be unrealistic and irrelevant when initially working with a Black family whose basic needs are the primary concern for therapy. Nevertheless, after the family's basic needs are realized, the process of "differentiation of self" may be helpful to those Black families who experience transactional difficulties that have cultural or intergenerational implications. Basic to personal or interpersonal problems is the individual's feeling of powerlessness. Once an individual learns that one of the greatest sources of power is from within, he or she can make decisions that are not patterned or rigid.

Bowen's focus on increasing differentiation by research methods and by genograms may be antithetical to the Black American's "present" orientation. Many Black Americans have experienced a painful past that they prefer to forget. For middle-class Black Americans who desire insight for personal growth and for resolving interpersonal problems with persons of different races, history taking and the use of genograms can be a penetrating tool toward self-differentiation.

Bowen's premise that the parental relationship dictates the entire nuclear family's emotional system is also applicable in work with Black families. However, his preference for singling out the couple relationship as a therapeutic target (Bowen, 1978, p. 175) may be premature for some Blacks who do not believe their couple relationship should take precedence over their children's concerns. Due to the shortage of Black males and their general unavailability at home, a therapist must be flexible and work with the mother individually or even include other significant adult family members, other than the child's biological father. If the biological father is available and is willing to be involved in therapy, the therapist should first focus on how the parents can interact differently in order to modify the child's behavior. As the parents modify their behavior in relating to their "problem" child, their relationship as a couple will improve.

The role of the therapist as that of a culture-broker (Bowen, 1978, p. 540) is highly desirable in work with Black families. It is important, however, that the therapist not assume the family's responsibility but assist them in using available resources and contacts to facilitate changes (Foley, 1975). Minuchin's differential applications of "joint techniques" (e.g., following the same family communication style) are helpful during the engagement phase of therapy with a Black American family. However, a great deal of caution should be exercised in employing such techniques, especially by a therapist who is not Black. Being a victim of a racist society, Black Americans are very observant and they are highly sensitive to behavior that is unreal. Hines and Boyd-Franklin (1982) suggest that sometimes it may be desirable for the non-Black therapist to acknowledge his or her difference in ethnic background and to discuss the family's feelings on this matter early in therapy. For an ethnic minority therapist, a good joining technique in work with a Black family may include sharing and agreeing with the family about the struggle each ethnic minority member in this society faces. Such empathic exchanges are consistent with the Black's humanistic orientation.

Minuchin's tracking technique aims to explore the content of family interaction and to analyze family structure. When using this technique, the therapist should keep in mind the strong kinship bonds of the Black family. For example, the amorphous spousal subsystem boundary might be caused by the husband's need to do extra work in order to support the family. Interpreting the less intense spousal interaction as pathological is premature, insensitive, and irrelevant. In addition, the Black family's flexibility in assuming different family roles should not be misconstrued as role confusion and family disorganization. It should be recognized and respected as a unique strength among Black families. To analyze a Black family structure without taking into consideration the strong extended family ties can do the client injustice and disservice. Hence Minuchin's system boundary-making and restructuring techniques are helpful, provided they are adapted to the Black family structured framework. In applying disequilibration (of boundary) techniques, Minuchin gives an example as to how a therapist can adapt his technique in work with a Black family whose structure includes a parental-child. Minuchin (1974, p. 98) suggests that "the therapeutic goal is to realign the family in such a way that the parental-child still helps the mother." The goal of the therapy is not to eliminate the child's parental role, which may be essential to the family's survival. Instead, the therapist needs to facilitate redistribution of the child's burdens and help the family make better use of the resources available to them.

Minuchin's "joining techniques" are generally sensitive to the Black American family structure, but his family restructuring techniques, such as escalating stress (by emphasizing differences), utilizing the symptom (by exaggerating it), and manipulating mood (by escalating the emotional intensity), are highly emotional and confrontational. Some Black families may be confused by these techniques and interpret them as a means to undermine their authority, integrity, and respect. These techniques should not be attempted prior to developing a trusting relationship. Their strategic application will be illustrated in the case illustration (Part 3) in this chapter.

The cultural values and structure of the Black American family were explored in the preceding pages. The communication and structural family therapy theories were reviewed along with their application in therapy with Black American clients. Attention will now be directed to culturally relevant techniques and skills in three phases of therapy: beginning, problem solving, and termination-evaluation.

PART 2: CULTURALLY RELEVANT
TECHNIQUES AND SKILLS IN
THERAPY PHASES

Beginning Phase

The engagement phase of therapy is a very critical period for Black American clients. Many Black clients distrust the therapists who represent mainstream society and utilize therapy only as a last resource to their problems. Blacks' strong endurance of suffering, religious beliefs, strong kinship bonds, and limited financial resources make family therapy less attractive and responsive to their needs. However, there are recent signs that Blacks are beginning to utilize psychological services and family therapy more, particularly lower-class Blacks. They are finding therapy action-oriented, short-term, and with a focus on changing concrete behaviors (Sattler, 1977).

The following discussion attempts to apply and integrate the cultural knowledge of Black Americans and communication and structural family theories used during the beginning phase of family therapy. Specifically, five major skills and techniques are considered essential in therapy with a Black American family in the beginning therapy phase. These skills and techniques include (1) engaging the client/family, (2) cultural transitional mapping and data collection, (3) mutual goal setting, (4) selecting a focus/system for therapy, and (5) the use of an eco-map.

Engaging the Client/Family

Learning how to engage a Black client/family begins with comprehending the circumstances under which the therapist-client contact takes place. Therapist-client contact is usually predicated by referrals from other health, social, and court-related agencies. The client's distrust is reinforced when the therapist is White and represents the establishment and the mainstream society. It is important that the therapist adopt a genuine and respectful "joining technique" by openly recognizing the strength that the family demonstrates by coming to therapy (Ho and McDowell, 1973). As a means to "accommodate" the family, the therapist needs to explore with the family their feelings or potential resentment toward seeking therapy. Because many Black families have past negative experiences with other health- and social service-related agencies, the therapist needs to define for the family the nature of his or her service and the role the family therapist plays. Hoehn-Sarie et al. (1964) and Acosta et al. (1982) have demonstrated the efficacy of orienting ethnic minority families.

Race is a major factor undermining the Black client's sense of powerlessness. The White therapist, therefore, may need to explore with the family the racial differences between the therapist and the family (Ho and McDowell, 1973). Some families may capitalize upon this opportunity to vent their anger in regard to discrimination and oppression, but the therapist should not react defensively or perceive this as a personal attack. Instead, helping the family to explore and express such repressed anger is an essential step in successfully engaging a Black family, regardless of its socioeconomic status (Bagarozzi and Wodarski, 1978, p. 163).

To be sensitive and empathic to the Black family's feelings of powerlessness does not imply that the therapist should take a less active role during this stage of therapy. Black families look for and expect the therapist to be strong. They look for the type of therapist strength that is "conveyed by an authoritative stance that communicates ability to interact vigorously but not oppressively, and understanding of the necessary stamina and commitment" (Pinderhuges, 1982, p. 121). Regardless of the nature of the family problem(s), Black families are likely to be most responsive to problem-solving, time-limited family therapy approaches. Often the family is so overwhelmed by multiple problems and the anxiety associated with seeking help that informing them at the engagement phase that therapy will be long term and difficult is self-defeating for the therapist and the family (Foley, 1975).

Transitional Mapping and Data Collection

While the family communication theory focuses on analyzing the here and now transactions of the family, family structure theory focuses on the family structure and functions in the present *and* in the past. Despite the Black family's responsiveness to problem-focused short-term therapy, some family problems cannot be successfully resolved without understanding the historical perspectives of the family. The circumstances surrounding the development and maintenance of the Black family have resulted in different life-styles among Black families.

In assessing the black family, experiential information is more important than chronological-developmental data. Important experiential information includes the experiences of the parents as children growing up in their families of origin; the couple relationship, their perspectives in child rearing; and the impact of social, economic, and political forces. Data collection has to be guided by the presenting problem. For example, both parents' rigid child-rearing practices must be examined historically in order to resolve their child's current socialization difficulty. The data collection process will be incomplete if the extended family system is not also included. The genogram is a useful tool for gathering information about forces that affect the current structure and functioning of the family. The Black family is strongly "present-oriented," so the therapist should explain carefully to the family how such information may help them analyze and resolve present problems. The genogram should not be constructed during the early stage of therapy or before a rapport has been developed. The therapist should look for an opportunity or opening to gather the desired information, rather than scheduling an agenda of data collection that the family might find insensitive and intrusive.

Black family genograms, when informal adoption has occurred, seldom conform completely to bloodlines (Hines and Boyd-Franklin, 1982). To obtain accurate information, the therapist needs to inquire who is in the family as well as who lives in the home. To inquire about the family's support system, the question, "Who can you depend on for help when needed?" should disclose significant individuals in the family's support system. It is important that the therapist be sensitive to the painful past many Black families have endured. Pinderhuges (1982) has suggested that the opportunity to replace gaps in knowledge with information, the feelings of shame with pride, and the identity confusion with a sense of integration and continuity through time have a profound therapeutic impact on Black families.

Mutual Goal Setting

Regardless of racial differences, all humans are goal-directed. Black American families share the same goals with their White counterparts (Berger and Simon, 1974; Scanzoni, 1971). However, Black American families find their attainment of goals more difficult than Whites due to discrimination and prejudice inherent in many social, cultural, and economic institutions in the United States. Discrimination can also affect the internal dynamics of a Black family. Scanzoni (1971) found that Black wives often become dissatisfied with their spouses' economic earning potential, and this becomes a major source of marital discord. The process of mutual goal setting with a Black family requires the therapist to assume an "ecostructural" approach that considers a family's environment and community (Aponte, 1979). The ecostructural reality or condition of poor Black families frequently includes welfare, the courts, schools, Medicaid, food stamps, and public housing. These families may face overwhelming socioeconomic problems, and survival needs should take precedence over family conflicts. Minuchin (1967) affirms that where patterns of change in the family are out of phase with the realities of extrafamilial systems, therapy will fail. Harris and

Balgopal (1980) advise focusing simultaneously on the problems and realities that are posed by external systems, as well as on the way the family manages its relationship with them.

Because of the Black's unfamiliarity with family therapy and high level of distrust toward the therapist, Aponte (1979) emphasizes the need to help a family experience therapy as a process that can produce immediate changes in their lives. Black families also need immediate success to help them sustain motivation for further structural changes in the family (Foley, 1975). Their positive response to success is related to their achievement need.

In formulating goals with the family, the therapist needs to pursue information in a problem-focused manner. Emphasis should be on the conditions maintaining the problem and how these conditions can be changed. Minuchin's tracking (data collection) technique is relevant in assisting the family to arrive at a goal that will ameliorate their immediate problem. This problem-focused approach should prevent the family's being overwhelmed with data and can maximize the therapist's selection of a therapeutic goal congruent with the family's identified needs.

Selecting a Focus/System
Unit for Therapy

Black families face multiple problems, so it is important that the therapist assess rapidly and accurately how to reduce family stress. In locating the proper system unit for therapy, the following guidelines are suggested.

Ecostructurally, a therapist needs to ascertain what systems are supportive or destructive to the present family problems(s). These systems may include external social systems such as school, social agencies, or extended family, friends, ministers. The discriminatory practice on the mainstream society toward Blacks is well-documented. This system may well be the primary focus for the reduction of stress in the family. The strong kinship bonds among Blacks sometimes are a source of family conflicts. McAdoo (1977) has described how inter-ference from extended family members may create marital difficulties when family members are unable to say "no" to unreasonable demands made by their kind and relatives. If such is the case, the system unit may include helping the clients to differentiate between their extended and nuclear families and to develop healthy boundaries between each. To achieve these goals, Minuchin's structure approach requiring seeing the family member and his or her kin in separate sessions is recommended. Once family boundaries are clarified, the therapist can focus on repairing or developing new boundaries within the nuclear family.

Second, external systems and kinship bonds are integral for the survival of a Black family. Flexible boundaries between the family and external systems must exist to incorporate the appropriate external supports. Third, there must be a congruence in perceptions of roles among family members. Such congruence may be interrupted by societal discriminatory practices, family life cycles, or idiosyncratic problems. Minuchin's (1974) list of different stressors (extrafamilial forces, family transitional points, and idiosyncratic problems) affecting the family is a useful framework for assessing factors that are responsible for the confusion of roles among family members. Finally, there must be a stabilized power balance within the nuclear family system. An egalitarian relationship does not imply lack of leadership, which can cause disorganization inherent in many multiproblem families.

The Use of an Eco-Map

Selecting a focus for therapy can be facilitated by the use of an eco-map. The eco-map, as developed by Hartman (1979), is a paper-and-pencil simulation that portrays in a dynamic way the ecological system whose boundaries include the client or family in the life space. It identifies and characterizes the significant nurturant or conflict-laden connection between the family and the environment. It makes available a more comprehensive picture of the major themes and patterns that give direction to the planning process and keeps both therapist and family from getting lost in detail. The actual use of an eco-map will be illustrated in the case illustration (Part 3) section of this chapter.

Specifically, an eco-map provides three major criteria for the family and the therapist to select a plan or a unit of intervention. These criteria include

(1) The family in relation to the ecological environment—the kinds of significant resources that are available or unavailable in the family's world and information pertaining to the relationships (strong, stressed, and so on) between family and environment also are important.

(2) The family-environment boundary as measured by the number and quality of transactions—to protect against discriminatory practices,

some Black families isolate themselves from the community environment. Such families may be closed off from new sources of energy and in
danger of moving toward a state of entropy, that is, of randomization,
disorganization, and ultimately dissolution.

(3) Relationship within the family and its connection with the outside
world—for example, unemployment outside of the home on the part of
the Black father will affect his role as husband and father. Similarly, for
a mother, working two jobs and being overly active in church affairs will
affect her relationship with her husband and children. An eco-map is
particularly relevant in work with Black families who are less verbal but
more visual and responsive to activity-oriented intervention (Foley,
1975).

Problem-Solving Phase

The following discussion focuses on the problem-solving phase of
therapy with Black American families and considers the cultural norm,
family structure, traditional help-seeking behavior, and capacities of
this particular population. Additionally, the application of communication and structural family theories has been integrated into the
therapeutic process. Specific skills and techniques that are of particular
relevance in the problem-solving phase of therapy include mobilizing
and restructuring the social and extended family network; self-observation as a tool for family restructuring; role-restructure for problem
solving; religiosity as a therapeutic tool; employing a role model,
educator, and advocate role; and the team approach.

Mobilizing and Restructuring the Social and
Extended Family Networks

In therapy with Black families, a therapist must recognize the survival
issues that often take precedence over family conflicts. With such
families, the therapist should define him- or herself as a system guide or
broker (Bowen, 1978) and help families learn skills to negotiate the
complexities of the bureaucratic system and social service agencies.

Robert, an excellent student with unusual musical talent, was
suspended from school when the music teacher claimed that he
continued to violate the rule of not having his practice card signed daily
by his parents. Robert's father was a truck driver who was away from
home much of the time. Robert's mother was a relief nurse and she

worked an irregular schedule. Both parents worked hard at their jobs, and they had high expectations for Robert's academic achievement. They were disappointed about Robert's school suspension. Robert's appeal to the teacher to make an exception to the rule was not successful. Trapped in this dilemma, Robert lost interest in music and his performance in other school subjects suffered. Robert's parents, partly due to busy work schedules and partly due to their lack of trust and experience in dealing with school personnel, blamed Robert for his problems. Robert developed severe headaches and the physician's diagnosis was that it was caused by stress. The therapist arranged a meeting between Robert, his parents, and the music teacher in an effort to resolve Robert's school problem. His parents were most apprehensive about the meeting and feared that the teacher regarded them as "unfit" parents. The therapist reassured them of their concern and competence as parents, and he also rehearsed the questions the teacher might raise at the meeting with them. The meeting with the teacher went smoothly, and the teacher cooperated in resolving Robert's situation.

Hansell (1976) has outlined three major attachments to various resources that can be instrumental in helping the Black family cope with the type of distress that is usually experienced in bicultural adjustment and in the loss of social supports. These attachments include (1) appropriate sources of information in which the therapist can connect the family with individuals, or organizations, as illustrated in Robert's case; and (2) resources that will enable the family to realize its identity as a functioning unit. The therapist's task is to help the family establish connections with other families, or other persons, with whom members can share mutual interests and activities; and (3) groups of people who regard the family as members. These might include religious groups that have the capacity to assist the family with various tasks.

When support systems are disrupted, the task of the therapist is to effect connections where indicated. The main objective is to connect the Black family with others who "speak the same language" and with whom family members can feel comfortable, build trust, and gain a sense of self-esteem and a feeling of security.

Self-Observation as a Tool for
Family Restructuring

Black clients often exhibit general distrust, unwillingness to express their feelings verbally, and pragmatic differences in communication styles. A therapeutic process solely dependent on verbal exchange may fall short in helping the client understand and alter his or her way of interacting with others. The self-observation techniques of focusing on a client's here-and-now transaction with other family members vividly illustrates behavioral patterns requiring change or restructuring. The following case illustrates how self-observation can alter the wife's perception and behavior with her spouse.

In an attempt to persuade her husband to take a more active part in disciplining their teenage son, Mrs. Boren accused Mr. Boren of not wanting to do anything. When Mr. Boren finally explained how his effort was constantly undermined by his wife, Mrs. Boren would repeatedly interrupt her husband before he could finish what he had to say. The therapist's attempts to block Mrs. Boren's interruptions were unsuccessful. The therapist then explained he would sit next to Mr. Boren and dramatize how Mr. Boren might feel when he was interrupted. The couple agreed to this plan. As Mr. Boren continued to explain to his wife how much he resented her treating him like one of the kids, Mrs. Boren got angry and said, "As far as I'm concerned, the way you have been acting, you are worse than my kids." The therapist immediately dropped down on the floor and said nothing. As Mrs. Boren continued to berate Mr. Boren about his passivity and inability to hold a job outside the home, the therapist crawled toward the door and started pounding. This finally got Mrs. Boren's attention. She stopped and asked what the therapist's behavior was supposed to mean. The therapist redirected the question and asked if she could come up with an answer. After a short pause, Mrs. Boren reluctantly turned to her husband, "Did I really make you feel this bad?" Mr. Boren nodded, and said, "All the damn time!"

The therapist then empathized with Mrs. Boren's frustration at work and at home. A short-term goal was mutually arrived at whereby the therapist would teach the couple skills for effective communication. Other techniques to help clients gain self-observation and different perspectives include the use of a one-way mirror or audiotape and videotape playbacks.

Role Structure for Problem Solving

The role of the oldest sibling regardless of sex has long been a strength and a potential liability for Black families. The following case illustrates how the role of the oldest daughter was restructured in consonance with the values and needs of a Black family.

Irene, aged 16, was the oldest of seven children in the Shaw family. Her father had been incapacitated and confined to a state mental hospital. Irene was an excellent student, and she also held a part-time job after school to supplement the family's income. Irene's mother, Mrs. Simpson, was irritated by her daughter's reluctance to take care of the younger siblings. The mother-daughter conflict finally came to blows when Irene was two hours late returning home from a date on weekend. Mrs. Simpson was so upset with her daughter's "irresponsibility" that she notified the police and filed a missing person report. The police officer referred the family to the transcultural family center for therapy.

At the first interview, Irene apologized for her irresponsible behavior and she volunteered that she sometimes hated to come home because of "endless chores" awaiting her. Irene explained that she didn't mind taking care of her younger brothers and sisters, but she just couldn't do the house chores along with her homework and part-time job. Mrs. Simpson agreed that perhaps Irene was burdened with too much work, but she insisted that she had to do the same when she was Irene's age. The therapist empathized with Mrs. Simpson's demanding responsibility and her "bringing up Irene the right way." He suggested other arrangements (role restructure) be considered so that the responsibilities at home were divided and shared and that Irene and her mother make an effort to get along better.

Mrs. Simpson explained that the family needed the extra income from Irene's part-time job and that the three-year-old child also needed proper care when the mother was away. Irene volunteered that she didn't mind taking care of the three-year-old, but she just could not be responsible for keeping the house clean and clothes washed in addition to everything else. The therapist asked if other siblings could help out by performing some of these house chores. Mrs. Simpson paused and reflected, "Perhaps other children need to chip-in and help out." Considering Irene's age and her developmental needs, ideally she should not be burdened by part-time employment outside the home while she was still a student. Unfortunately, the financial need of the family requires that Irene work to supplement the family income. It is important that the therapist not impose his or her values in deciding "proper" or "improper" roles for each family member. The therapist's role as culture researcher or coach (Bowen, 1978) is to facilitate solutions that are compatible with the needs and structure of the Black family.

Religiosity as a Therapeutic Tool

Religion plays a vital role in the lives of many Black families, yet some family problems, unfortunately, emanate from a family's interpretation and rigid adherence to certain religious beliefs. For example, the biblical principle, "spare the rod, spoil the child," interpreted literally by some Black families can be a potential source of physical abuse to children. A therapist may not share the same beliefs with the family, but he or she should respect and appreciate the family's religious beliefs. Larsen (1976) suggests that the therapist who is familiar with scriptural passages can cite biblical authority to support recommendations and can draw to some extent on the immense prestige of the Bible. A therapist who conveys no acceptance of the family's religious beliefs may find he or she is not respected by the family. A religious Black family may refuse to associate with an outsider who detours them from "God's path and God's will."

If a therapist is unfamiliar with the family's religious beliefs and if these beliefs are contributing to the family problem, he should consult the minister with whom the family has close contact and respects. In some instance, the minister can be cotherapist for family therapy. In cases where the therapist intervention is too threatening to a family, the minister can be used as a therapist-helper (Landau, 1981). This approach allows the therapist to avoid direct confrontation with the family. The therapist-helper approach also ensures that therapeutic changes on the part of the family are congruent with the family's cultural and religious background.

Employing Role Model, Educator Role, and
Advocate Role

Black families usually exhibit a positive response to problem-focused, present-oriented, short-term therapy. A family therapist can effectively use him- or herself as a role-model to demonstrate how certain behaviors can produce positive changes in a familial relationship. Minuchin (1967) has observed that transactions among disadvantaged Blacks tend to have an all-or-nothing emotional expression. The therapist may alienate himself from the family if he attempts to intellectualize their interactional style. Instead, the therapist should role model by immediately identifying exchanges when they occur. For instance, if parents accuse their misbehaving child of "never" minding them, the therapist can stop the conversation and point out to the parents the child's recent considerate acts. Second, if a family fails to display appropriate behavior, the therapist needs to point out his observations at the particular moment. For example, when one family related the death of a loved one with no apparent change of affect, the therapist pointed out to the family that their unusual calmness probably did not reflect their inner feelings of sadness. Third, the therapist may use his own feelings to make a point as a means to role model appropriate behavior. For example, if parents are calmly reflecting the injustice they receive from their children, the therapist can comment, "that angers me," or "I can't stand that." By modeling for the family, the therapist demonstrates that it is possible to be loving without being controlling, and critical without being punitive.

In addition to role modeling, a family therapist also needs to assume an educator role. He should teach families about the role the social system plays in their family problems. For example, a family can be commended for their efforts to protect their child from a hostile environment, yet they also need to be shown that such overprotection can retard their child's normal development. It is important that the therapist's educative approach recognize the family's sincere effort to resolve its problem. Such recognition neutralizes any negative interpretations the family might perceive as cultural insensitivity or disrespect from the therapist. Black families' responsiveness to a therapist's educator role is usually consistent with their achievement orientation.

The role as an advocate is congruent with a family therapist's training as a system expert. At times, a Black family's space can be invaded with well-intentioned but uncoordinated, inappropriate, and even destructive interventions. For example, a family with a school child who receives service from a guidance clinic can be inundated by recommendations from a speech therapist, a nurse, a social worker, a substance-abuse counselor, and a psychologist. While the speech therapist says the child's speech problem is caused by emotional stress, the nurse may advise the parents to be more permissive. Meanwhile, the social worker could be taking the parents for job interviews as a means to meet their basic needs, but the substance-abuse counselor may insist that the father's drinking problem be treated by attending Alcoholics Anonymous. The psychologist may recommend joint family therapy as the most effective tool to combat the child's school problems.

As an advocate of the family, the therapist needs to help the family prioritize and coordinate all these services so they will not fragmentize the family. At times, the therapist may need to assume a biased position to help the family negotiate and arrive at a workable solution to its problem. In view of the family's general feelings of powerlessness, it is important that the therapist's advocating efforts be realistic.

Team Approach

Some Black families face multiple problems. When intensive work is required to assist a family in interacting with the environment, a team of therapists is recommended. The team approach offers several advantages. First, it simultaneously attends to the family unit's needs as well as to various family members' needs. Second, a therapist team with different personalities, skills, and sensitivities maximizes the likelihood that each family member will be emotionally connected with at least one therapist. This is particularly important in the engagement stage of therapy when the dropout rate is generally high. Third, a therapist team can provide the family with a role model for interaction and for problem solving (Norlin and Ho 1974). Such learning through observation is most relevant when working with Blacks who are activity-oriented. Fourth, team therapists generally can provide a more accurate assessment plan, and they are more effective with the implementation of strategies (Mostwin, 1981). Fifth, team therapists ensure continuity of therapy should one therapist become unavailable. Finally, team therapists avoid potential professional burnout, which is heightened when working with Black families who live under oppressive conditions.

If team therapists fail to work collaboratively or experience conflict, it can further fragmentize the family organization. Other drawbacks to team therapy are that it is time-consuming and costly.

Evaluation and Termination Phase

In evaluating the outcome goal of family therapy with Black clients, it is important to distinguish between the goals of the family and the goals of the therapist. Family goals often focus on one member of the family who is the "identified patient." As therapy progresses, the family and the therapist often renegotiate and arrive at a "compromised" goal(s). There may be a wide range of goals for which a Black family needs therapy.

Kramer (1974) takes the position that a necessary goal of therapy with any family is the reduction or elimination of the presenting problems.

To determine if a specific goal has been accomplished through family therapy with a Black client, the ecological framework of assessment and therapy is particularly helpful. This framework consists of four major categories including family/environment interface, family structure, family processes (communication/interaction), and individual symptoms and/or character traits.

Family/environment interface. Goals to be evaluated during family/environment interface are the extent to which the family's basic needs (income, school, and shelter; safe neighborhoods; adequate health and medical resources; transportation; social connections with extended kin network or friends; shared ethnic cultured activities; employment; and so on) are met. Different individual member's adaptive balance with the environment is important as is the overall adaptive relationship between the family and its environment.

Family structure. Two aspects of family structure are particularly important in family therapy with Black Americans: family rules and programs and family roles and boundaries. Family rules are relationship agreements (conscious and unconscious) that prescribe and limit a family member's behavior over a wide variety of content areas. The egalitarian relationships orientation of Blacks under stress can confuse such family rules. Haley (1963) has indicated the importance of stabilizing the spousal subsystem as a means to effect a productive parent-child relationship. Minuchin (1974) emphasizes the importance of intrafamilial role boundaries, and sees most families who come for therapy as falling at one of two extremes on a continuum of boundary rigidity-flexibility. For Black families who need family therapy, the structure is a combination of disengagement and enmeshment (Foley, 1975). For example, a highly enmeshed subsystem of mother and children sometimes includes the father, who becomes disengaged in the extreme. According to Minuchin, a major goal of family therapy is improving family structure by recalibrating subsystem boundaries.

Family processes. Communication and conflict resolutions are two key concepts in evaluating family processes with a Black family. As a result of successful family therapy, communication should become clear, congruent, noncontradictory, direct, and honest (Satir, 1967). More open and spontaneous expression of feelings, wishes, ideals, and goals should occur (Ackerman, 1961). Conflict resolution as a result of therapy includes changes in the frequency, quality, and methods of handling intrafamilial conflicts (Aponte, 1979). However, Hines and Boyd-Franklin (1982) caution that family therapy goals with "conflict-avoidant" Black families should aim to increase the frequency of overt expression of conflict while simultaneously decreasing the frequency of covert conflict expression.

Symptoms and character traits of individual members. As a result of family therapy, the identified client is expected to have reduced frequency and/or intensity of symptoms or the complete disappearance of symptoms (Haley, 1963). Also, the identified client should become more differentiated. Bowen (1978) defines differentiation as a process in which a person comes to assume responsibility for his or her own happiness and comfort and avoid thinking that tends to blame and hold others responsible for one's own unhappiness or failure. To be differentiated does not imply total separation from one's family or ethnic cultural group. Contrarily, a differentiated individual possesses a sense of mature dependency in which he or she needs to feel belonging and to validate self-worth.

Additionally, in assessing therapeutic goals relating to family/environment interface, family structure and processes, and individual symptoms, a therapist needs to be cognizant of the unique cultural perspectives of Black Americans. Black American culture defines family structure and processes differently than Anglo culture. Any evaluation of therapeutic goals should be considered in the appropriate cultural context.

Black Americans usually display strong feeling of interdependence, humanism, and fatalism (Foster and Perry, 1982). This, coupled with their priority for survival and possibly a lack of physical energy or a reluctance to burden the therapist, may cause a family to terminate therapy before the goal is realized. The therapist needs to reassure and to point out to the family the potential negative consequences associated with premature termination. On the other hand, the Black American client's value of humanism and kinship bonds may delay the termination process with a therapist who is accepted as a trusted kin. It is important that a therapist be comfortable with this element of cultural and human inclusiveness and make termination a natural and gradual process.

The preceding discussion should be helpful in understanding Black American families and applying family structure and communication theories and culturally relevant emic-based principles. Part 3 of this chapter offers a case example to explicate and delineate how these family theoretical perspectives and emic-based practice principles can be integrated in actual therapy with a Black American family.

PART 3: CASE ILLUSTRATION

Mr. Jackson, a 52-year-old Black man was referred to us (Transcultural Family Study Center) by a Black minister. Mr. Jackson, a retired military man, is working irregularly as construction worker. When not working, Mr. Jackson has a tendency to drink heavily. He is married with four children, but has a habit of not returning home when he drinks. Mr. Jackson has two "fairly close" female friends whom he refers to as "drinking buddies," adding "they don't mean much." Over the past two weeks, Mr. Jackson had two rather serious car accidents, and he was found asleep in his car on a cold night. The minister suggested that Mr. Jackson might be suicidal and in need of therapy. Mr. Jackson refused to go to the mental health clinic for therapy, claiming that he was not crazy and "those folks [counselors] know nothing."

Recognizing strength.

When I first met Mr. Jackson, he looked suspicious and extremely anxious. I introduced myself to him and he asked if I was Korean. I remarked that he was close, but I am Chinese. As I was thanking him for taking time to visit with me, he interrupted

Joining to help client feel at ease.

me by informing me that he once was stationed in Seoul, South Korea. I *encouraged him to relate to me* his overseas experience. Mr. Jackson volunteered that his experience in Korea was the best time of his life. I sensed some sadness in his voice,

Tracking.

so I *empathized by saying,* "Life is full of happy times as well as sad times." Mr. Jackson picked up my lead and said, "I have been living in hell the past few years, especially the past several months." I *en-*

Data collection.

couraged Mr. Jackson to *elaborate* on his present situation. He sighed and explained that since his retirement from the army two years ago, things had been going downhill. Mr. Jackson volunteered that on the surface, he had a "good all-American family." He and his family were blessed with *no*

Basic needs not a problem source.

financial constraints and that income from

Problem identification.

Strenuous family relationship.

Joining.

Respect for client.

Identify strength in family.

Crisis intervention.

Problem identification.

his wife, a Licensed Practical Nurse, his retirement benefits, and his on-and-off construction jobs helped "to pay the bills all right." His two oldest children, a son aged 31 and a daughter aged 28, are married and live out-of-state. Two of his younger children, aged 17 (girl) and 15 (boy), are still at home. Both are excellent athletes and students. They are very involved with their friends at school. The family's eco-map and genogram is described in Figure 5.2.

Mr. Jackson continued, "My wife Gloria is an excellent mother and a busy body working all the time and attending church activities at least 4-5 times a week." "You seem to have a happy family," I remarked. "Yes, for everybody except me." I asked if he would explain what he meant by that statement. "I feel out of place . . . in my own home. Nobody notices me . . . except when I am not there for a couple of days. Then all hell breaks loose . . . sometimes I have a feeling that they [family members] are ashamed of me and want to have nothing to do with me." Mr. Jackson broke into tears. I *empathized* by saying that nobody likes to be alone especially in one's own home. After Mr. Jackson finished venting his frustration and disappointment toward his family, I *asked him if I could arrange* a joint meeting with him and his family. I briefly explained to him the joint meeting was to reunite everybody for I sensed there was a *great deal* of love lost in this family. Mr. Jackson hesitated and asked if I would contact his wife for the meeting. I agreed.

The family meeting *took place three days later*. Although Mrs. Jackson and the children, Terri and Jason, appeared anxious and apprehensive, they were extremely polite and cooperative. After I thanked them for coming, I *asked if they understood the purpose behind the meeting*. Mrs. Jack-

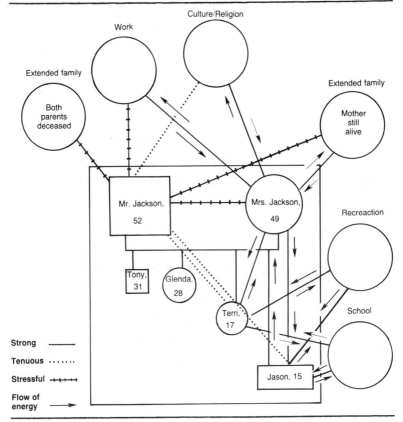

Figure 5.2 Eco-Map and Genogram

Blaming the victim.

Shift from individual to family focus.

Attempt family restructure.

Assist Mr. Jackson to reenter into family structure.

son responded immediately that she was glad that *her husband finally sought help*. To avoid focusing (blaming) on Mr. Jackson, I *asked how everybody got along at home*. Mrs. Jackson again responded by stating that everybody except her husband got along just fine. I then turned to Terri who said that she wished her father was more a "part of the family." Jason nodded also. I *asked what each of them was willing to do to involve* their father. They looked at each other and at their mother and said, "I don't know." I then directed my attention to Mr. Jackson by asking him how he felt when his children wished to involve him. Mr. Jackson hesitated and said, "Perhaps

Reframing.

Changed family process.

Summary evaluation.

New family process.

Family restructuring, father peripheral role shifts.

it was all my fault . . . when I was in the service, I was not home often, and I really did not get to know my children." "You didn't get to know me either, for that matter," Mrs. Jackson interrupted angrily. Before he had a chance to retaliate, I *reframed by asking* Mr. Jackson how he felt upon learning that his wife wanted to get to know him and be close to him. Mr. Jackson appeared to be surprised and he said that he *never realized that his family*, especially his wife, *wanted to be close to him.* Mrs. Jackson was very angry at this moment, and she began to enumerate the many occasions in which Mr. Jackson was indifferent and inconsiderate toward her including countless embarrassments involving his drinking and being with other women. "You have pushed me and the children away from you," cried Mrs. Jackson.

In defense of his drinking and being with other women, Mr. Jackson complained about the disappointment and disrespect he experienced, and how he felt like a stranger in his own home. Before the session ended, I asked the family *what they had gotten* out of the session. Mrs. Jackson commented that she was tired of this kind of bickering, but *she did realize how lonely her husband might* have felt. I commented that she also might be feeling alone. Mrs, Jackson nodded and said, "Especially when the children are all grown."

Mr. Jackson commented that he felt bad for letting the family down, but he was comforted to see that the family still had love for him.

Terri said that she was saddened by what had happened to her father but was relieved that the family "is talking" again.

Jason asked his father *if he could attend his* basketball game Friday night. Realizing that family restructuring attempts to reenter the father into the nuclear family had just begun, and that the spousal subsystem

Focusing on a subsystem.

boundary needs special attention, I suggested meeting only *with Mr. and Mrs. Jackson* for the next few sessions.

During the next meetings, the emphasis was to "restructure" the Jackson's marital subsystem. A brief review of the couple's genogram reveals that Mrs. Jackson was a *firstborn* from a female-headed family. She was a parental-child to her mother who had "had no respect for men." Mrs. Jackson had always excelled at whatever she did and ran the household "single-handedly" when she was only a teenager. She had had no role model as to how a wife should interact with her husband, and even at this

Intergeneration transmission.

moment, she still recalls her *mother's injunction* that "men are not to be trusted." Mrs. Jackson maintains close contact with her mother. As her children grow older, she finds herself alone and occupies herself with church activities.

Mr. Jackson, on the other hand, came from a two-parent family. Both of his parents died and he had no contact with his

Emotional cutoff from extended family.

other relatives due to geographic location. After retiring from the military, he lost his role identity. He dislikes construction work and is in the process of looking for some-

Strenuous person/environment and person/family relationship.

thing more challenging. His *dissatisfaction* with his current role, retirement, present work, and familial relationship caused him to drink excessively and to mingle with friends who would accept him.

The first marital therapy session was spent helping the Jacksons get reacquainted with each other. Their accusations and criticisms toward each other *were relabeled as want-*

Reframing.

ing to be close to each other but without knowing how.

Spousal restructuring.

The second marital therapy session was devoted to assisting the couple in redefining their *roles as husband and wife* and their parental role in dealing with children. Mrs. Jackson, as expected, was reluctant to relinquish her central role and position with the family, especially in dealing with

Educative role.

her children. In addition, she needed *to*

acquire "mature dependency" in relation to becoming vulnerable in seeking love and affection from her husband. Mr. Jackson, on the other hand, needed directives in becoming more assertive in dealing with his wife. He also needed to forsake his passive-aggressive behavior by not drinking and staying away from home to get attention.

The third and fourth marital sessions were spent in helping the couple creatively resolve conflicts. Effective problem-solving skills and styles were introduced.

Evaluation.

Improved family relationship.

Improved individual symptoms.

Improved environmental support.
Improved relationship with work world.

The sixth and final session was spent in therapy with the whole family. Both *children reported* marked changes in the behavior of their father and mother, and that the whole family started doing things together more. Mr. Jackson volunteered that he "carried on" his drinking *only one time* over the last two months and that he had never been absent from home since therapy started. "I even get him to to to *church with me*," quipped Mrs. Jackson. As the therapy ended. Mr. Jackson requested information about attending *vocational training* school.

This case study demonstrated that even without financial constraint, Black families still have problems like all families do. Such problems manifest themselves in personal conflict and alcohol abuse as in the case of Mr. Jackson. The therapist's sensitivity to the client's ethnic background, his transaction with work environment and his family relationship, help to transform the presenting problem from individual- to family-focused. The therapist capitalizes upon the family's strength in kinship bond as well as Mr. Jackson's motivation to be a part of the family. Through culturally relevant techniques such as joining, tracking, reframing, educating, and restructuring, the client is helped to reenter the family system successfully, which once again become intact.

The therapist's skill in conveying proper respect for Mr. Jackson reassures the latter that he is not "crazy." The therapist further capitalizes upon the family's humanistic orientation and flexibility in family roles that later become the curative factors for Mr. Jackson's personal and family problems. By applying culturally relevant marital therapeutic techniques such as genogram, communication and problem-solving skills, and environmentalal support, the couple's marital relationship is improved and change in family relationship is stabilized.

PART 4: CULTURALLY RELEVANT TECHNIQUES AND SKILLS FOR SPECIFIC THERAPY MODALITES

Marital Therapy

In view of the Black American cultural characteristics that emphasize strong kinship ties, flexibility of roles, egalitarianism, and religiosity, it may be assumed that marriage among Blacks is stable. Statistics reflect just the opposite. As a group, the Black's divorce and separation rate is twice as high as the Whites (U.S. Bureau of the Census, 1977). There are several possible explanations to this phenomenon. First, Black males historically have been the major victims of discrimination that makes it difficult for them to seek and maintain gainful employment. This undermines their ability to function in an egalitarian relationship with their wives, who are comparatively less discriminated against in the work world, and who normally have the emotional support of the nuclear family as well as the extended family. There is relatively little pressure for wives to assume leadership roles. Hence Black females are less threatened by their wifely role in the family.

Contrarily, Black husbands are strongly influenced by the mainstream society that prescribes that their role in the family is to lead. This is often inconsistent with their earning capacities greatly hampered by discrimination. The husband's disillusionment about work and dissatisfaction at home make a marital relationship highly vulnerable. Second, the husband-wife conflict may escalate when the wife is disappointed with their inability to maintain an egalitarian relationship. This then casts the husband in a passive or peripheral role in the family. The husband's disappointment in himself and in his family role function may push him to seek confirmation and reassurance of manhood outside the family. This availability coincides with the large number of single Black females, which, in turn, further lessens a husband's commitment to a marital relationship. Third, the past four centuries have witnessed the gradual erosion of the traditional family system consisting of both parents. Many disadvantaged Blacks have not seen a close daily interaction between their parents. These Blacks lack husband-wife interactive role model experience. Because a great deal of energy has to be devoted to daily survival needs, these Blacks do not have energy left to resolve conflicts inherent in a husband-wife relationship. Fourth, the Black's general distrust of therapists makes marital therapy the last resort they will seek for their intimate personal family problems. The therapists's general lack of knowledge and insensitivity toward Black culture and ecology-related marital problems also hinders therapy. Keeping the above information in mind, the following specific guidelines are suggested while providing marital therapy to a Black American couple.

Improving Couple Relationship Through
Improved Parent-Child Relationship

With the exception of middle- and upper-class Black clients, most Blacks enter family therapy because of their child's problems. These couples are often more conscientious about their role as parents than their role as husband and wife. Partly due to the shortage of Black males, most Black wives are not willing to risk a marriage failure. Therefore, marital therapy focusing exclusively upon a couple's marital relationship is too threatening to the couple, especially the wife. Additionally, the couple may feel selfish or guilty should they perceive that their marital needs precede their child's needs. Therefore, it is important that the therapist not employ marital therapy prematurely as a means to resolve parent-child problems. Obviously, according to structural framework, a child's problems cannot be satisfactorily resolved without first repairing or realigning the parental or spousal subsystem (Minuchin, 1974; Satir, Stachowiak, and Taschman, 1975). However, the spousal subsystem can be repaired directly or indirectly by focusing on the parents' newly learned alternative transaction with the child. For example, if the child's problem is related to mother triangulating with the child against the father who is peripheral, the therapist can suggest to the parents joining forces (restructuring the mother-son dyad to father-mother dyad) to provide a more unified firm and consistent structure for their child who may be seeking generational boundaries and directives.

Teaching Communication and Problem-Solving Skills

Both Minuchin (1967) and Foley (1975) have observed that transactions among disadvantaged Blacks tend to have an "all-or-nothing" emotional expression about them. Furthermore, communication among Black families tends to be in generalities more than in specifics. Regardless of whether the couple is from a disadvantaged or middle-class background, communication skills required in conflict resolution and problem solving must go beyond generalities. Specific and open exchange of affects and intentions are required. To specify one's message in communication, Satir et al. (1975) suggests the couple learn when and how to use "I" statements. In addition, Miller, Nunnally, and Wackman (1975) suggests the couple learn when and how to make senses (informational data) statements, interpretation statements, feeling statements, intention statements, and action statements. They need to learn communication feedback techniques and a transactional style that is congruent, direct, and open (Satir, 1967).

In view of the Black American's present and activity orientation, marital therapy processes focusing upon self-observation and immediate feedback through audio tapes or videotapes are recommended. The use of cotherapists of both sexes can also provide a model for effective communication (Norlin and Ho, 1974).

Religiosity as a Source of Strength in Marriage

A great deal has been written about the importance that religion and church play in the lives of Black families (Hines and Boyd-Franklin, 1982). Yet, family therapists have yet to integrate this component of strength with marital therapy. For a religious Black client, no amount of knowledge and measure of communication skills can substitute for the level of marital commitment derived from religion. Without religious faith, a Black client is weakened in his or her internal strength, spirit, and commitment essential to becoming a happy individual and to achieving a successful marriage. Statistics on divorce consistently reveal that divorced couples show more religious indifference than married couples, and most family therapists will agree that religious couples tend to work harder to solve their marital problems than nonreligious couples (Ho, 1984). A therapist needs to appreciate and respect the influence of religion on the well-being of a Black couple. When a couple allows their religious faith to be a vital part of their marriage, they not only gain added strength and hope, but also a model of love to guide their interactions. When religious faith is present in the couple's marriage, they become more fully aware of their responsibilities for themselves and for each other. Equality and problem solving in marriage can be pursued in open discussions, negotiations, and compromise.

During marital therapy, one partner may attempt to use certain biblical scriptures as a means to entice the therapist to side with him or her. The therapist should avoid being triangulated by such unproductive intellectual or philosophical maneuvers. Instead, the therapist needs to help the couple focus on the issue to be solved.

Divorce Therapy

Black clients, particularly those from lower socioeconomic levels, seldom actively seek divorce therapy. This may be due, in part, to the shortage of Black males, and Blacks' traditionally strong commitment to religious convictions that discourage divorce. The majority of divorce therapy clients seek help during moments of crisis, such as when the husband abruptly decides to end the marriage, or the wife contemplates ending the relationship because of repeated physical or mental abuse. Hence divorce therapy generally is crisis-oriented, time-limited, and extremely stressful for clients. The following recommendations are offered when divorce therapy is conducted with Black clients.

Exploring Divorce Experiences and Consequences

Black clients who grew up in a single-parent female-headed family seldom seek divorce therapy as a means to end a marriage. A couple's relationship may be deteriorating, but the wife's strong desire to maintain a two-parent family generally is so strong that divorce is viewed as the last solution to a couple's problems. Many Blacks consider divorce as "following the devil's trap" because of their religious views (Staples, 1978). While the therapist should consider and respect the client's decision about divorce, it is his or her responsibility to help the client point out the family problem(s) or physical abuse problems causing unresolved marital stress. Under no circumstances should a therapist be judgmental about the client's decision.

Extended Family and Social Support

The strength of family ties among Black Americans is a valuable resource to clients experiencing divorce. Extended families are the natural resources for emotional support and can often provide financial help, child care, house chores, and so on. The therapist at this stage should assist the client in taking advantage of the extended family system. The important objective is to help the client to make the necessary transitions and connections with the extended family without abdicating personal responsibility and allowing the extended family system to overstep the nuclear family system boundary. This may be difficult for a dependent client who during stressful time regresses to greater dependency on the family of origin. Bowen's (1978) theoretical concept of differentiation is applicable in helping the client to negotiate the family/extended family interface. Such negotiation may require conjoint sessions with extended family members. For clients who are experiencing divorce but because of geographical barriers or inter-personal conflicts are unable to utilize extended family help, the therapist's task is to link the family's needs with appropriate community resources. Such resources may include a human service department, health department, women's resource center, child-care center, and so on. Because of the urgency of the client's need at the time of divorce, the therapist's role can be that of a resource mediator, child specialist, educator, and supporter to the client. The frequency and intensity of therapist-client contact at the time of divorce requires the therapist's flexibility in scheduling and in conducting home visits and field activities.

Postdivorce Adjustment and New Relationships

Divorce can be a traumatic experience for both female and male clients. The female divorcée generally has the support of the children and the extended family, and the male divorcée is often left totally without support. It is generally the female's responsibility to be with the children after divorce, so she generally receives more attention from various support sources, including the therapist. A female divorcée is frequently confronted with economic survival, which Black females seem better prepared to deal with than White females, *even though* they face economic and employment discrimination (Peters and deFord, 1978). After divorce, the mother must often do extra work outside of the home and will have less time to spend with the children. The firstborn of the siblings can easily be colluded with assuming the parental-child role (Minuchin, 1974). While empathizing with the mother to assign more responsibilities to the firstborn, the therapist also needs to point out to the mother the developmental needs of all children, including the parental-child.

Divorce usually is a devastating experience that can reactivate a person's feelings of unworthiness. A therapist needs to assess where the client is developmentally and the level of negative affect, which the divorce experience may have on the individual. Again Bowen's (1978) differentiation concept is very helpful to ascertain how emotionally divorced the client is and the area(s) of "unfinished business" the client may possess. A divorcé may perceive his or her experience as unique or unforgivable. A divorce support group can be very beneficial to such a client (Barry, 1979).

Single-Parent Therapy

Increased divorce and separation, as well as decisions to have children and not marry, have increased the number of female-headed families among Black Americans. Between 1974 and 1977, the number of female-headed Black families increased 16% (from 1.8 million to 2.1 Million), while the number of female-headed White families rose by 13% (from 4.9 to 5.5 million) (National Urban League, 1978). Beal (1980, p. 242) notes that "every family must establish an income, maintain a household, develop social and emotional relationships in the neighborhood and at work, and relate to children in a way that makes them productive members of society." For Black single-parent families, there are even fewer institutionalized sources of support informing them how to accomplish these tasks. Statistics on the income levels of female-headed households support the idea that economic need is the greatest problem facing these single-parent families. Almost one-half of all Black single parents live below the poverty line (Smith, 1980). Divorced and separated mothers experience a 43% and 51% decline in family income, respectively (Beal, 1980). Many Black single parents fit the description of the "at-risk" population who Pett (1982) describes in her research findings as a single parent who

is feeling depressed, hopeless, and out of emotional control. She is in receipt of Aid to Dependent Children and is of low socioeconomic status. This custodial parent reports poor relations both with her own family and that of the former spouse. She tends to be socially isolated and feels that there are few, if any, persons available to help the family in time of emergencies.

The following suggestions aim to assist these high-risk single-parent Black families.

Mobilizing the Support System

The extended family can be a significant source of support and self-esteem for a Black single parent. It can be especially critical in providing emotional and instrumental assistance and can reduce feelings of loneliness and isolation. Statistics show that, increasingly, single-parent families take advantage of the strong Black extended family ties. Between 1969 and 1975, the proportion of Black children living in households composed of their mothers and other relatives increased from 22% to 39% (U.S. Bureau of the Census, 1978).

The family of origin network is important in providing the single-parent family with child care, finances, household chores, and emotional support. Geographical barriers or emotional strains may deny many Black single parents assess to this valuable resource. In such cases, other extended network resources should be found. These can be new friendship ties, especially other single mothers, women's support groups, and social activity groups that can help the single-parent family adjust to this transitional period.

Mobilizing and Involving the Conjugal Network

When the father is absent from the family, a key male figure, or spouse-equivalent, may be present in the single-parent household (McLanahan et al., 1981). This individual may or may not live with the mother in the single-parent household, yet he may have a great deal of influence in the daily transactions of the single parent and her children. Whether a single parent utilizes such a conjugal network depends on the personality, value orientation, and sex-role orientation of the single mother. The therapist's task is to explore with the single parent the value and need of having such a network. If the therapist is aware of the conjugal partner, he or she can introduce the option of involving this individual in matters that concern the welfare of the single parent or child-rearing practices of the children. Stack (1974) reported that the lower-class Black male contributes to the welfare of the family more than is commonly acknowledged and plays an important role as a substitute father to her children.

Restructuring the Family

The absence of the father from the family requires family renegotiation and a restructuring of the family system boundary (Minuchin, 1974). Robert Weiss (1979) noted two major changes that can occur in the transformation from a two-parent to a single-parent family. First, the "echelon structure" collapses, with children being promoted to junior partner status and becoming more involved in decision making. Second, decompensation of the authority structure increases communication among family members. This situation may also be prompted by Black's egalitarian authority orientation. As a result of these structural changes, enmeshment between the single parent and the children can occur resulting in parent-child conflict or idiosyncratic symptoms.

In view of the traditional closeness of the mother-child relationship within the Black family, the concept of enmeshment should be addressed only if it relates to the immediate problem to be solved. For example, in the case of parent-child conflict involving the single parent's unawareness or unwillingness to allow her teenage son to have peer relations, enmeshment should be explored. New structural arrangement needs to be developed to maintain the closeness of a parent-child relationship without emotionally suffocating the parent and child in the case of enmeshment.

Reconstituted Family Therapy

The remarriage family is identified as a high-risk group for which society has not as yet established norms. Individuals with children who remarry are heirs to specific problems for which, on the whole, they are unprepared. The Black's strong sense of kinship and humanistic individualism can produce split loyalties between members of a remarriage. The following suggestions are offered in providing family therapy for a reconstituted Black American family.

Focus on Parental Coalition

There is a consensus among all family therapy theorists that a strong spousal subsystem is essential to all family functioning. In view of the number of family members involved and their loyalties toward the spouse or in-laws of previous marriages, strong spousal subsystems of a reconstituted family are much more crucial. However, emphasizing the spousal subsystem to a reconstituted family experiencing parent-child conflict or child-related problems may be insensitive to the Black family's expectation for therapy. The task of the therapist is to assist the parents to work collaboratively for sake of their children and stepchildren. If the parents' differences remain unresolved, any treatment may at best result in a temporary resolution of the symptoms that will have a high tendency to reappear in the future in the same manner or in a disguised form.

Interviewing the parents separately may help repair or establish the parental coalition. Both parents should be encouraged to express their feelings about their previous marriages and the legal settlement involving custody, visitation, and financial arrangements. They also need to be encouraged to discuss their child-rearing practices. To many parents, such a discussion can be highly informative and educational. To lessen the parent's sense of guilt and defensiveness, the therapist needs to adopt an educative approach during this stage of therapy. As the therapy progresses, the therapist may need to shift to a more confrontational therapeutic role in order to modify the parent's rigid pattern acquired from the past.

The parental coalition emanates from the couple's commitment to function as a marital unit. It is important that the couple explore the motives or reasons behind their remarriages. Once their motives are identified, the couple should see more clearly the nature of their marital problem and how it affects the behavior of their children or stepchildren.

At the second interview, Mrs. Peters admitted that she decided to remarry simply because she wanted her two children to have an adult male figure at home. As she was growing up, she always regretted that there was not an adult male at home, and her grandfather and uncles lived out of state and had infrequent contact with the family. Mrs. Peters was afraid to confront Mr. Peters, her second husband, fearing that he might leave home as her first husband had done. Mrs. Peters was resentful and "unfeeling" toward Mr. Peters, whom her children from the previous marriage disliked. Mr. Peters was dissatisfied with his present marriage with Mrs. Peters and increasingly resented his stepchildren, whom Mrs. Peters claims is her "number one priority and responsibility." At the fourth interview, Mrs. Peters began to see that she could enable Mr. Peters to be more loving toward her children by giving him more attention and affection.

Define Roles and Expectations

Most Black children of divorced persons retain relationships with the parent outside their current household. This may be attributed to strong kinship ties or perhaps as a means to defend against a hostile external environment. This is the one permanent tie that links the present marriage with the previous marriage(s). Other areas of linkage include financial ties, previous in-laws, other relatives, and friends. Hence the reconstituted family is more vulnerable to role confusion and stress than is a first marriage (Kahn, 1974). Despite Black Americans' general flexibility in assuming different family roles, role ambiguity and overload tend to create tensions and conflicts. Moreover, split loyalties can leave some instrumental and nurturing roles unfilled and the entire family disorganized.

In addition to helping the reconstituted family redefine essential roles, the parental subsystem boundary also needs to be clarified so that the executive functions can be carried out with continuity and cohesion.

As a strategy to decentralize the stepmother's role with her children in the reconstituted family, some authors (Haley, 1976; Minuchin, 1974; Carter and McGoldrick, 1980) suggest that she take a passive role, leaving the father/stepfather to take charge of the children. This directive may be antithetical to Black American culture, which prescribes that a woman's responsibility is to care for her children on a day-to-day basis. To strengthen the spousal subsystem or father-stepchild subsystem will automatically dilute the mother-child enmeshment. To encourage husband-wife and father-child interaction is more consistent with Black culture of strong kinship bonds.

Involve Extended Family Members

The strong family ties of Black Americans can also become a problem for the reconstituted family whose loyalties are divided by more than one set of in-laws and relatives. On the other hand, in-laws and relatives can be added resources for the reconstituted family. If they are unsympathetic and uncooperative toward the reconstituted family, it can create unending demands and stress on the reconstituted family, especially on the stepparent. Inferences from in-laws and relatives from a previous marriage may be unintentional. But reconstituted families often experience complexities around unspoken loyalties. The use of an eco-map and genogram is a practical tool to portray to the reconstituted family their sources of strength and liability emanating from their contacts with their extended families. It is important that the therapist constantly focus upon the problem to be solved within the reconstituted family. The nature of the kinship relationship should not necessarily be weakened, but it should be restructured to augment the functioning of the reconstituted family. If a child in the reconstituted family is unable to adjust, the extended family can be a viable temporary resource and shelter for the child. This is a common practice among Black American families (Norton, 1983).

PART 5: CONCLUSION

In view of the diversity of Black life-styles and socioeconomic factors, any discussion pertaining to therapy with Black families risks over-generalization and stereotyping. Yet, there are specific factors that set them apart from the dominant society and from other ethnic minority groups. This chapter represents an initial attempt to further the development of family therapy with Black Americans from an incubator stage to an early infancy stage (Foley, 1975).

Family therapy with Black Americans requires therapists to expand the context of their intervention and to redefine their own role. Family therapists must be willing to explore the impact of the social, political, socioeconomic, and broader environmental conditions on the families they serve. Inasmuch as the Black family is affected by the victim system, discrimination, and injustice, it has a rich cultural heritage and possesses enormous strength and potential. Family therapy with Black Americans must take this into account and provide culturally relevant techniques and skills in order to serve clients effectively.

6

Family Therapy with
Ethnic Minorities:
Similarities and Differences

A family therapist usually has the opportunity to work with many different ethnic minorities. With the exception of such agencies as ethnic culture centers that limit their services to a specific client group, most agencies and private practitioners provide family therapy to cross-cultural populations. It is not uncommon for a family therapist to provide therapy to many different ethnic minority families. The major objective of this chapter is to highlight and analyze the similarities and differences of therapy with different ethnic minority families at different therapeutic phases. Specifically, at the pretherapy phase, therapy similarities and differences pertaining to ethnic minority family structure are analyzed along with application of system structure and communication theories. The similarities and differences in family therapy with various ethnic minority families at the beginning, problem-solving, and evaluation phases are examined and contrasted together with the techniques skills for specific therapy modalities, such as marital, divorce, single-parent, and reconstituted therapy.

PART 1: PRETHERAPY
PHASE CONSIDERATIONS

The Ethnic Minority
Family Structure

Cultural Values in Relation to
Family Structure

Family therapy with ethnic minorities must be directed at the system of conflict, anxiety, and defense systems within the individual and/or the family. The ecological approach maintains that imbalance and conflict within a family may arise from any point in the individual or the family's transaction with the environment. For ethnic minority families undergoing acculturation and survival in a mainstream society, cultural values should be the focus from which to begin the therapeutic process.

According to Kluckhohn, "A value orientation is a generalized and organized conception, influencing behavior of time, of nature, of man's place in it, of man's relation to man, and of the desirable and undesirable aspects of man, environment, and interhuman transactions" (Kluckhohn and Strodtbeck, 1961). By focusing on the ethnic minority family's value orientation, a therapist gains understanding and insight of the family's view of the nature of the world and its problems, their feelings about their problems, and the direction the family adopts to resolve problems.

The major cultural values of selected ethnic minority families are summarized in Table 6.1 along with the middle-class White American cultural orientation, which can serve as an informative guide for the family therapist.

Man to nature/environment. Middle-class, White American cultural values place man in control of his nature or environment. In contrast, ethnic minority groups emphasize man's harmony with his environment. According to the Asian Confucian system, man's quest for spiritual fulfillment is to achieve harmony in this world through observing five basic relationships that demand loyalty and respect toward each other, especially the old in the family (Keyes, 1977, p. 195). American Indians hold nature as extremely important for they realize that they are but one part of a greater whole. They believe the growing things of the earth and all animals have spirits or souls, and that they should be treated as humanely as possible. A Black American's cultural value of keeping harmony with the environment manifests itself in strong kinship bonds and collectivity above individualism (Clark, 1972, p. 13). Their strong religious or spiritual orientation is also a way to keep them in harmony with nature. They view emotional difficulties as "wages of sin," and interpersonal conflicts as not following the "Lord's teachings." The Hispanics' strong sense of hierarchy keeps them in harmony with the environment. They believe in a world of two class systems: high and low, as fixed and natural as the parts of their bodies. In pursuit of spiritualism as a means to maintain harmony with nature, Hispanics believe the visible world is surrounded by an invisible world inhabited by good and evil spirits who influence human behavior (Delgado, 1978). In order to be protected by good spirits, an individual is expected to

TABLE 6.1

Cultural Value Preferences of Middle-Class White Americans and Ethnic Minorities: A Comparative Summary

Area of Relationships	Middle-Class White Americans	Asian/Pacific Americans	American Indian Alaskan Native	Black Americans	Hispanic Americans
Man to nature/ environment	Mastery over	Harmony with	Harmony with	Harmony with	Harmony with
Time orientation	Future	Past-present	Present	Present	Past-present
Relations with people	Individual	Collateral	Collateral	Collateral	Collateral
Preferred mode of activity	Doing	Doing	Being-in-becoming	Doing	Being-in-becoming
Nature of and bad man	Good and bad	Good	Good	Good and bad	Good

NOTE: For cultural value orientation, see Kluckhohn and Strodtbeck (1961).

produce good and charitable deeds in a secular world. Because a Hispanic is not preoccupied with mastering the world, he or she feels a keen sense of destiny and a sense of divine providence governing the world.

Ethnic minority cultural values of harmony with nature see no clash between humans and nature. Family problems develop when we have not attended properly to or kept our lives in balance with all sources of influence (heavens and earth). A therapist's "mastery-over-nature" orientation, assuming that there are few (if any) problems that cannot be solved, may conflict with the values of ethnic minority clients. Recognizing this value difference, the therapist needs to respect and learn from the family how it views family problems and their solution.

Time orientation. Time in the mainstream society is oriented to the future, worshipping youth and making sacrifices for a "better" tomorrow. Other ethnic groups view the time orientation differently. Asian Americans worship their ancestors and emphasize the past, which represents respectability and wisdom. American Indians, on the other hand, are very much grounded in what is happening in their lives at the moment, rather than making specific plans for future endeavors. They view events moving through time in a rhythmic, circular pattern and consider artificial impositions of schedules disruptive to the natural pattern. In view of the slavery period and historical suffering, most Blacks prefer to forget the past and concentrate on what is happening at the present. The strong hierarchical sense of the Hispanics reminds them of the importance of the past, while their value on personalism makes their present encounters a spontaneous activity. In view of the overall present time-orientation of most ethnic minorities, concrete immediate problems and their solution will likely be more relevant than future-oriented, abstract philosophical goals.

Relations with people. Most middle-class White Americans prefer individual autonomy, while ethnic minorities prefer collectivity. The individual in traditional Asian/Pacific culture is protected securely in a wide network of kinship. He or she is clearly reminded that other social relationships or friendships should be secondary to the needs of family. In Asian/Pacific societal structures, where interdependence is stressed, the actual or threatened withdrawal of support may shake a person's basic trust and cause him or her considerable anxiety over the thought of facing life alone. American Indians believe in getting along with each other: the family and group take precedence over the individual. This concept of collaterality reflects the integrated view of the universe, where all people, animals, plants, and objects in nature have their place in creating a harmonious whole. Black Americans' strong kinship bonds and the extended family ties are heavily influenced by traditional African culture, which valued collectivity above individualism. Studies have revealed that kinsmen help each other with financial aid, child care, house chores, and other forms of mutual support. Within the Hispanic American culture, the importance of family membership and belonging cuts across caste lines and socioeconomic conditions. An individual's self-confidence, worth, security, and identity are determined by his relationships to other family members. During good times or during crisis, the family's name and family member's welfare always come first.

Ethnic minority American's adherence to collaterality is sure to conflict with the dominant culture's stress on individualism and competition. Children of ethnic minority groups are often mistakenly seen as "unmotivated" due to their reluctance to compete with peers in the classroom or on the playground. Ethnic minority workers also are mistakenly labeled as "lazy" or "unproductive." However, their cooperative spirit can be revitalized and capitalized on in the problem-solving process during a family crisis.

Preferred mode of activity. In the activity dimension, the "doing" orientation is basic to the middle-class White American life-style. Thus competitiveness and upward mobility are the trademarks connected with Doing. Asian/Pacific American's doing orientation is manifested in their ability to exercise self-discipline, which involves controlling one's feelings in order to fulfill properly one's responsibility and thus gain recognition not for oneself but for the family. To "gaman" for a Japanese is to evince stoicism, patience, and uncomplainingness in the face of adversity and to display tolerance for life's painful moments. Black Americans share a similar doing orientation with Asian/Pacific Americans. Black Americans endure suffering and often view education as an essential path to minimize discrimination and to succeed in life.

American Indians prefer a "being-in-becoming" mode of activity. They value what the human being is rather than what he or she can achieve. They do not wish to manipulate nature and situations for their comfort, convenience, or economic gain. They believe that to attain maturity, which is learning to live with life, its evil as well as its good, one must face genuine suffering. Hispanic Americans also prefer a "being-in-becoming mode" of activity. A Hispanic defines his self-worth in terms of those inner qualities that give him self-respect and earn him the respect of others. He feels an inner dignity (dignidad) and expects others to show respect (respeto) for that "dignidad."

The preferred mode of activity has important implications in family therapy with different ethnic minority groups. For example, a Hispanic or an American Indian who believes in "being-in-becoming" also believes that every individual has some sense of personal dignity and will be sensitive about showing proper respect to others and demanding it for him- or herself. This expectation is intensified when the client first encounters a non-Hispanic or non-American Indian and interprets the latter's insensitivity as personal insult or disdain. Hence a Hispanic or an Indian family may seek and perhaps benefit from family therapy not because of agency affiliation or the professional training of the therapist, but simply because of the therapist's skill and ability to convey this sense of "being-in-becoming" when dealing with the family. "Being-in-becoming" translated into practice principle simply means to respect the client's right for self-determination and noninterference.

Nature of man. Both Black Americans and Hispanic Americans share with middle-class White Americans the view that the nature of man basically is that of neutrality: he is neither good nor bad, but more of a product of the physical and nurturing environment. This explains the achievement orientation of these minorities, especially if they are members of the middle class. Because they believe the environment can influence the nature of man, they tend to be more receptive to environmental sources for changes or improvement.

Asian Americans and American Indians, on the other hand, believe that man basically is good. The Asian Buddhist canons state that qualities essential to harmonious living include compassion, a respect for life, moderation in behavior, and selflessness. An Indian believes that human nature is always good. His misbehavior or problem is thought to result from lack of opportunity to be and to develop fully. There are always some people or things that are bad and deceitful. However, in the end, good people will triumph just because they are good. The Asian American's belief of the nature of man informs them that the best healing source for their problem is within the family and not outside sources. Similarly, American Indians believe that because man basically is good, if he is allowed to be left alone with people within his own nurturing environment, his goodness will outweigh his evil.

These cultural value orientations significantly influence ethnic minority family organization and structure. A discussion of how these values affect subunits and overall family interaction follows.

Traditional Family Structure and
Extended Family Ties

To provide an informative guide for the family therapist, the traditional family structures of selected ethnic minority families are summarized in Table 6.2 along with the middle-class White American family structure.

Studies indicate that ethnic minority extended family ties are more cohesive and extensive than kinship relationships among the White population (Padilla, Carlos, and Keefe, 1976; Stack, 1974; Martin and Martin, 1978; Shimkin et al., 1978). The extended family of all ethnic groups includes lifelong friends also. One example is the "compadrazgo," a Filipino system, in which trusted friends and allies can be recruited to serve as godparents to children (Ponce, 1977). Through a Catholic baptismal custom, a Hispanic child can acquire a godmother (madrina) and godfather (padrino) who directly share responsibility for the child's welfare and thus form coparent (compadre) bonds with the child's parents. Nonkin in an American Indian family can also become a family member through a namesake for a child (Wahrhaftig, 1969). This individual then assumes family obligations and responsibilities for child rearing and role modeling.

Kinsmen of extended families provide essential functions for a family member or members experiencing a crisis. For example, transferring children from one nuclear family to another within the extended family system is a common practice among all ethnic minorities. Unless the practice is regarded as a problem by the family, a therapist should not criticize or attempt to alter such arrangements. The extended family network represents a relational field characterized by intense personal exchanges that have unending effects upon one's perception, value system, and behavior. It has immense practice implications in therapy with ethnic minority families. It sometimes represents the only natural source through which the family will seek help and benefit; it can also be the major source of blockage impeding the client's or family's progress for problem solving.

Mate selection and husband/wife relationship. In the area of mate selection and husband/wife relationship, there are a great deal of similarities among the Asian/Pacific Americans, the American Indians, and the Hispanic Americans. While the tradition of arranged marriage is gradually disappearing among these ethnic minority groups, the choice of mate is still heavily influenced by the families of both sides. In

TABLE 6.2
Family Structure of Middle-Class White Americans and Ethnic Minorities: A Comparative Summary

Family Structural Relationships	Middle-Class White Americans	Asian/Pacific Americans	American Indians/ Alaskan Natives	Black Americans	Hispanic Americans
Kinship tie	Nuclear	Extended family	Extended family	Extended family	Extended family
Husband/wife	Egalitarian	Patriarchal	Patriarchal/ matriarchal	Egalitarian	Patriarchal
Parent/child	Hierarchical/ egalitarian	Hierarchical	Egalitarian	Hierarchical	Hierarchical
Siblings	Hierarchical	Hierarchical by age and sex	Egalitarian	Hierarchical	Hierarchical by age and sex

view of the influence of extended family ties, many Indian tribes strongly encourage their young people to marry within their tribal group.

Traditionally, a young Hispanic man interested in a young woman was expected to speak to the parents of the girl, particularly the father, to declare his intentions. A serious courtship could never even begin if the families disapproved. The patriarchal system of Asian/Pacific Americans, some American Indians, and Hispanic Americans places the wife in a low status in the family structure. Within a traditional Asian/Pacific American family, a wife's position, in addition to being lower than that of her husband and her husband's parents, is also lower than that of her oldest son. American Indian women, independent for the most part, played a submissive, supportive role to the husband (Hanson, 1980).

Traditionally, Eskimo men treated their wives as inferior and were reluctant to have close interpersonal contact (Hippler, 1974). While the Hispanic husband assumes the instrumental dominant role of provider and protector of the family, his wife assumes the expressive role of homemaker and caretaker. Because it is the wife's responsibility to care for the home and to keep the family together, the husband is not expected to assume household tasks or help care for the children. The Indian Hopi say that "the man's place is on the outside of the house." This role arrangement sometimes results in wives assuming power behind the scenes, while overtly supporting their husband's authority (Stevens, 1973; Brown and Shaughnessy, 1982; Hsu, 1972).

Partly due to the high unemployment of Black males and the Black female's wage earning ability, the husband-wife relationship of a Black couple has been more egalitarian than the other three ethnic minority groups, and even more so than for the White American couple. When the Black male/husband is at home, he is more capable and willing to assume a flexible role and responsibilities. Women of all ethnic minority groups consider motherhood a more important role than that of a wife (Hsu, 1972; Stevens, 1973; Brown and Shaughnessy, 1982; Bell, 1971). Given that it is the existence of children that validates and cements the marriage, motherly love is a much greater force than wifely love.

During therapy with ethnic minority families, the marital subsystem may be the cause of the problem but it should not receive the initial emphasis. An egalitarian relationship preferred by some middle-class White Americans may not be the desired transactional relationships for minority couples. The romantic, egalitarian relationship should not be the criterion used to measure an ethnic minority couple's marriage and parental subsystem boundary. The couple should always be encouraged to communicate with each other clearly and effectively.

Parent-child relationship. The parental functions of both Asians and Hispanics follow the cultural prescriptions for the husband-wife relationship. The father disciplines and controls, while the mother provides nurturance and support. The child's responsibility at home is to obey and to be deferent to his or her parents. Love and affection are displayed openly when the child is an infant. The Hispanic father generally is relaxed and playful with younger children and more stern and strict with older children, especially daughters (Fitzpatrick, 1981, p. 209). Within an American Indian family, the basic parental disciplinary role may be shared among relatives of several generations. The biological parents are thereby afforded the opportunity to engage in fun-oriented activities with their children. Hence the American Indian parent-child relationship is less pressured and more egalitarian than that of other ethnic groups, including the dominant culture. While a Black father's involvement with his children may be hindered by economic restrictions, a Black mother is generally recognized for her devotion and care of her children. The effects of the absence of a Black father on the child is partly compensated for by male kinsmen in the extended family network. In fact, one unique strength characteristic of all ethnic minorities is the involvement of the extended family in the rearing and guidance of children. Most ethnic minority children grow up in the midst of adults, not only their parents, but also members of the extended family. Ethnic minority children are seldom left at home with baby-sitters or other adults unknown to them.

Parents of Asian, Hispanic, and Black children usually engender the respect of their children through complementary transactions. They would not expect or want to be friends with their children. In disciplining the children, Black parents may use physical force, but this is done with love and care. Conversely, American Indian parents seldom order or physically punish their children (Lewis, 1970). The high status that the child is afforded in American Indian families is evidenced in some tribes where the mother and the daughter may be referred to by the same term (Brown and Shaughnessy, 1982, p. 30). A daughter would properly address her mother as "mother-sister," the mother would properly address the child as "child-sister." In terms of practice implications, a therapist must follow the authority stance of Asian, Hispanic, and Black families, which places the child in a subservient and

obedient role. Free and open expression characteristic of conjoint
family therapy should take into consideration the pragmatics of the
ethnic minority background. These three ethnic groups believe in firm
discipline of their children. A therapist should not automatically assume
that children from female-headed families lack adult male influence or
models. Having been exposed to the companionship of many adults in
an extended family, an ethnic minority child is more aware of what
socially approved patterns of behavior should be, as well as what other
people think of them.

   Sibling relationship. The sibling relationship within all ethnic
minority families is influenced by the extended family network. Asians
and Hispanics further distinguish themselves in a vertical hierarchical
structive and male sex-role dominance. Historically, through a son,
Asian parents could be assured that the family's name and the memory
of ancestors would continue. Due to the egalitarian orientation of
Blacks and the different matrilineal and patrilineal patterns among
Indian tribes, there is no distinct favoritism afforded to the American
Indian or Black child. Parents of all ethnic minorities typically accord
authority to older siblings and delegate supervisory and caretaking
functions to them. The oldest son of an Asian family is expected to be a
role model and to provide continuous guidance to his younger siblings
not only when they are young but throughout their adult lives. Given the
one down position of Black woman in White American society, the
oldest daughter of a Black family is expected to be self-sufficient and
independent early in life. Among Asians, Hispanics, and American
Indians, cross-sex sibling companionship is curtailed at adolescence and
is replaced by complementary functions such as girls doing household
chores and boys working outside of the home and chaperoning the girls.
Black adolescents are taught, however, that such traits as nurturing and
assertiveness are desirable for any individual, regardless of sex. Because
all ethnic minority children are taught respect, cooperation and control
of aggression (Rothenberg, 1964; Sollenberger, 1962; Hippler, 1974) at
an early age, there is little sibling rivalry. The emotional support,
guidance, and practical help among siblings continues during adulthood.
Family therapy with ethnic minorities should consider the significance
of the sex, age, and sibling order factors of children at the assessment
phase. The intergenerational parent-child boundary within an ethnic
minority family is often influenced by factors different than in the White
middle-class family. The therapist should take care not to use the latter
as his frame of reference.

Intermarriages. The process of acculturation and social interaction and increased tolerance of ethnic or racial differences are responsible for the gradual increase of intermarriage between members of ethnic minority groups and with the White American majority. Generally, upward mobility has been cited as positively associated with intermarriage (Grebler et al., 1970). Although a great deal has been written about the "abnormal" psychological characteristics of those involved in intermarriages, research indicates just the opposite (Porterfield, 1978). Nevertheless, in view of diverse cultural backgrounds and family patterns of the ethnic minorities and the dominant culture, intermarried couples may experience a high rate of conflict. The effects of intermarriages in family therapy also depend upon how other relatives view the marriage. Some see intermarriage as one channel through which equality can be achieved; others feel that such a marital union may weaken nationality ties and the family of origin. Hence most traditional older members of the respective ethnic minority families oppose intermarriage. Their strong sentiment against intermarriage can make a couple's marriage vulnerable. Family therapists can play a role in intermarriage by becoming more knowledgeable about and by professionally analyzing this phenomenon so as to dispel the fears, myths, misconceptions, and prejudice historically associated with intermarriages.

Divorce and remarriage. National research data have consistently supported the fact that the divorce rate among Asian and Hispanic Americans is lower than that for Anglo populations (Schwertfeger, 1982; Alvirez et al., 1981). Reasons include social ostracism, a female's realistic expectations of the wife's subservient role, and the predominant Catholic religion among Hispanics, which has a strong prohibition against divorce. Conversely, American Indians and the Blacks have a higher divorce rate. In 1975, the Black's divorce and separation rate doubled that of Whites (U.S. Bureau of the Census, 1977). Diversity of tribal cultures that conflict with the dominant culture, unemployment, poverty, and a shortage of males contribute to the high divorce rate among these two groups. While an Asian or Hispanic American divorcée may risk social ostracism, American Indian and Black divorcées have fewer problems with their families and extended families after divorce. Divorce and remarriage are more acceptable within American Indian culture than among dominant culture families (Price, 1981). The strong support of the extended family and multiple households offer the divorcée a place in the family. Family therapists who work with these ethnic groups should be cautious of the various implications and consequences that divorce has upon different ethnic minority members. They should be empathic with the Asian and Hispanic Americans' reluctance to end their marriages. Should the marriage end in divorce, the strong support system among American Indians and among Blacks should be capitalized on to ensure a smooth transition. Different ethnic minorities view divorce differently. Many therapeutic implications including mobilizing the extended family and social support system exist for the future adjustment of the divorcée in terms of single-parenthood and remarriage.

Immigration, Migration, Political, and Cultural Adjustments

Both Asian and Hispanic Americans experience similar patterns of immigrational, political, and cultural adjustments. There are two interrelated levels of adaptive cultural transition that both Asian and Hispanic American families in the process of immigration must face: (1) the physical or material, economic, educational, and language transition, and (2) the cognitive, affective, and psychological (individual members and family as a unit) transition. Immigration and migration produce a transitional crisis in the family with predictable stages of resolution (Sluzki, 1979). Membership change within the family during immigration may necessitate that a family restructure its roles, functions, and transactions. The traditional hierarchical role structure of both Asian and Hispanic families members may conflict with the husband/father who becomes unemployed. This coupled with the wife's working outside of the home can disrupt the traditional male dominant role in the marriage. The faster acculturation rate of the children can threaten authoritarian parents who may have to depend on their children to translate for them when they deal with community agencies, immigration authorities, and health care sources. Lack of support outside the family system and fear of crime, drug addiction, and more permissive sexual mores often cause parents to be overly strict with their children who, in turn, rebel against them. The children also reject their parents' traditional customs, which they consider inferior to American mores.

American Indians and Blacks are less affected by distant geographical separation and are seldom cutoff from their family of origin or experience language problems. They are victims, however, of federal programs and policies that deprive them of the opportunities and benefits entitled to all United State citizens. The statistics for income, education, mental health, and crime among Blacks and urban Indians present a bleak picture. Living against such ecological stresses and daily survival threats, the life of an Indian or Black family is certain to deteriorate rapidly. In an attempt to survive the oppressive victim system, some Indians and Blacks adapt a value orientation that, when translated behaviorally, can lead an individual to seek immediate gratification, manipulative relationships, and passive-aggressive, rebellious, or aggressive actions. These characteristics may be adapted as a reaction to powerlessness but they can be stressful to mental health and destructive to family relationships.

Thus family therapy with ethnic minorities must recognize the impacts of immigration, political discrimination, and cultural adjustments. The therapist's role extends beyond a therapeutic function; it includes the roles of educator, cultural translator, mediator, and model to help families form an open system with available community resources. The old natural support systems and the newly established network based on mutual aid developed by the therapist can provide needed economic, emotional, and educational assistance to families in cultural transition.

Family Help-Seeking Patterns and Behaviors

Ethnic minority clients and families do not consider mental health services a solution to their emotional and family problems (Kleinman and Lin, 1981; Casas and Keefe, 1978; De Geyndt, 1973; McAdoo, 1977). Reasons for their underutilization of health and mental services include (1) distrust of therapists, especially White therapists; (2) cultural and social class differences between therapists and clients; (3) an insufficient number of mental health facilities and professionals who are bicultural; (4) overuse or misuse of physicians for psychological problems; (5) language barriers; (6) reluctance to recognize the urgency for help; and (7) lack of awareness of the existence of mental health clinics. All ethnic minorities consider the family and extended family their primary source of support. Reliance on natural support systems produces fewer feelings of defeat, humiliation to self and to the family, and powerlessness. When natural support systems are unavailable, most ethnic minority clients or families consult their folk healers, priests, or religious leaders. When all these fail, the family may seek help from the mainstream family and health care system. The ethnic minority client's fear and mistrust of therapists are caused by past oppression and discrimination and negative experiences with helping professionals from the mainstream institutions. When minorities do seek mental health or family-related services, they see the therapist as a physician who prescribes medication or gives directives.

Help-seeking patterns of ethnic minorities closely correspond to their specific needs and family types. Both Asian and Hispanic American families can be categorized into three types: (1) recently arrived immigrant families, (2) immigrant-American families, and (3) immigrant-descendent families. Newly arrived immigrant families need information, referral, advocacy, and English-language instruction. Due to cultural and language barriers, they seldom seek personal or family therapy.

Immigrant-American families characterized by cultural conflict may need help in resolving generational conflicts, communication problems, role clarification, and renegotiation. Native or immigrant-descent families usually are acculturated, speak both languages at home, and can seek help from mainstream social and mental health agencies, including private practice family therapists. Red Horse's (1980b) classification of American Indian families also indicates that bicultural families are the ones most receptive to family therapy.

Neither traditional nor pantraditional families are receptive to the idea of family therapy. Knowing the similarities and differences of help-seeking patterns among various ethnic minority groups, a therapist is informed generally what to expect especially during the initial contact phase with the client. Variations within each ethnic minority group also inform and remind the therapist of the need for individualization in therapy with ethnic minority families.

Applying Culturally Sensitive Family Theories, Models, and Approaches

Family Communication Theory

Family communication theory pertaining to the daily interactions among family members has a great deal of relevance and applicability in therapy with ethnic minority families. The following discussion focuses on the contribution of family communication theory and is organized into two sections. The first section describes the principles of family behavior from the perspective of family communication theory. The second section describes practice principles derived from communication theory.

Communication principles of family behavior as they relate to understanding ethnic minority families. In analyzing the pragmatics of communication as they relate to ethnic minority families, the behavioral principle that all behavior is communicative is applicable to all groups. When American Indians are confronted or under stress, they communicate their anxiety through silence (Lewis and Ho, 1975). Hispanics, governed by their hierarchical structure, may display no overt sign of displeasure when confronted, but they may not return for the next scheduled session (Falicov, 1982). Some Asians communicate their stress and displeasure through a physical symptom, which is acceptable in their culture. Blacks, however, respond to anxiety by either saying nothing or becoming loud, threatening, and abusive (Cheek, 1976, p. 65).

The process of metacommunication, defined as information containing a command (Haley, 1963), is further complicated by the process of immigration and acculturation among Asian and Hispanic Americans. Traditionally, these groups interact according to a prescribed vertical and hierarchical role structure, which is determined by age, sex, generation, and birth order of family members. American Indians' use of indirect communication also is a form of metacommunication that requires sensitivity and reciprocity from others. When indirect communication is not properly received and reciprocated, there is a threat to that relationship. When a Black family's basic security and safety needs are threatened, metacommunication among family members in the manner of distrust is likely to occur.

The principle of the "punctuation" of the communicational sequences (Bateson, 1972) is experienced in an intergenerational parent-child conflict among various ethnic minority families. The principle of "punctuation" of the communicational sequences usually is triggered or related to "internal" stressors affecting the family" (Minuchin, 1974), such as a family member's illness or parents coping with adolescent child problems. For an ethnic minority family, "punctuation" of the communicational sequences may be caused by cultural value conflict, the acculturation process, or discriminatory practices by mainstream society.

The communication concept of digital (verbal) and analogic (non-verbal) communication has important implications in therapy with all ethnic minority families. Although most ethnic minority clients are bilingual, some traditional Asian, Hispanic, and Indian families are more comfortable with their native language when dealing with crises or problem-solving issues. Clients who speak English with difficulty may have the added demands of decoding and encoding (Pitta, Marcos, and Alpert, 1978). Some Black families communicate mostly through paraverbal channels in the pitch, tempo, and intensity of the verbal messages and the accompanying kinesthetic modifiers (Minuchin, 1967, p. 206). Difficulties in digital and analogic communication can cause problems in deciding the extent to which there is congruence between the message and the way it is delivered.

Other communication concepts such as syntaxis (the grammatical properties), semantics (meaning of communication), and pragmatics (behavioral effects of the communication) may hinder an ethnic minority member's ability to resolve family conflicts. Because these concepts are closely related to different family members' levels of acculturation, these concepts also partly explain why so many ethnic minority clients hesitate to speak during therapy, especially if the therapist is not a member of their ethnic group.

The principle of schismogenesis (Bateson, 1958) states that cumulative interaction between individuals tends to result in progressive change. The cultural transitional process and the strong influences of the egalitarian couple relationship of the dominant culture have greatly affected the traditional complementary (dominant/submissive) relationship of Asian and Hispanic couples. While the husband struggles to maintain a complementary transaction, the wife may try to negotiate a symmetrical (equal) relationship. Conversely, while the American Indian and Black husbands try hard to maintain a symmetrical relationship with their wives, the latter may have difficulty complying due to their increased financial earning power and central role within the family. As the schismogenesis between husband and wife shifts, other aspects of the family emotional relationship change, thus creating dysfunctional transactions such as triangulation and scapegoating.

Satir's classification of family behavior for a family member under stress (Satir, Stachowiak, and Taschman, 1975) can explain an Asian or a Hispanic husband/father's behavior during acculturation and other stressful periods. When a family transaction is out of (hierarchical) "structure," a husband/father easily falls into the blamer role, finding fault in others as a means to "save face" or reaffirm his "machismo." The in-between position (husband and children) occupied by the wife often places her in a placator role of agreeing, pleasing, and apologizing. The consistent unemployment status of many Black males and the occupationally displaced status of many American Indian males often force them to assume placator roles in their families. As they become "demoralized" by assuming the placator role, they shift into an "irrelevant" role, which, in turn, places them in a peripheral position in transactions with the children and other family members.

The principles of behavior derived from communication theory have contributed significantly to understanding the dynamics and interaction of ethnic minority families. The following discussion aims to explicate the matter in which these principles can be applied in actual therapy with various ethnic clients.

Communication practice principles as they relate to work with ethnic minority families. To communicate with Asian and Hispanic American families, a therapist needs to consider the prescribed vertical and hierarchical role structure as determined by age, sex, generation, and birth order of family members. The hierarchical role structure places the father in a spokesman role that cannot be openly challenged, especially by his own children. Hence it is advisable that beginning family therapy sessions with Asian and Hispanic families be divided between the spouse subsystem and sibling subsystem. Further, to respect the authoritarian parental position, parents should be interviewed first and the siblings second. When the parents are ready to be interviewed with their children (assuming the therapist is bilingual), their native language can be used to communicate with the parents and English can be used with the children. An interchange of language is useful for delineating blurred generational boundaries (Falicov, 1982, p. 158).

Conversely, because of the egalitarian power orientation within an Indian or a Black family, the father should not be expected to lead the discussion during therapy. Furthermore, the therapist may need to align the authority or relationship concept with a collateral, mutually respected, and responsible phrase. For example, instead of instructing the family members exactly what to do, the therapist can suggest different alternatives to improve relationships with other family members.

The role of the therapist, as defined by Haley, is that of a "metagovernor of the family system," thus requiring intense active participation and at times manipulation. The therapist's active leadership role may easily be interpreted by the ethnic minority family as an unwelcome intrusion. Hence the therapist's activity should be guided by the cultural values of each group. This is particularly important at the engagement phase of the therapy. For example, in therapy with Hispanics, the therapist should use the formal form of the pronoun "you"(usted) with adults to indicate respect. Children can be addressed with the familiar form (tu). Similarly, in therapy with a Black family, a therapist should not assume familiarity with adult family members without asking their permission.

The technique of relabeling/reframing (by emphasizing the positive or behavior that can be changed) is consistent with the Black American culture's emphasis on humanistic orientation and harmonious living. The Asian and Hispanic cultures emphasize respect, interdependence, and compassion. American Indian culture stresses respect and individuality. The technique for prescribing the symptom (encouraging the usually dysfunctional behavior) may be perplexing at best and disrespectful at worse to most ethnic minority families. However, paradoxical messages (double bind) are often effective in work with an authoritarian Hispanic or Asian father or overly protective Indian or Black mother who rigidly reinforces what is expected of her culturally. By joining the parent's resistance, through recognizing his or her effort to carrying out parental duties, a therapist can help him or her explore alternate ways to fulfill obligatory parental roles.

Satir's (1967) emphasis on "good feelings" within the family and among family members is consistent with Asian Buddhists' teachings of harmonious living and compassion, Hispanics' emphasis on familism and respect, American Indians' teaching of collaterality and "goodness" of man, and the Blacks' humanistic orientation. Her cognitive approach to "teaching" family members to recognize and restructure rules appeals to ethnic minorities' needs for concreteness. Sculpting technique suggested by Satir may also be appealing to all ethnic minority families who learn by observation and participation. Satir's emphasis on communication skills essential for congruent communication and effective feedback should also be taught to all ethnic minority families who need constant renegotiation of expectation of roles within the family. Her utilization of family history, which she calls the "family life chronology" (Satir, 1967), can help ethnic minority clients, especially Asians and Hispanics, to be proud of their past traditions.

Family Structure Theory

A theoretical discussion of family structure theory and its comparison with family communication theory has been presented in Chapter 1. The discussion of family structure theory here centers on behavioral principles and family practice principles. The first section examines behavioral principles of family structure theory. The second section presents family practice principles of structure family theory as they relate to assessment and therapy with ethnic minority families.

Behavioral principles of structure family theory as they relate to understanding ethnic minority families. Structural family theory strongly adheres to the system outlook and was primarily developed and advanced by Bowen (1976) and Minuchin (1974). The societal projection process (Bowen, 1976) creates societal scapegoats with which all ethnic minorities have been identified. Through the societal projection process, one group (the White society and benefactors) maintains the illusion of competence at the expense of "unfortunates" by "helpfulness and benevolence." The benefactors (White society) assume the blamer role and the unfortunates (ethnic minorities) are forced to assume the victim role. Thus a homeostasis social system is maintained. Such a social system resembles the family projection process.

Given the reality that most ethnic minority families are embedded in a complex kinship network of "blood" and unrelated persons, the process of "triangulation," which involves intense interaction among three people within a relatively long period, may not have the same meaning and intensity for an ethnic minority family. However, the process of immigration and migration affecting the Asian and Hispanic families and the Black and American Indian families' responses to the external threats by a racist society may cause an ethnic minority family to protect itself by maintaining a rigid closed system. Asian and Hispanic male dominance and typical mother-child bond and the unemployed Black father's less than consistent involvement with the family can cause these families to be highly susceptible to the process of triangulation with mother-child siding against the father. In a multiple household of an extended American Indian family, where a child's interaction with parents is greatly shared by other extended family members, the triangulation process may occur and involve extended family members other than the typical parent-child dyad. In order to survive the victim system, parents in ethnic minority families are determined to create a better future for their children. They will sacrifice for their children, whom they expect to earn greater rewards from the opportunity structure than they themselves were unable to achieve. Parents' intense wish for their children to achieve and to behave accordingly corresponds closely to Bowen's concepts of "family projection process" and the "multigenerational transmission process." Again, the traditional extended family structure of ethnic minorities needs to be considered in relation to the impacts of these processes. For example, at times the close relationship between a child and grandparents within an American Indian family may have more to do with the family projection process than the shallow relationship between the child and his or her biological parents.

Asian and Hispanic families must cope with acculturation; Blacks and American Indians must cope with economic survival, which may necessitate their moving away from their extended families and close friends. Such processes make "emotional cutoff" a reality for many ethnic minority families. Yet, the strong kinship bond within these groups can be a source of strength to be capitalized on in therapy with ethnic families.

To survive biculturally in a dominant White society, Bowen's central concept of "differentiation" has great implications for the well-being of all ethnic minority groups. Ethnic minority members' adherence and loyalties to nationality, race, and origin of birth and extended families make them culturally unique. Such visible or invisible loyalties at times can be dysfunctional especially when an ethnic minority family is interacting with the dominant White society. Bowen's concept of "self-differentiation" coincides with the ethnic minority concept of individuality, which allows uniqueness to become the richness of life. Hence a differentiated person is not a self-centered person, but an individual who values her past, including ethnic heritage and family background. A differentiated acculturated person is one who is intellect (reason) and goal-directed instead of overwhelmed by emotion or feeling. Such an individual can build his or her own life without feeling disloyal and still remain emotionally tied to the family of origin, or can be geographically close without being trapped emotionally in intense family relationships. However, the level of differentiation in an individual may not be determined strictly by the differentiated level of one's parents, by sex, or by sibling position as advocated by Bowen. The reason behind such uncertainty is that the typical ethnic minority child experiences a broader sphere of interaction with extended family members as compared to an Anglo child's limited interaction with only nuclear family members. Hence the importance that parental role, sex, and sibling position play in an individual's level of differentiation varies from one ethnic family to another. Thus in the assessment of an ethnic minority family relationship and an individual family member's level of differentiation, greater attention should be focused on extended family relationships and framework.

Family structure theory focusing on the family system's structural (contextual) dynamics, especially the creation, maintenance, and modification of boundaries (Minuchin, 1974, p. 53), is highly useful in work with ethnic minority families. Under normal conditions, the traditional ethnic minority family structure characterized by familism, collaterality, and extended family ties can produce cohesion conducive to the developmental growth of all family members. As Minuchin points out, however, "the stressful contact of the whole family with extra familial forces" (1974, p. 63) can produce role confusion and power conflict within the family. Because both husband and wife must often work outside the home, the couple system within the ethnic minority family may shift toward "disengagement" where a relationship is too rigid and distant. Such is also true for the parent-child subsystem. The maintenance of a couple system is further complicated by some American Indian tribal customs that treat mother and daughter alike (Brown and Shaughnessy, 1982, p. 30). By focusing upon the extrafamilial forces, Minuchin is sensitive to the political, economic, social, and cross-cultural processes of poverty and discrimination faced by many ethnic minority families.

In defining family structure and system boundaries, Minuchin points out that the dominant culture family structure places husband and wife in an equal relationship with different levels of authority over their children (Minuchin, 1974, p. 52). However, a therapist working with Asian and Hispanic families should not assume that the spouse boundary is diffuse just because the spousal system of these two family group is structured differently (hierarchical instead of egalitarian). The same also applies to an American Indian couple who considers too much authority detrimental to the development of a child's individuality. An ethnic minority family generally is large, and parents are usually burdened with meeting the economic survival needs of the family. Older siblings are assigned the responsibility of caring for the young children and assisting with other household duties. A therapist should avoid interpreting this as boundary diffusion and should not label an older child as "parental-child" (Minuchin, 1974, p. 53). This unique complementary accommodation between spouses and between parents and children characterizes a unique strength of the ethnic minority family structure.

Family structure practice principles in therapy with ethnic minority families. Bowen's societal process, which places the ethnic minorities in a victim role, suggests the therapist be a culture-broker (Bowen, 1978, p. 540) who is open to exploring the impact of the social, political, socioeconomic, and broader environmental conditions of ethnic minority families. Family group interaction characteristic of all ethnic minority cultures normally should be conducive to conjoint (with every family member present) family therapy. Yet, the unnaturalness of the formal family therapy format with the therapist in charge may be too threatening for many ethnic minority families. They often believe family problems should be resolved within the family itself. Bowen's technique of focusing upon one individual, usually the more differentiated or respected member in the family, should be useful. Bowen's detached but interested, rational, calm, low-key approach to problem solving corresponds closely to the Asian, Hispanic, and American Indian cultural emphasis on moderation, patience, and self-discipline. Other techniques employed by Bowen to help a spouse define and clarify his or her relationship by speaking directly to the therapist instead of the other spouse is applicable to therapy with these ethnic groups.

Bowen's preference for singling out the couple relationship as a therapeutic target (Bowen, 1978, p. 175) may alienate the parents of all ethnic minorities. The ethnic minority mother often feels more challenged to perform as a good mother than as a wife. Bowen's efforts in taking careful family history reflects his sensitivity and respect of the intergenerational perspectives and cultural nurturing system, the migration process, and the need for individualizing each family. Yet, this approach may be antithetical to the ethnic minority's "present" orientation and their reluctance to examine the painful past. His heavy reliance on the client to be active and to do the research, assessment, and differentiation process may not be congruent with the ethnic minority client's need and perception of the therapist as an expert.

Minuchin's differential applications of "joining techniques" are especially helpful during the beginning phase of therapy with ethnic minority families. Application of these techniques reflects Minuchin's sensitivity to individual family differences and the wisdom that structural change in a family usually requires time and patience. In the joining process, Minuchin also is mindful of the ethnic minority family's need to accept the therapist with a leadership role aspired to and expected by all ethnic minority families. The strategic use of the "maintenance" technique enables the therapist to adhere to the transactional process of a particular ethnic minority family system. For example, in therapy with a three-generation Asian or Hispanic American family adhering to a rigid hierarchical structure, the therapist may find it advisable to address the grandfather first. For some American Indian tribes who follow matriarchal practices, the grandmother is the person to whom the therapist should speak. The technique of "tracking" also is helpful for the therapist to explore the content of family interaction and to analyze family structure. Here the therapist should keep in mind how ethnic minority family structures differ from the dominant culture. In view of their inclusive involvement with extended family ties, the degree of intensity within each subsystem usually varies from the dominant culture. For example, while the ethnic minority spouse subsystem is not as strong and intense as that of the dominant culture, the ethnic minority minority siblings subsystem and the extended family subsystem are much stronger and more involved. Likewise, to eliminate totally the Black "parental-child's" parental role may be totally insensitive to the family's basic survival need.

In applying Minuchin's disequilibration technique, which aims to reestablish clear family subsystems and cross-generational boundaries, the therapist needs to use different modalities including interviewing the parental sybsystem separately, using native language (assuming the therapist is bilingual) to communicate with the parents or grandparents, and using English when speaking to the children. While Minuchin's joining, maintenance, and tracking techniques are compatible with ethnic minority family values and structure, his "disequilibration techniques" or family restructuring techniques need to be applied with caution. These techniques, including escalating stress (by emphasizing differences), utilizing the symptom (by exaggerating it), and manipulating mood (by escalating the emotional intensity), are much too abstract, antithetical to ethnic minority cultures that emphasize interdependence, harmonious living, and moderation of behavior.

The preceding discussions aim to analyze, compare, and integrate the cultural values and family structure of ethnic minority families. The communication and structural family therapy theories have been reviewed along with their application in therapy with different ethnic client groups. Attention will now be directed to comparison and integration of culturally relevant techniques and skills with different ethnic minority families in three phases of therapy: beginning, problem solving, and evaluation-termination.

PART 2: CULTURALLY RELEVANT TECHNIQUES AND SKILLS IN THERAPY PHASES

Beginning Phase

The beginning phase of therapy is a critical period for all ethnic minority clients and families. The reason for this phase of therapy being so important is due to several factors. All ethnic minority families utilize family therapy only if all other traditional help-seeking attempts have failed. They have no knowledge of what family therapy is about. To rely on a family therapist who is considered an outsider to resolve private family problems is antithetical to filial piety and a betrayal of ancestors (Asian/Hispanics). It is an unwelcome intrusion to self-determination and individuality (American Indians/Blacks). Most ethnic minority clients distrust therapists who represent the mainstream society that oppresses them and perpetuates their sense of powerlessness. Most ethnic minority clients are uncomfortable with "talk" therapy and are self-conscious of their English language deficiency. They often lack the financial resources to seek continuous therapy help. Many ethnic minority clients have contact with family therapists only because they are referred by mainstream societal agencies such as schools, mental and health care agencies, the court, or social service agencies. If this beginning phase of therapy is not "properly" conducted, the first interviews will most likely be the last time the therapist will have contact with the client or family. Five major skills and techniques are essential in therapy with ethnic minority clients and families in the beginning therapeutic phase. These skills and techniques include (1) engaging the client/family, (2) cultural transitional mapping and data collection, (3) mutual goal setting, (4) selecting a focus/system for treatment, and 5) the use of an eco-map. Although these skills and techniques are considered generic and applicable to all ethnic minority groups, the following discussion attempts to draw some comparisons and conclusions of their strategic application in the beginning phase of therapy with different ethnic minorities.

Engaging the Client/Family

Because of their long history of discrimination, ethnic minority Americans find it difficult to trust a family therapist who represents the majority system. The level of mistrust is compounded by the fact that some Asians and Hispanics do not have the proper documents to reside in this country. It is important that the therapist defines his or her role with the client early. Most ethnic minority clients (Asians and Blacks) perceive the role of a family therapist as that of a physician, a medicine man (American Indians), or a folk healer (Hispanics). There is a need to orient ethnic minority families to how to make use of family therapy (Hoehn-Sarie et al., 1964; Acosta et al., 1982). Such orientation includes exploring with the families their expectations of the therapy goals, the role of the therapist, and their involvement during the therapeutic process.

To foster an element of trust, a therapist can help the client feel comfortable by displaying in her office objects, pictures, or symbols of different ethnic minority cultures. Race is a major factor undermining the ethnic minority client's sense of powerlessness. During this early stage of therapy, the therapist, therefore, may need to explore with the family the racial differences between the therapist and the family (Ho and McDowell, 1973).

A therapist needs to be sensitive to English language deficiencies, especially by older traditional clients who are Asians, Hispanics, and American Indians. Using children as translators may reverse the authority structure of these families and threaten the parents, especially the fathers. When there are no native-speaking therapists available, an adult interpreter is recommended (Kline et al., 1980).

Because the therapist is perceived as an authority figure, she or he needs to assume an active role in the beginning phase of the therapy process. Minuchin's joining technique is most applicable because the therapist can be accepted with a "quota of leadership" (Pinderhughes, 1982, p. 121). To minimize the unnaturalness of the initial therapist-family contact, Minuchin's maintenance technique, which "requires the therapist to be organized by the basic rules that regulate the transactional process in a specific family system" (1974, p. 175), is helpful. For instance, given that the social interaction of the Hispanic American is governed by a hierarchical role structure, the therapist should address the father first. The therapist's willingness to answer personal questions and receive a small token or gift is consistent with the Asian's "interpersonal grace" and Hispanic's "personalism." Additionally, a therapist should allow herself and an American Indian family ample time to gather their thoughts and emotions before pressing on to a new topic. Often the ethnic minority family is so overwhelmed by multiple problems and the anxiety associated with seeking help that informing them at the engagement phase that therapy will be long term and difficult is self-defeating for the therapist and the family (Foley, 1975).

Transitional Mapping and Data Collection

The therapist should demonstrate personal interest in the family; this is consistent with the ethnic minority families' orientation of personalism and collaterality. Inquiries about the family's cultural background can shift the focus of the therapy session away from the "problem" or the "identified patient," and it also provides the family an opportunity to educate the therapist, who assumes the role of a researcher (Bowen, 1978). In ascertaining the family's connectedness with their birthplace, culture, or roots, the frameworks of Boszormenyi-Nagy and Krasner (1980) and Sluzki (1979) have been found helpful especially in therapy with Hispanic and Asian clients. The technique of cultural mapping and genograms are similar (Pendagast and Sherman, 1977). They provide insight into family member's intergenerational perspective and levels of "differentiation" (Bowen, 1978).

Many ethnic minority families, especially Hispanics, American Indians, and Blacks, practice informal adoption. Consequently, their genograms seldom confirm completely to bloodlines (Hines and Boyd-Franklin, 1982). Therefore, to obtain accurate information, the therapist needs to inquire who is in the family as well as who lives in the home. Many ethnic minority families have endured great pain in the past, so the therapist must be sensitive when asking questions. The therapist should look for an opportunity or a natural opening to gather the desired information rather than adhering to an inflexible schedule. Techniques in data collection with ethnic minorities require more than the usual question and answer mode of communication. The use of home visits, family photographs, albums, paintings, and native music can facilitate interaction and generate meaningful information (Ho and Settles, 1984).

Mutual Goal Setting

Therapeutic goals with ethnic minority families can be divided into three categories (Falicov, 1982, p. 154): (1) goal related to situational stress (e.g., social isolation, poverty, and so on) caused by interface between the family and the new environment; (2) goal related to dysfunctional patterns of cultural transition (e.g., parent-child role reversal, conflictual child-rearing practice); and (3) goal related to transcultural dysfunctional patterns (e.g., universal family problems such as developmental impasses, limited range of repetitive interactional behaviors, and so on). Minorities are forced to adjust to mainstream society. Goal setting with an ethnic minority requires an ecostructual approach (Aponte, 1979), which, in turn, considers the "incompleteness" (basic survival needs) that most ethnic minority families experience (Pollak, 1964).

The process of mutual goal formulation requires that the therapist adhere to the value orientation of a specific ethnic minority family. Individual psychologically oriented goals will not fit well with ethnic minorities' emphasis on familism and interdependence. Therapy goals that do not reflect a person's determinants or self-centeredness, but rather that emphasize the rehabilitation of physical or organic illness, will be acceptable to most ethnic minorities, especially Asian Americans. An ethnic minority client is often reluctant to formulate goals that benefit only him- or herself. Ethnic family structure places strong emphasis on the parent-child relationship. Early therapeutic goals emphasizing only improvement of the couple relationship will meet with resistance. Because of the family's involvement with the extended family, the process of goal formulation should involve all family members, including sometimes the extended family members. The hierarchical or egalitarian structure of the family should be recognized and capitalized on in the mutual goal formulation process.

Intergenerational perspectives can be influential; however, therapy goals should not dwell on the parents' families of origin or multi-generational transmission, because it may be too threatening, too time-consuming, and antithetical to the ethnic minorities "present" and "doing" orientation. This orientation, plus linguistic complexities and deficiency in the English language, requires that therapeutic goals be problem focused, structured, realistic, concrete, practical, and readily achievable (Marage and Johnson, 1974; Acosta et al., 1982; Edwards and Edwards, 1984). Minuchin (1967) affirms that when patterns of change in the family are out of phase with the realities of extrafamilial systems, therapy will fail. Aponte (1979) also emphasizes the need to formulate therapeutic goals that can produce immediate success (power) in the clients' lives.

Selecting a Focus/System Unit for Therapy

Once the problem is identified and the therapeutic goal is formulated, which system unit selected for therapy can determine the outcome. Understanding and respecting the ethnic minority family's cultural norms and present social context are perhaps the most important skills in selecting a subsystem unit for therapy. Considering the intense involvement that ethnic minority families have with their extended family, some family problems can be resolved simply by involving the extended family members, especially the spokesperson, who normally is the grandfather (Asian/Hispanic) or grandmother (Black and Indian). McAdoo (1977), however, points out that sometimes extended family kinship bonds can be a source of family conflicts. Regardless, resolution of family problems within the immediate nuclear family will probably need to involve some extended family members.

The family's need for privacy and the hierarchical and vertical structure of Asian and Hispanic American families discourage family members from showing their true thoughts and negative feelings. A separate session with siblings may be in order for negotiating issues they may not normally discuss in their parent's presence. The strengthening and the restructuring of the siblings subsystem can, in turn, extricate an overprotected child from the parental subsystem. A separate session with the parents need not focus exclusively on the marital relationship. Instead, emphasis can be on how the parents can relate to their child in a "united front" manner that fosters a harmonious living environment desired by all family members. Considering the importance that "machismo" (Hispanic) or "face" (Asian) play in the father's role as head of the family, conjoint family sessions with every family member or with wife present may be too threatening to the Asian or Hispanic father. Hence Bowen's therapeutic strategy of focusing on the differentiation of one person (preferably, the father) may be most appropriate. This approach is also relevant to working with underinvolved Black or American Indian fathers experiencing role peripherality within the family.

The Use of an Eco-Map

In view of immigration, the acculturational process, cultural and language barriers, and poverty factors, therapy with ethnic minority clients must employ an ecostructural approach. The eco-map developed and advanced by Hartman (1979) is a useful and practical technique that visually depicts the family's relationship with its environment. It identifies and characterizes the important supportive or conflict-laden connection between the family and the environment. It also identifies emotional and interactive relationships within the family and its connection with the outside world. The comprehensive picture of the family's major themes and patterns identified by an eco-map, in turn, gives direction to the planning process and keeps both the therapist and the family from getting lost in details. The eco-map is a paper-and-pencil simulation, therefore, it is visual, nonabstract, and easy to administer. It should be highly relevant to all ethnic minority families who are less verbal but more visual and responsive to activity-oriented processes (Foley, 1975).

Problem-Solving Phase

There are 12 generic techniques and skills that are particularly relevant in the problem-solving phase of therapy with ethnic minority families. These techniques and skills can be categorized according to the specific therapeutic goal to be accomplished. As stated earlier, there are three therapeutic goals characteristic of therapy with ethnic minorities (Falicov, 1982). These goals involve resolution of (1) situational stress, (2) cultural transitional conflicts, and (3) conflicts within the family. Table 6.3 presents goal-related techniques and skills in the problem-solving phase of therapy with ethnic minority families.

Techniques and Skills in Resolving Situational Stress

Four techniques and skills are relevant in assisting the ethnic minority family to resolve situational stress caused by the family's interaction with the dominant society. The techniques and skills include mobilizing and restructuring the extended family network; collaborative work with a medicine person, folk healer, and paraprofessional; home visits; and employing role models, the educator role, and the advocate role.

Mobilizing and restructuring the extended family network. One of the factors plaguing many ethnic minority families is the lack of extended family support due to the fact that the family has immigrated (Asian and Hispanic) or migrated (Indians and Blacks) from their native

TABLE 6.3

Goal-Related Techniques and Skills for Problem-Solving
Phase of Therapy with Ethnic Minority Families

| | *Therapeutic Goals* | |
Situational	*Cultural Transitional*	*Family Relationship*
Mobilizing and restructuring the extended family network	Indirectness Social-moral, and organic reframing	Self-observation as a tool for family restructuring Paradoxical intervention
Collaborative work with a medicine person, folk healer, or paraprofessional	Promoting interdependence, family obligation	Employing a therapist-helper
Home visits	Restructuring cultural taboos	Team approach
Employing role models, educator role, and advocate role		

environment where mutual inter- and intrafamily support was strong. Studies have indicated that ethnic minority families make use of the extended family network much more extensively than White American families (Hsu, 1972; Mindel, 1980; McAdoo, 1978, Red Horse, 1980b). A social support network is essential for ethnic minority Americans who need a place and a way to bridge the ecological deficit, to ventilate frustration, to learn acculturated social skills, to form friendships, and to reconnect with their culture of origin. In an effort to mobilize social networks, the therapist's role may become that of a "social intermediary" (Minuchin, 1974, p. 63), a system guide, or a broker (Bowen, 1978).

Collaborative work with a medicine person, folk healer, or a paraprofessional. Many ethnic minority families still resist certain aspects of the dominant culture, particularly a health care provider or family therapist. A medicine person, shaman, or spiritual leader plays a vital role in resolving situational stress in the lives of many Hispanic and American Indian families. Even among bicultural families, the need for a medicine person or spiritual leader is still prevalent. Hispanic folk practitioners have demonstrated the acculturational function of "espiritismo" (Douglas, 1974), problem-solving skills of "santeria" (De La

Cancela, 1978), and the reassurance of "curanderismo" (Kiev, 1968). Hence a family therapist should not hesitate to consult with a spiritual leader when the need arises. The spiritual leader should always be treated with professional integrity and respect.

Home visits. Many ethnic minority families lack specific knowledge about mental health services and family therapy. They may have limited financial resources and transportation problems. Home visits should be a logical and practical tool for reaching such clients. The advantages of home visits in therapy with ethnic minority families include seeing the family in their natural environment (Carter, 1976), personalizing and joining the family in an emotional sense (Spiegel, 1959), and helping the family feel at ease (Pitman et al., 1971). Home visits should be prearranged and conducted in a culturally appropriate manner that is nonintrusive but spontaneous and flexible.

Employing role models, educator role, and advocate role. Migration and acculturation often create confusion and disorganization for individual members as well as for the whole ethnic minority family. Traditional role-modeling might have been functional in the past, but it becomes dysfunctional as family members experience different cultural norms and life cycles. Many American Indians grew up and were educated in boarding schools and out-of-home placements. They lack clear parental role models. Many disadvantaged Blacks tend to have an "all-or-nothing" emotional expression that impedes communication. The therapist's role as cultural translator, mediator, and model (Anda, 1984; Minuchin, 1974) is vital to help the family resolve situational stress and form an open system with available community resources. Guided by the communication practice principles, a therapist can teach a family, through role modeling, the skills essential for open and congruent communication (Satir, 1967). Because many ethnic minority families are the victims of societal lags and intentional or unintentional indifference by agencies and institutions essential to their survival and well-being, the therapist may need to serve as an advocate for the family. Most ethnic minority families do not wish to draw public attention to themselves. It is important that the therapist's biased advocate role on their behalf not subject them to further agency humiliation or discrimination.

Techniques and Skills in Resolving Cultural Transitional Problems

To assist ethnic minority families in resolving dysfunctional patterns of behavior that are caused mainly by cultural conflict with the dominant society, four techniques and skills are identified. They include the use of indirectness; social, moral, and organic reframing; promoting interdependence, family obligation; and restructuring cultural taboos.

Indirectness. Ethnic minority families, especially Asians, Hispanics, and American Indians, are highly sensitive to authority figures (including the therapist). The pragmatic communication of these families should be respected and observed. Thus open, direct, congruent communication essential in problem solving may need some tempering, particularly during the early stage of therapy. Examples of direct communication such as, "Tell your wife what you really think of her," may need to be rephrased as, "Please comment on the things your wife does that contribute to the family." Such indirectness may be time-consuming and nonspecific, but it conveys moderation and respect, which all ethnic minority families cherish. Indirectness can be altered when the family decides to deal with problems directly.

Social, moral, and organic reframing/relabeling. Haley's and Minuchin's reframing/relabeling technique is extremely helpful and applicable in therapy with ethnic minority families whose problems involve cultural conflicts. Using this technique, the therapist can capitalize on the pragmatics and interdependence of ethnic minority cultures by emphasizing the positive aspects of behavior and redefining negative behavior as positive. During the course of a parent-child conflict or marital problem, the therapist can relabel the problem "socially" by pointing out to the family that the immigration or discrimination process is unsettling for every family. Similarly, psychosomatic illness resulting from unresolved interpersonal relationships can be reframed "morally" to put it beyond everybody's control. Moral reframing views illness as natural and it proceeds according to its own course of action. Reframing accentuates good feelings among family members and avoids holding a client directly responsible for the cause of problem.

Promoting interdependence, family obligation. Despite living in a bicultural world immersed with individualism, most ethnic minority clients still value what others, especially family members, think of them. Family centrality, loyalty, fairness, and responsibility can be capitalized on to promote change that is consonant with the native value system. During the family restructuring process, a therapist can challenge the family's obligation to maintain the family as a unit. Furthermore, the therapist can challenge family members to exercise the power of self-control inherent in all ethnic minority cultures. Promoting change as a means to fulfill family obligation must also include consideration of respective ethnic minority communication pragmatics. For example, instead of encouraging the Asian or Hispanic wife to challenge her domineering husband openly, the therapist can encourage the wife to suggest to her husband other alternatives in child rearing. This public support that the husband is receiving from his wife can reinforce his powerful role as patriarch, and, at the same time, make him more receptive to new ways of coping with his child's problem.

Restructuring cultural taboos. Each ethnic minority culture has strong cultural beliefs, including prohibitions and proper conduct rules for family members. The process of acculturation may not alter these prohibitions. The more traditional an ethnic minority family is, the more rigidly it will adhere to cultural taboos. When a therapist encounters cultural taboos, she or he should not categorically label them as just another form of client resistance. Instead, taboos should be carefully examined and respected. Moreover, the therapist may need to consult and work collaboratively with elders, religious leaders, or other indigenous healers for resolving family problems caused by cultural taboos.

Techniques and Skills in Resolving Family Relationship Problems

To assist an ethnic minority family in resolving internal relationship conflicts, four generic techniques and skills are presented. They are (1) self-observation, (2) paradoxical intervention, (3) employing a therapist-helper, and (4) team approach.

Self-observation. The family therapy process traditionally relies heavily upon verbal interaction. Such pragmatic communication may at times be inappropriate in therapy with ethnic minority clients who exhibit distrust, English language deficiencies, or a general reluctance to express feelings verbally. The self-observation technique, which aims at assisting a client to observe his or her own behavior that requires change, is applicable for it visually focuses on a client's here-and-now "doing" transactions with other family members. This technique has produced positive results in therapy with Blacks and Hispanics (Minuchin, 1974; Foley, 1975). It should not be used, however, until a trusting relationship has been established between the family and the therapist. The open, revealing nature of this technique when used in conjoint therapy session is sometimes threatening to parental figures, especially Asian, American Indian, and Hispanic fathers. The insight gained by this technique may not be strong enough at times to compensate for the "insult" the parents may experience when told their behavior has detrimental effects on other family members. Therefore, when this technique is used, a therapist should support the family member whose behavioral pattern needs examining and changing.

Paradoxical intervention. Coping with a hostile external environment and the immigration process and the lack of a supportive extended family system can rigidify the role structure and transaction of an ethnic minority family. Because of the family's different cultural orientation, it may be suspicious of the therapist's attempt to intervene. The implicit message of the family usually is "take care of our problems, but don't change us or anything else." The ethnic minority family is proud of its traditional family structure and traits it feels are essential to maintaining the family itself.

Given that ethnic minority parents (especially mothers) highly value their parental roles, they may not be receptive to any therapeutic effort to restructure the "enmeshed" parent-child relationship. The same parent-child conflict can also be manifested in an Asian or Hispanic father's rigid discipline against a son or daughter. The parent's persistence in maintaining the old pattern of behavior may be so entrenched that the usual therapeutic techniques are ineffective. Paradoxical intervention may be the only technique for such "resistant" or "stuck" families. The strength and cultural relevance of this technique lies within the therapist's alliance and trusting relationship with the family. By using paradoxical intervention, the family relationship is explained in positive and supportive terms that describe how the identified problem (behavior) may be helping the family. It leaves the therapist with a "no lose" situation: The family feels supported or "accommodated" if they decide not to change, or should the family reject the therapist's hypothesis, the family structure or problem will thus be altered.

Employing a therapist-helper. The therapist-helper approach is indicated when an ethnic minority family is persistently uncooperative, adheres rigidly to cultural norms and behavior, is unfamiliar with the concept of family therapy, and when there is a definite language barrier between the therapist and the family. Additionally, this approach provides the family with a normal course of problem solving, and an acculturation direction uninfluenced by the therapist. Consistent with cultural norms and expectations, a bicultural mature male may be compatible in therapy with a Hispanic or Asian American family.

Grandparents of either sex may work well with a Black or Indian family. In some instances, the therapist-helper does not need to be a member of the extended family but could be a highly trusted and respected individual. Extensive planning and supervisory sessions with the therapist-helper are needed in order to make this technique a success.

Team approach. The team approach is especially helpful in therapy with an ethnic minority family of multiple members who have numerous problems. Advantages of this approach include spontaneously meeting different family members' needs, provision of emotional and affective bondage with different family members, provision of a role model for problem solving, development of a more accurate assessment and treatment plan, assurance of continuity of therapy, and avoidance of professional burn-out. Potential disadvantages of the team approach in work with ethnic minority families include disorganization and fragmentation, its time-consuming nature, therapists' conflicts, and excessive cost.

Evaluation and Termination Phase

To determine if a specific goal has been accomplished through family therapy with an ethnic minority family, the ecological framework of evaluation is particularly helpful. This framework consists of four major categories including family/environment interface, family structure, family processes (communication/interaction), and individual symptoms and/or character traits. In assessing therapeutic goals relating to dysfunctional patterns of cultural transition or transcultural dysfunctional patterns, a therapist needs to be cognizant of the unique perspectives of each ethnic minority culture. The intense interactive subsystem relationship characteristic of a nuclear family in a dominant society should not be used as a yardstick in evaluating the functional structure and transaction of an ethnic minority family. Instead, the inclusive extended family framework should be kept in mind when evaluating a family's functioning.

Ethnic minority Americans may not verbally express the progress they make in therapy. Hence the therapist may need to maximize his or her observational skills in evaluating the family's progress. A therapist may need to participate in and be a part of the family's activities, including home visits, participation in seasonal ceremonies (Asian, American Indians, and Hispanic), and other rituals.

Ethnic minority Americans usually display strong feelings of obligation, interdependence, self-control, and fatalism. They have a tendency
to deemphasize the extent of their family problem. The family usually is
so considerate of the therapist's time and effort that they prefer not to
burden the therapist but to terminate therapy prematurely. The
therapist needs to reassure and to point out to the family the potential
negative consequences associated with premature termination.

The termination process should take into consideration the ethnic
minority client's concept of time and space in a relationship. Some
families may never want to end a good relationship and they learn to
respect and love the therapist as a member of their family. It is important
that a therapist be comfortable with this element of cultural and human
inclusiveness and make termination a natural and gradual process.

PART 4: CULTURALLY RELEVANT
TECHNIQUES AND SKILLS FOR
SPECIFIC THERAPY MODALITIES

Marital Therapy

The divorce rate among Asians and Hispanics is relatively low
compared to American Indians (Byler, 1977) and Blacks (U.S. Bureau
of the Census, 1977). Nevertheless, the process of acculturation and the
changed roles and status of both husband and wife make marital
adjustment extremely vulnerable. Factors contributing to the high
divorce rate among Blacks and American Indians include high unemployment rate of husbands, husbands' inability to adjust to an
egalitarian relationship, absence of an effective parental interactive
model, insufficient energy reserved for problem solving, and underutilization of mental therapy for problem solving.

Marital therapy with ethnic minorities must consider the extended
family system framework. Couple enmeshment (Minuchin, 1974) may
take place between one spouse with his or her family of origin. Bowen's
intergenerational perspective can be used to assist the enmeshed partner
to redefine and restructure a new relational boundary. Working
collaboratively with the respected extended family members (e.g.,
padrino of the Hispanic family), the couple's conflict can be resolved in a
culturally relevant manner. Couple therapy for problem solving with an

ethnic minority family is a totally new concept to most ethnic minority couples. Only the upper or middle class and more acculturated couples may seek marital therapy for their family problems (Falicov, 1982). Because of the hierarchical role structure of the Asian and Hispanic couple relationship, the wife is usually reluctant to challenge her authoritarian husband openly in the therapist's presence. Individual interviews can be used to bridge the gap. Advantages of using the individual interview at the beginning phase of couple therapy include development of rapport (face saving for Asians and personalism for Hispanics) and trust, and the disclosure of intimate information such as extramarital affairs or incest, and so on. Bowen's calm, unemotional, but interested approach can be most effective in assisting the individual spouse to gain a cognitive understanding of the problem.

Ethnic minority parents (especially the wife/mother) feel a strong responsibility to their children. The therapist should not employ marital therapy prematurely as a means to resolve parent-child problems. The spousal subsystem can be repaired directly or indirectly by focusing on the parents' newly learned alternative transactions with the child.

The nuclear family system created by the process of migration and cultural change forces the ethnic minority couple to interact intimately for daily problem solving. Often, the couple is ill-prepared, particularly American Indians and Blacks. Additionally, most Asian and Hispanic couples are limited by their rigid male-dominant role expectations and dyadic complementary style of communication. Effective communication and problem-solving skills (Satir, 1967; Miller et al., 1977), have proven effective in assisting the ethnic minority couple to "feel good" and to solve problems effectively. To help the Asian and Hispanic husbands rectify prior learning of male-dominant traits or "machismo," cognitive awareness training has been found beneficial. Consistent with an ethnic minority client's learning style of observation and active participation, a cotherapist model (Norlin and Ho, 1974) is also helpful. Advantages of a cotherapist team approach include an effective interactive role model, resemblance of a natural extended family system interaction, and provision of a warm and secure environment in which to learn affective and expressive skills.

Divorce Therapy

In addition to such factors as the breakdown of extended family ties, high rate of unemployment, unmet physical and economic needs, poor physical and mental health, high rate of alcoholism and attempted suicides, and intermarriages, American Indians' and Blacks' traditional respect for individuality, a person's right to make his own decisions, and their strong belief in noninterference make divorce a more socially acceptable behavior with very little negative stigma attached. Conversely, Asian Americans consider divorce a family disgrace. The strong Catholic influence upon Hispanics contribute to their relatively low divorce rate. The attitude of different ethnic groups toward divorce greatly affects the decision for divorce and the adjustment of the divorcées. For instance, American Indian's and the Black extended families' unconditional acceptance of a divorce greatly facilitates the adjustment to a divorce. Contrarily, an Asian or Hispanic divorcée may risk ostracism from the extended family or the Catholic church, making the adjustment more traumatic and difficult.

Usually only the more acculturated and financially capable ethnic minority couples will seek divorce therapy. The majority of the divorce therapy clients seek help during moments of crisis, such as when the husband abruptly decides to get a legal divorce, or the wife decides to divorce her husband because of excessive physical abuse. In either instance, divorce therapy with ethnic minority clients is often conducted under extremely stressful circumstances. It requires quick decisions on the part of the client and therapist.

The strength of family ties among ethnic minorities is a valuable resource to clients experiencing divorce. Extended families are the natural resources for emotional support and can often provide financial help, child care, household help, and so on. The therapist at this stage should assist the client in taking advantage of the extended family system. Some families, especially among Asians and Hispanics may withdraw support and sympathy from the client. The therapist's role is often to be a systems-broker by helping the client secure new support systems, preferably with other divorcées who have shared similar experiences. Considering the relative nonromantic involvement in most traditional ethnic minority marriages, especially among Asians, Hispanics, and American Indians, emotional termination and adjustment to life without the previous spouse may be less traumatic than in romantic marriages. An ethnic minority divorcée, despite facing economic and employment discrimination, often seems better prepared to deal with survival and financial issues than White female divorcées (Peters and deFord, 1978). They should be cautioned against possible collusion with their older siblings thus creating intergenerational boundary diffusion problems.

Single-Parent Therapy

The process of immigration and acculturation, increased divorce and separation, as well as decisions to have children and not marry have increased the number of female-headed families among ethnic minority Americans (Fitzpatrick, 1981; National Urban League, 1978). Many such females fit the description of the "at-risk population" characterized as recipients of Aid to Dependent Children, emotionally depressed, socially isolated, and experiencing crisis emergencies (Pett, 1982). Although ethnic minority American women are known for their hard-working attitude and resourcefulness (Hanson, 1980), the demands of single-parenthood may far exceed the single parent's ability to cope.

The extended family can be a significant source of support and self-esteem for an ethnic minority single parent (Stack, 1974; Redhorse, 1980a; Fitzpatrick, 1981; Hsu, 1972). However, for recently arrived immigrants (Asians and Hispanics), family support systems may not be readily available. Unemployment, pride, geographical location, and strained relationships with parents can cause single parents not to return to their relatives after divorce. In such cases, other support network resources should be found. These can be new friendship ties, especially other single mothers, women's support groups, and social activity groups that can help the single-parent family adjust during this transitional period.

Among ethnic minority families, it is not unusual for a key male figure, such as uncle, grandfather, or other spouse-equivalent, to be present in the single-parent household (McLanahan et al., 1981; Stack, 1974). If the therapist is aware of this individual or conjugal partner, he or she can introduce the option of involving this person in matters that concern the welfare of the single parent or in child-rearing practices.

The absence of the father from the family requires family renegotiation and a restructuring of the family system boundary (Minuchin, 1974). The traditional closeness of the mother-child relationship within an ethnic minority family should be considered in determining enmeshment or a parental-child structural relationship. Due to the acculturation process (Asians and Hispanics) and single parent's potential lack of parenting skills, a therapist needs to adopt an educative role in assisting any single parent who is experiencing this transitional period. The collateral orientation of many ethnic minority clients who are single parents necessitate the therapist's focusing the attention, first, on the child (or children) and, second, on the care of the mother.

Reconstituted Family Therapy

All ethnic minority families have a strong ties, obligations, and loyalties to the family of origin. Problems abound when an ex-spouse with children remarries. Some ethnic minority Americans remarry because of love and affection for their children and a strong desire to do what is best for their children. Problems arise when children encounter conflicts with their stepparent or stepbrothers or sisters. If children are no longer happy, as originally anticipated by the parents, the second marriage may dissolve.

Many ethnic minority families (American Indians, Blacks) have experienced living in extended families and households. The reconstituted family phenomenon should present fewer problems for them than it does for dominant culture families whose past references are limited to the single-household nuclear family. It has also been a common practice among Hispanic Americans for adults to raise children who are not their own (Garica-Preto, 1982).

In therapy with a reconstituted ethnic minority family, the focus should be on repairing or strengthening the parental subsystem (Satir, 1967; Duberman, 1975). The therapist may encounter resistance, for most ethnic minority mothers are more devoted to motherly love for their children than maintaining a close relationship with their husbands. It is important that the therapist emphasize to parents, especially the mother, that a strong marital coalition is a prerequisite to ensure the healthy and normal development of all children in a reconstituted family. Interviewing the parents separately has been found helpful in repairing or establishing the parental bond. Feelings about each previous marriage(s) and the legal settlement involving custody, visitation, financial support, and current child-rearing practices need to be expressed and discussed by the couple. Some ethnic minority couples, especially Asians, American Indians, and Hispanics, may need help in problem-solving skills characteristic of an egalitarian relationship. As a strategy to decentralize the stepmother's role with her children in the reconstituted family, some authors (Haley, 1976; Minuchin, 1974; Carter and McGoldrick, 1980) suggest that she take a passive role, thus allowing the stepfather to take charge of the stepchildren. This directive may be in indirect conflict with all ethnic minority cultures that prescribe that a woman's responsibility is to care for her children. A more culturally relevant directive that aims to dilute the mother-child enmeshment is strengthening the spousal subsystem or father-stepchild subsystem. Extended family ties of the reconstituted couple can be a source of interference prohibiting the couple from forming a strong coalition or effectively rearing the children. The therapist may need to mediate between the reconstituted family and the extended family members of previous marriages.

PART 5: CONCLUSION

A close examination and analysis of the different ethnic minority families' cultural values and family structure clearly indicate that while the traditional family therapy model based upon middle-class White American culture generally is helpful and applicable, it can sometimes be impractical, ineffective, and at times harmful. Certain commonalities are shared by middle-class White American families and by different ethnic minority families, but vast differences also exist. These differences include the extent to which each ethnic minority family has to struggle daily with political discrimination, unemployment, poverty, poor physical and mental health, immigration and acculturational problems, and the English language. Among ethnic minority groups themselves, there are both differences and similarities, including how each family group is structured, how it copes with a hostile external environment, negotiates differences, adjusts to changes, resolves problems, and responds to family therapy. This chapter represents an attempt to synthesize and systematize the degree of interethnic minority group variance regarding cultural orientation and the effect of this variance on the family therapy process and outcome for four ethnic groups: Black Americans, Asian Americans, Hispanic Americans, and American Indians.

The interventive principles of system communication and family structure theories have been demonstrated to be quite relevant in explaining how an ethnic minority family responds to society and interacts with each other within the family. The practice principles of these two family system theories need further exploration, elaboration, and specification to make them culturally and ethnic specific. In addition, the ecological, systemic, and emic approaches must be the guiding framework by which to intervene effectively and prevent problems generally plaguing ethnic minority families.

The effectiveness of a family therapist also depends on the therapist's self-awareness of his or her own ethnic background, and how this affects therapy with different ethnic minority groups. The need for bicultural and bilingual therapists is obvious. Effective family therapy with ethnic minority families requires that the therapist be sensitive and flexible in responding to the clients' time and space limitations. The routine 50-minute session within the 8 a.m. to 5 p.m. time frame conducted in an office no longer is viable and responsive to all minority clients' needs. Instead, a block of time of two to three or more hours for a session in the client's own home environment may become more of a rule than exception in therapy with ethnic minority families. The extra time and effort demanded of a therapist can easily cause professional burn-out. Hence ethnic sensitive agency administrators or supervisors also need to provide therapists with reduced caseloads, greater flexibility of time, and more autonomy.

Family therapy with ethnic minority families still is in an infancy stage. A great effort is needed to continue to explore, explicate, and systematize family therapy knowledge and practice principles that are culturally and ethnically specific.

REFERENCES

Abad, V. and E. Boyce. 1979. "Issues in Psychiatric Evaluations of Puerto Ricans: A Socio-Cultural Perspective." *Journal of Operational Psychiatry* 10:28-30.

Abad, V., G. Ramos, and E. Boyce. 1974. "A Model for Delivery of Mental Health Services to Spanish Speaking Minorities." *American Journal of Orthopsychiaïy* 44:585-495.

Ackerman, N. 1961. *The Psychodynamics of Family Life.* New York: Basic Books.

Acosta, F. 1977. "Ethnic Variables in Psychotherapy: The Mexican American." In *Chicano Psychology,* edited by G. Martinez. New York: Academic Press.

————et al. 1982. *Effective Psychotherapy for Low-Income and Minority Patients.* New York: Plenum Press.

Alvairez, R. 1981. "The Psycho-Historical and Socio-economic Development of the Chicano Community in the United States." *Social Science Quarterly* 53:920-942.

Alvirez, D. et al. 1981. "The Mexican American Family." In *Ethnic Families in America,* edited by C. Mindel and R. Habenstein. New York: Elsevier.

Anda, D. 1984. "Bicultural Socialization: Factors Affecting the Minority Experience." *Social Work* 29:101-107.

Aponte, H. 1979. "Family Therapy and the Community." In *Community Psychology: Theoretical and Empirical Approaches,* edited by M. Gibbs and J. Lachenmeyer. New York: Gardner Press.

Attneave, C. 1982. "American Indians and Alaska Native Families." In *Ethnicity and Family Therapy,* edited by McGoldrick M. et al. New York: Guilford.

Auerswald, E. 1968. "Interdisciplinary Versus Ecological Approach." *Family Process* 7:202-215.

————1971. "Family, Change and the Ecological Perspective." *Family Process* 10:263-280.

Badillo-Ghali, S. 1974. "Culture Sensitivity and the Puerto Rican Client." *Social Casework* 55:100-110.

Bagarozzi, D. and J. Wodarski. 1978. "Behavioral Treatment of Marital Discord." *Clinical Social Work Journal* 6:135-154.

Baraka, I. 1973. *A Black Value System in Contemporary Black Thought: The Best from the Black Scholar.* Indianapolis: Bobbs-Merrill.

Barlett, A. 1958. "Toward Clarification and Improvement of Social Work Practice." *Social Work* 3:3-9.

Barnett, L. D. 1963. "Interracial Marriage in Los Angeles, 1948-1959." *Social Force* 25:424-427.

Barrera, M. 1978. "Mexican-American Mental Health Service Utilization: A Critical Examination of Some Proposed Variables." *Community Mental Health Journal* 14:35-45.

Barry, A. 1979. "A Research Project on Successful Single-Parent Families." *American Journal of Family Therapy* 7:65-73.

Barth, F. 1969. *Ethnic Groups and Boundaries*. Boston: Little, Brown.

Bateson, G. 1958. *Haven*. Stanford, CA: Stanford University Press.

———1972. *Steps to an Ecology of Mind*. New York: Ballantine.

Baumrind, D. 1972. "An Exploratory Study of Socialization Effects on Black Children: Some Black-White Comparisons." *Child Development* 43:261-267.

Bayer, A. 1972. "College Impact on Marriage." *Journal of Marriage and the Family* 34:600-610.

Beal, E. 1980. "Separation, Divorce, and Single-Parent Families." In *The Family Life Cycles*, edited by E. Carter and M. McGoldrick. New York: Gardner Press

Bell, R. 1971. "The Relative Importance of Mother and Wife Roles Among Lower Class Women." In *The Black Family: Essays and Studies*, edited by R. Staples. Belmont, CA: Wadsworth.

Bennett, J. 1975. *The New Ethnicity: Perspectives from Ethnology*. St. Paul: West.

Berger, A. and W. Simon. 1974. "Black Families and the Moynihan Report: A Research Evaluation." *Social Problems* 22:145-161.

Bernal, G. and Y. Flores-Ortiz. 1982. "Latino Families in Therapy." *Journal of Marital and Family Therapy* 8:357-365.

Billingsley, A. 1968. *Black Families in White America*. Englewood Cliffs, NJ: Prentice-Hall.

Blanchard, E. 1983. "The Growth and Development of American and Alaskan Native Children." In *The Psychosocial Development of Minority Group Children*, edited by G. Powell et al. New York: Brunner/Mazel.

Bontemps, A. 1975. "National Poll Reveals Startling New Attitudes on Interracial Dating." *Ebony* 30:144-151.

Boszormenyi-Nagy, I. and B. Krasner. 1980. "Trust Based Therapy: A Contextual Approach." *American Journal of Psychiatry* 137:767-775.

Boszormenyi-Nagy, I. and G. Spark. 1973. *Invisible Loyalties: Reciprocity in Intergenerational Family Therapy*. New York: Harper & Row.

Bowen, M. 1976. "Theory and Practice of Psychotherapy." In *Family Therapy*, edited by P. Guerin. New York: Garden Press.

———1978. *Family Therapy in Clinical Practice*. New York: Jason Aronson.

Brown, A. and D. Forde. 1967. *African Systems of Kinship and Marriage*. New York: Oxford University Press.

Brown, E. and T. Shaughnessy. 1982. *Education for Social Work Practice with American Indian Families*. Washington, DC: U.S. Department of Health and Human Services.

Bureau of Indian Affairs. 1971. *Information Office Statistics*. Washington, DC: Author.

Burkhardt, V. 1960. *Chinese Creeds and Customs*. Vol. 3. Hong Kong: South China Morning Post.

Bustamante, J. and A. Santa Cruz. 1975. *Psiquiatra Transcultural*. Havana: Editorial Cientifico-Technica.

Bryde, G. 1971. *Modern Indian Psychology*. Vermillion: University of South Dakota.

———1972. *Indian Students and Guidance*. Boston: Houghton Mifflin.

Byler, W. 1977. "The Destruction of American Indian Families." In *Destruction of American Families*, edited by S. Unger. New York: Association on American Indian Affairs.

Cahn, E., ed. 1979. *Our Brother's Keeper*. New York: New American Library.

Carter, E. 1976. "Family Therapy in the Family Therapist's Own Home." In *Family Therapy: Theory and Practice*, edited by P. Guerin. New York: Gardner Press.

———and M. McGoldrick, eds. 1980. *The Family Life Cycle: A Framework for Family Therapy*. New York: Gardner Press.

Casal, L. et al. 1979. "The Cuban Migration of the Sixties in Its Historical Context." In *Black Cubans in the United States*, edited by L. Casal. Miami: Office of Latin America and the Caribbean.

Casas, S. and S. Keefe. 1980. *Family and Mental Health in Mexican American Community*. Los Angeles, CA: Spanish Speaking Mental Health Research Center.

Chadwick, B. and J. Strauss. 1975. "The Assimilation of American Indian into Urban Society: The Seattle Case." *Human Organization* 34:4.

Cheek, D. 1976. *Assertive Black . . . Puzzled White*. San Luis Obispo, CA: Impact.

Chestang, L. 1976. "The Black Family and Black Culture: A Study of Coping." In *Cross Cultural Perspectives in Social Work Practice and Education*, edited by M. Satomayor. Houston: University of Houston, Graduate School of Social Work.

Chin, R. 1982. "Conceptual Paradigm for a Racial-Ethnic Community: The Case of the Chinese American Community." In *The Pluralistic Society: A Community Mental Health Perspective*, edited by S. Sue and T. Moore. New York: Human Sciences Press.

Clark, C. 1972. "Black Studies or the Study of Black People." In *Black Psychology*, edited by R. Jones. New York: Harper & Row.

Combs, D. 1978. *Crossing Culture in Therapy*. Monterey, CA: Brooks/Cole.

Costo, R. and J. Henry. 1977. *Indian Treaties: Two Centuries of Dishonor*. San Francisco: Indian Heritage Press.

DeGeyndt, W. 1973. "Health Behavior and Health Needs in Urban Indians in Minneapolis." *Health Service Reports,* 88:360-366.

De La Cancela, V. 1978. "Culture Specific Psychotherapy." Pp. 128-152 in *Proceedings of the Fourth Annual Spring Conference of the New York Association of Black Psychologists*. New York: NYABP.

Delgado, G. 1978. *Steps to an Ecology of Mind*. New York: Ballantine.

Deloria, V., Jr. 1969. *Custer Died for Your Sins: An Indian Manifesto*. New York: Macmillan.

Devore, W. and E. Schlesinger. 1981. *Ethnic-Sensitive Social Work Practice*. St. Louis: C. V. Mosby.

DeVos, G. 1978. "Selective Permeability and Reference Group Sanctioning: Psychological Continuities in Role Degradation." Paper presented at Seminar on Comparative Studies in Ethnicity and Nationality, University of Washington, Seattle.

D.I.A.N.D. 1975. *The Canadian Indian: Statistics*. Ottawa: Indian Affairs.

Douglas, F. 1974. "Prescientific Psychiatry in the Urban Setting." *American Journal of Psychiatry* 131:280-281.

Dreyfuss, B. and D. Lawrence. 1979. *Handbook for Anti-Racism*. Norman: University of Oklahoma Press.

Duberman, L. 1975. *The Reconstituted Family: A Study of Remarried Couples and Their Children*. Chicago: Nelson-Hall.

Edwards, D. and M. Edwards. 1984. "Minorities: American Indians." In *Encyclopedia of Social Work*. Washington, DC: National Association of Social Workers.

Eggan, F. 1966. *The American Indian: Perspectives for the Study of Social Change*. Chicago: Aldine.

Falicov, C. 1982. "Mexican Families." In *Ethnicity and Family Therapy*, edited by M. McGoldrick et al. New York: Guilford.

Farris, C. 1973. "A White House Conference of the American Indian." *Social Work* 18:80-86.

Fei, H. 1962. *Peasant Life in China: A Field Study of Country Life in the Yantze Valley.* London: Routledge & Kegan Paul.

Feldman, L. 1985. "Integrative Multi-Level Therapy: A Comprehensive Interpersonal and Intrapsychic Approach." *Journal of Marital and Family Therapy* 11:357-372.

Fitzpatrick, J. 1981. "The Puerto Rican Family." In *Ethnic Families in America*, edited by C. Mindel and R. Habenstein. New York: Elsevier.

Fogleman, B. 1972. *Adoptive Mechanisms of the North American Indian to an Urban Setting.* Ann Arbor: University Microfilms.

Foley, V. 1975. "Family Therapy with Black Disadvantaged Families: Some Observations on Roles, Communications, and Technique." *Journal of Marriage and Family Counseling* 1:29-38.

Foster, M. and L. Perry. 1982. "Self-Valuation Among Blacks." *Social Work* 27:60-66.

Frisbie, W., E. Bean, and R. Eberstein. 1978. "Patterns of Marital Instability Among Mexican Americans, Blacks, and Anglos." In *The Demography of Racial and Ethnic Groups*, edited by E. Bean and W. Frisbie. New York: Academic Press.

Fujii, S. 1976. "Elderly Asian Americans and Use of Public Service." *Social Casework* 57:202-207.

Garcia-Preto, N. 1982. "Puerto Rican Families." In *Ethnicity and Family Therapy*, edited by M. McGoldrick et al. New York: Guilford.

Garrison, V. 1977. "Puerto Rican Syndrome." In *Psychiatry and Espiritism: Case Studies in Spirit Possession*, edited by V. Garrison. New York: John Wiley.

Germain, C. 1968. "Social Study: Past and Future." *Social Casework* 49: 403-409.

———1973. "An Ecological Perspective in Casework Practice." *Social Casework* 54:323-330.

Giordano, J. 1974. "Ethnics and Minorities." *Clinical Social Work Journal* 2:207-219.

Gonzales-Wippler, M. 1975. *Santeria: African Magic in Latin America.* New York: Anchor.

Gonzalez, J. 1978. "Language Factors Affecting Treatment of Schizophrenics." *Psychiatric Annals* 8:68-70.

Gordon, W. E. 1969. "Basic Constructs for an Integrative and Generative Conception of Social Work." In *The General Systems Approach: Contributions Toward an Holistic Conception of Social Work*, edited by G. Hearn. New York: Council on Social Work Education.

Green, J. 1982. *Cultural Awareness in the Human Services.* Englewood Cliffs, NJ: Prentice-Hall.

Grebler, L., J. Moore, and R. Guzman. 1970. *The Mexican American People: The Nation's Second Largest Minority.* New York: Free Press.

———1973. *The Family: Variations in Time and Space.* In *Introduction to Chicano Studies*, edited by L. Duran and H. Bernard. New York: Macmillan.

Grier, W. and P. Cobbs. 1968. *Black Rage.* New York: Basic Books.

Guerney, B. 1977. *Relationship Enhancement.* San Francisco: Jossey-Bass.

Gurman, A. S. and D. G. Rice 1975. "Emerging Trends in Research and Practice." In *Couples and Conflicts: New Directions in Marital Therapy*, edited by S. G. Alan and G. R. David. New York: Jason Aronson.

Haley, J. 1963. *Strategies of Psychotherapy*. New York: Grune and Stratton.

———1976. *Problem-Solving Therapy: New Strategies for Effective Family Therapy*. San Francisco: Jossey-Bass.

Halpern, T. 1970. "The Role of Agency in Supporting Black Male Adolescents." *Social Work* 18:53-58.

Hansell, B. 1976. *The Person in Distress*. New York: Human Science Press.

Hanson, W. 1980. "The Urban Indian Woman and Her Family." *Social Casework* 61:476-484.

———1981. "Grief Counseling with Native American Indians." In *Human Services for Cultural Minorities*, edited by R. Dana. Baltimore: University Park Press.

Hardy-Fanta, C. and E. MacMahon-Herrera. 1981. "Adapting Family Therapy to the Hispanic Family." *Social Casework* 62:138-148.

Hare, B. 1975. "Relationship at Social Background to the Dimensions of Self-Concept." Ph.D. dissertation, University of Chicago.

Harris, O. and P. Balgopal 1980. "Intervening with the Black Family." In *Family Treatment in Social Work*, edited by C. Janzen and O. Harris. Itasca: Peacock.

Hartman, Ann. 1978. "Diagrammatic Assessment of Family Relationships." *Social Casework* 59:465-76.

———1979. *Finding Families: An Ecological Approach to Family Assessment in Adoption*. Newbury Park, CA: Sage.

Hawkes, G. and M. Taylor. 1975. "Power Structure in Mexican and Mexican American Farm Labor Families." *Journal of Marriage and the Family* 31:807-811.

Heer, D. 1974. "The Prevalence of Black-White Marriage in the United States, 1960 and 1970." *Journal of Marriage and the Family* 36:246-258.

Hernandez, J., L. Estrada, and D. Alvirez. 1973. "Census Data and the Problem of Conceptually Defining the Mexican American Population." *Social Science Quarterly* 53:671-687.

Hill, R. 1972. *The Strength of Black Families*. New York: Emerson-Hall.

Hines, P. and N. Boyd-Franklin. 1982. "Black Families." In *Ethnicity and Family Therapy*, edited by M. McGoldrick et al. New York: Guilford.

Hippler, A. 1974. "The North Alaska Eskimos: A Culture and Personality Perspective." *American Ethnologist* 1:449-469.

Ho, M. 1976. "Social Work with Asian Americans." *Social Casework* 57:195-201.

———1980. "Model to Evaluate Group Work Practice with Ethnic Minorities." Paper presented at the Social Work with Group Symposium, Arlington, Texas.

———1982. "Building On the Strength of Minority Groups." *Practice Digest* 5:6-7.

———1984. *Building a Successful Intermarriage*. St. Meinrad, IN: Abbey Press.

———and E. McDowell. 1973. "The Black Worker-White Client Relationship." *Clinical Social Work Journal* 1:161-167.

Ho, M. and A. Settles. 1984. "The Use of Popular Music in Family Therapy." *Social Work* 29:65-67.

Hoehn-Sarie, R. et al. 1964. "Systematic Preparation of Patients for Psychotherapy: Effects on Therapy, Behavior, and Outcome." *Journal of Psychiatric Research* 2:267-281.

Holmes, T. and M. Masuda. 1974. "Life Change and Illness Susceptibility." In *Stressful Life Events: Their Nature and Effects*, edited by B. Dohrenwend and P. Dohrenwend. New York: John Wiley.

Homans, G. 1964. "Contemporary Theory in Sociology." In *Handbook of Modern Sociology*, edited by R. Faris. Chicago: Rand McNally.

Hopkins, T. 1973. "The Role of Agency in Supporting Black Manhood." *Social Work* 18:53-58.

Hsu, F. 1972. *American Museum Science Book*. Garden City, NY: Doubleday.

Huffaker, C, 1967. *Nobody Loves a Drunken Indian*. New York: David McKay.

Jackson, A. 1973. "Psychotherapy: Factors Associated with the Race of the Therapist." *Psychotherapy: Theory, Research and Practice* 10:273-277.

Jackson, D. 1967. *Communication, Marriage and Family*. Palo Alto, CA: Science and Behavior.

———ed. 1968. *Therapy, Communication, and Change*. Palo Alto, CA: Science and Behavior.

Jackson, J. 1972. "Comparative Life Styles and Family and Friends Relationships Among Older Black Women." *Family Coordinator* 21:477-486.

———1973. "Family Organization and Ideology." In *Comparative Studies of Blacks and Whites in the United States*, edited by D. Miller. New York: Seminar Press.

Jones, D. 1974. *The Urban Native Encounters the Social Service System*. Fairbanks: University of Alaska.

———1977. "The Mystique of Expertise in the Social Service." *Journal of Sociology and Social Welfare* 3:332-346.

Josephy, A. 1971. *The Indian Heritage of North America*. New York: Alfred Knopf.

Kagan, S. and R. Buriel. 1977. "Field Dependence-Independence and Mexican-American Culture and Education." In *Chicano Psychology*, edited by J. Martinez. New York: Academic Press.

Kahn, R. 1974. "Conflict, Ambiguity and Overload." In *Occupational Stress: Three Elements in Job Stress*, edited by A. McLean. Springfield, IL: Charles C. Thomas.

Kernberg, O. 1975. *Borderline Conditions and Pathological Narcissism*. New York: Jason Aronson.

Keyes, C. 1977. *The Golden Peninsula*. New York: Macmillan

Kiev, A. 1968. *Curanderismo: Mexican American Folk Psychiatry*. New York: Free Press.

Kikumura, A. and H. Kitano. 1973. "Interracial Marriage: A Picture of the Japanese Americans." *Journal of Social Issues* 29:67-81.

Kim, B. 1978. *The Asian Americans: Changing Patterns, Changing Needs*. Montclair, NJ: Association of Korean Christian Scholars in North America.

King, C. 1967. "Family Therapy with the Deprived Family." *Social Casework* 48:206-207.

Kitano, H. and W. Yeung. 1982. "Chinese Interracial Marriage." In *Intermarriage in the United States*, edited by G. Crester and J. Leon. New York: Haworth Press.

Kleinman, A. and T. Lin, eds. 1981. *Normal and Deviant Behavior in Chinese Culture*. Hingham, MA: Reidel.

Kline, F., W. Austin, and F. Acosta. 1980. "The Misunderstood Spanish Speaking Patient." *American Journal of Psychiatry* 137:1530-1533.

Kluckhohn, F. 1951. "Values and Value Orientations." In *Toward a General Theory of Action*, edited by T. Parsons and E. Shils. Cambridge, MA: Harvard University Press.

———and F. Strodtbeck. 1961. *Variations in Value Orientations*. New York: Harper & Row.

Kohut, H. 1972. "Thoughts on Narcissism and Narcissistic Rage." *Psychoanalytic Study of the Child* 27:360-400.

Kramer, R. 1974. "Conflict, Ambiguity and Overload." In *Occupational Stress*, edited by A. McLean. Springfield, IL: Charles C. Thomas.

Kunkel, P. and S. Kennard. 1971. *Spout Spring: A Black Community*. New York: Random House.

Landau, J. 1981. "Link Therapy as a Family Therapy Technique for Transitional Extended Families." *Psychotherapeia* 7:390.

Lapuz, L. 1973. *A Study of Psychopathology*. Quezon City: University of the Philippines Press.

Larsen, J. 1976. "Dysfunction in the Evangelical Family: Treatment Consideration." Paper presented at the American Association of Marriage and Family Counselors, Philadelphia.

Lee, E. 1982. "A Social System Approach to Assessment and Treatment for Chinese American Families." In *Ethnicity and Family Therapy*, edited by M. McGoldrick et al. New York: Guilford.

Levande, D. 1976. "Family Therapies as a Necessary Component of Family Therapy." *Social Casework* 57:271-295.

Lewis, C. 1970. *Indian Families of the Northwest Coast: The Impact of Change*. Chicago: University of Chicago Press.

Lewis, D. 1975. "The Black Family: Socialization and Sex Roles." *Phylon* 2:221-237.

Lewis, R. 1984. "The Strength of Indian Families." In *Proceedings of Indian Child Abuse Conference*. Tulsa: National Indian Child Abuse Center.

———and M. Ho. 1975. "Social Work with Native Americans." *Social Work* 20:379-382.

Lin, T., T. Donetz, and W. Goresky. 1978. "Ethnicity and Patterns of Help-Seeking Culture." *Medicine and Psychiatry* 2:3-13.

Loo, C. and C. Yu. 1980. "Chinatown: Recording Reality, Destroying Myths." Paper presented at a symposium at the American Psychological Association Convention, Montreal.

MacLanahan, S. et al. 1981. "Network Support, Social Support and Psychological Well-Being in the Single-Parent Family." *Journal of Marriage and the Family* 43:601-612.

Madsen, W. 1964. *The Mexican-American of South Texas*. New York: Holt, Rinehart & Winston.

Marishima, J. 1978. "The Asian American Experience: 1850-1975." *Journal of the Society of Ethnic and Special Studies* 2:8-10.

Martin, E. and J. Martin. 1978. *The Black Extended Family*. Chicago: University of Chicago Press.

Martinez, D. 1978. "Protestant Ministries Increasing." *Agenda* 8:8.

Mass, A. I. 1976. "Asian as Individuals: The Japanese Community." Social Casework 57:160-164.

Merian, L. 1977. "The Effects of Boarding Schools on Indian Family Life: 1928." In *The Destruction of American Indian Families*, edited by L. Merian. New York: Association on American Indian Affairs.

McAdoo, H. 1977. "Family Therapy in the Black Community." *Journal of the American Orthopsychiatric Association* 47:74-79.

———1978. "The Impact of Upward Mobility of Kin-Help Pattern and the Reciprocal Obligations in Black Families." *Journal of Marriage and the Family* 4:761-776.

McGoldrick, M., J. Peonce, and J. Giordano, eds. 1982. *Ethnicity and Family Therapy*. New York: Guilford.

Mead, G. 1934. *Mind, Self and Society*. Chicago: University of Chicago Press.
Medicine, B. 1978. *The Native American Woman: A Perspective*. Austin: National Education Lab.
Merton, R. 1957. *Social Theory and Social Structure*. New York: Free Press.
Miller, P. et al. 1977. *Annual Report: Formative Evolution of the Innovative Demonstration Projects in Child Abuse and Neglect*. Washington, DC: CPI Associates.
Miller, S., E. Nunnally, and D. Wackman. 1975. *Alive and Aware*. Minneapolis: Interpersonal Communication Program.
Miller, W. 1959. "Implications of Urban Lower-Class Culture of Social Work." *Social Service Review* 33:219-236.
Mindel, C. 1980. "Extended Familism Among Urban Mexican Americans, Anglos, and Blacks." *Hispanic Journal of Behavioral Sciences* 2:21-34.
————and R. Habenstein, eds. 1981. *Ethnic Families in American: Patterns and Variations*. New York: Elsevier.
Minuchin, S. 1967. *Families of the Slums*. New York: Basic Books.
————1974. *Families and Family Therapy*. Cambridge, MA: Harvard University Press.
Mizio, E. 1979. *Puerto Rican Task Report-Project on Ethnicity*. New York: Family Service Association.
————and A. Delaney, eds. 1981. *Training for Service Delivery to Minority Clients*. New York: Family Service Association of America.
Moll, L. et al. 1976. "Mental Health Services in East Los Angeles." In *Psychotherapy with the Spanish Speaking: Issues in Research and Service Delivery*, edited by M. Miranda. Los Angeles: Spanish Speaking Mental Health Research Center.
Momaday, N. 1974. "I Am Alive." In *The World of the American Indian*, edited by N. Momaday. Washington, DC: National Geographic Society.
Morales-Dorta, S. 1976. *Puerto Rican Espiritismo: Religion and Psychotherapy*. New York: Vantage.
Morey, S. and O. Gilliam, eds. 1974. *Respect for Life*. Garden City, NY: Waldorf Press.
Morishima, J. 1978. "The Asian American Experience." *Journal of the Society of Ethnic and Special Studies* 2:8-10.
Mostwin, D. 1981. "Multidimensional Model of Working with the Family." *Social Casework* 55:209-215.
Mouseau, J. 1975. "The Family, Prison of Love." *Psychology Today* 9:53-58.
Moynihan, D. 1965. *The Negro Family: The Case for National Action*. Washington, DC: Office of Policy Planning and Research, U.S. Department of Labor.
Muguia, E. 1982. *Chicano Intermarriage*. San Antonio: Trinity University Press.
Munson, C., ed. 1980. *Social Work with Families*. New York: Free Press.
Murase, T. and F. Johnson. 1974. "Naikan, Morita and Western Psychotherapy." *Archives of General Psychiatry* 31:121-128
Murillo, N. 1971. "The Mexican American Family." In *Chicanos: Social and Psychological Perspectives*, edited by N. Wagner and M. Huag. St. Louis: C. V. Mosby.
National Urban League. 1978. *The State of Black America 1977*. New York: Author.
Native American Research Group. 1979. *American Indian Socialization to Urban Life*. Final Report, N119H Grant MH 22719 (D. Miller, Principal Investigator). San Francisco: Scientific Analysis Corp.
Nobles, W. 1974. "African Root and American Fruit: The Black Family." *Journal of Social and Behavioral Sciences* 20:52-64.

Norbeck, E. and G. DeVos. 1972. "Culture and Personality: The Japanese." In *Psychological Anthropology in the Behavioral Sciences*, edited by F. Hsu. Cambridge, MA: Schenkman.

Norlin, J. and M. Ho. 1974. "Co-Worker Approach to Working with Families." *Clinical Social Work* 2:127-134.

Norton, D. 1978. "Black Family Life Patterns, the Development of Self and Cognitive Development of Black Children." In *The Psychosocial Development of Minority Group Children*, edited by G. Powell et al. New York: Brunner/Mazel.

Ortiz, C. 1972. "The Chicano Family: A Review of Research." *Social Work* 18:22-23.

Padilla, A. and R. Ruiz 1973. *Latino Mental Health: A Review of Literature*. DHEW Publication No. (HSM) 73-9143. Washington, DC: Government Printing Office.

Padilla, A., M. Carlos, and S. Keefe. 1976. "Mental Health Service Utilization by Mexican American." In *Psychotherapy with the Spanish-Speaking: Issues in Research and Service Delivery*, edited by M. R. Miranda. Los Angeles: Spanish Speaking Mental Health Research Center, University of California

Papajohn, J. and J. Spiegel. 1975. *Transactions in Families*. San Francisco: Jossey-Bass.

Parsons, T. 1951. *The Social System*. New York: Free Press.

Pearce, J. and L. Friedman, eds. 1980. *Combining Psychodynamic and Family Systems Approaches*. New York: Grune and Stratton.

Pedersen, P. V., ed. 1985. *Handbook of Cross-Cultural Counseling and Therapy*. Westport, CT: Greenwood Press.

Penalosa, F. 1968. "Mexican Family Roles." *Journal of Marriage and the Family* 30:680-689.

Pendagast, S. and R. Sherman. 1977. "Diagrammatic Assessment of Family Relationships." *Social Casework* 59:465-476.

Peters, M. and C. deFord. 1978. "The Solo Mother." In *The Black Family, Essays and Studies*, edited by R. Staples. Belmont, CA: Wadsworth.

Pett, M. 1982. "Predictions of Satisfactory Social Adjustment of Divorced Single Parents." *Journal of Divorce* 5:1-17.

Pike, K. 1954. *Language in Relation to a Unified Theory of the Structure of Human Behavior*. Glendale, CA: Summer Institute of Linguistics.

Pinderhughes, E. 1976. "Afro-Americans and Economic Dependency." *Urban and Social Change Review* 12:24-27.

———1982. "Afro-American Families and the Victim System." In *Ethnicity and Family Therapy*, edited by M. McGoldrick et al. New York: Guilford.

Pitta, P., L. Marcos, and M. Alpert. 1978. "Language Switching as a Treatment Strategy with Bilingual Patients." *American Journal of Psychoanalysis* 38:255-258.

Pittman, F. et al. 1971. "Therapy Techniques of the Family Therapy Unit." In *Changing Family-A Family Therapy Reader*, edited by J. Haley. New York: Grune and Stratton.

Pollak, O. 1964. "The Broken Family." In *Social Work and Social Problems*, edited by N. Cohen. New York: National Association of Social Workers.

Ponce, D. E. 1977. "Intercultural Perspectives on Mate Selection." In *Adjustment in Intercultural Marriage*, edited by W. Tseng et al. Honolulu: University Press of Hawaii.

Porterfield, E. 1978. *Black and White Mixed Marriages: An Ethnographic Study of Black-White Families*. Chicago: Nelson Hall.

President's Commission on Mental Health. 1978. *Report to the President*. Vol. 1. Washington, DC: Government Printing Office.

Price, J. 1981. "North American Indian Families." In *Ethnic, Families in America*, edited by C. Mindel and R. Habenstein. New York: Elsevier.

Purdy, B. et al. 1970. "Mellaril or Medium, Stelazine or Seance? A Study of Spiritism as it Affects Communication, Diagnosis and Treatment of Puerto Rican People." *American Journal of Orthopsychiatry* 40:239-240.

Rainwater, L. 1966. "The Crucible of Identity: The Lower Class Negro Family." *Daedalus* 95:258-264.

Ramirez, R. 1979. "Machismo: A Bridge Rather than a Barrier to Family Counseling." In *La Frontera Perspective: Providing Mental Health Services to Mexican Americans*, edited by P. Martin. Tucson, AZ: La Frontera Center.

Red Horse, J. 1980a. "American Indian Elders: Unifiers of Indian Families." *Social Casework* 61:490-493.

———1980b. "Family Structure and Value Orientation in American Indians." *Social Casework* 61:462-467.

Reiss, D. 1981. *The Family Construction of Reality*. Cambridge, MA: Harvard University Press.

Ritter, E., R. Ritter, and S. Spector. 1965. *Our Oriental Americans*. New York: McGraw-Hill.

Rogler, L. and A. Hollingshead. 1965. *Trapped: Families and Schizophrenia*. New York: John Wiley.

Rosen, P. and D. Proctor. 1978. "The Study of the Family." *Family Process* 4:1-20.

Rosenberg, M. 1979. *Convicting the Self*. New York: Basic Books.

Rothenberg, A. 1964. "Puerto Rico and Aggression." *American Journal of Psychiatry* 20:962-970.

Rubin, R. 1974. "Adult Male Absence and the Self-Attitudes of Black Children." *Child Study Journal* 4:33-44.

Ruiz, R. 1977. *The Delivery of Mental Health. Report of the Task Panel on Special Population*. Vol. IV. Washington, DC: Government Printing Office.

Russell, G. and B. Satterwhite. 1978. "It's Your Turn in the Sun." *Time* October 16:48-61.

Satir, V. 1967. *Conjoint Family Therapy*. Palo Alto, CA: Science and Behavior Books.

———J. Stachowiak, and H. Taschman. 1975. *Helping Families to Change*. New York: Jason Aronson.

Sattler, J. 1977. "The Effects of Therapist-Client Racial Similarity." In *Effective Psychotherapy*, edited by A. Gurman. New York: Pergamon.

Scanzoni, J. 1971. *The Black Family in Modern Society: Patterns of Stability and Security*. Chicago: University of Chicago Press.

———1975. "Sex Roles, Economic Factors and Marital Solidarity." *Journal of Marriage and the Family* 37:130-144.

Schwertfeger, M. 1982. "Interethnic Marriage and Divorce in Hawaii." In *Intermarriage in the United States*, edited by G. Crester and J. Leon. New York: Haworth Press.

Scott, J. 1979. "Polygamy: A Futuristic Family Arrangement for African Americans." *Black Books Bulletin* 8:127-132.

Shon, S. and D. Ja. 1982. "Asian Families." In *Ethnicity and Family Therapy*, edited by M. McGoldrick et al. New York: Guilford.

Shimkin, D. et al., eds. 1978. *The Extended Family in Black Societies*. The Hague: Mouton Publishers.

Sluzki, C. 1979. "Migration and Family Conflict." *Family Process* 18:379-39.

Smith, M. 1978. "Black Females' Perceptions on the Black Male Shortage." M.A. thesis, Harvard University.

——1980. "Economic Conditions in Single-Parent Families: A Longitudinal Perspective." *Social Work Research and Abstract* 16:20-24.

Sollenberger, R. 1962. "Chinese-American Child-Rearing Practices and Juvenile Delinquency." *Journal of Social Psychology* 74:13-23.

Solomon, B. 1976. *Black Empowerment*. New York: Columbia University Press.

Speck, R. and C. Attneave 1974. *Family Networks*. New York: Vintage.

Spencer, F., G. Szapocznik, D. Santisteban, and A. Rodrigues. 1981. "Cuban Crisis. 1980: Mental Health Care Issues." Paper presented at the Southeastern Psychological Association, Atlanta, March.

Spiegel, J. 1959. "Some Cultural Aspects of Transferences and Counter-Transferences." In *Individual and Family Dynamics*, edited by G. Masserman. New York: Grune and Stratton.

——J. 1971. "Transactions Inquiry: Description of Systems." In *Transactions: The Interplay between Individual, Family and Society*, edited by J. Papajohn. New York: Science House.

Spindler, G. and L. Spindler. 1971. "Male and Female Adaptations in Culture Change." In *Man in Adaptation: The Institutional Framework*, edited by G. -and L. Spindler. Chicago: Aldine-Atherton.

Stack, C. 1974. *All Our Kin*. New York: Harper & Row.

Staples, R. 1976. *The Black Family: Essays and Studies*. Vol. 2. Belmont, CA: Wadsworth.

Stein, I. 1974. *Systems Theory, Science, and Social Work*. Meterchen: Scarecrow Press.

Stevens, E. 1973. "Marianismo: The Other Face at Machismo." In *Female and Male in Latin America*, edited by A. Pescatello. Pittsburgh: University of Pittsburg Press.

Stewart, J. and J. Scott. 1978. "The Institutional Decimation of Black American Males." *Western Journal of Black Studies* 2:82-92.

Stuart, P. 1977. "United States Indian Policy." *Social Service Review* 47:451-63.

Stuart, R. 1980. *Helping Couples Change. A Social Learning Approach to Marital Therapy*. New York: Guilford.

Sue, S. and H. McKinney 1975. "Asian Americans in the Community Mental Health Care System." *American Journal of Orthopsychiatry* 45:111-118.

Sue, S. and J. Morishima 1982. *The Mental Health of Asian Americans*. San Francisco: Jossey-Bass.

Sue, S. et al. 1974. "Delivery of Community Mental Health Services to Black and White Clients." *Journal of Consulting and Clinical Psychology* 42:794-801.

Sung, B. 1967. *Mountain of Gold*. New York: Macmillan.

Szapocznik, J., M. Scopetta, and W. Tillman. 1978. "What Changes, What Remains the Same, and What Affects Acculturation Change in Cuban Immigrant Families." In *Cuban American: Acculturation, Adjustment, and the Family*, edited by J. Szapocznik. Washington, DC: COSSMHO.

Thomas, E. and R. Carter. 1971. "Instigative Modification with a Multi-Problem Family." *Social Casework* 52:444-455.

Thomas, R. 1969. "Lecture on Nationalism." In *The American Indian Reader*, edited by G. Wikerson. Albuquerque: National Indian Youth Council.

Tinker, J. 1972. "Intermarriage and Ethnic Boundaries. The Japanese American Case." Paper presented at the meeting of the Pacific Sociological Association, Portland, Oregon.

Tolson, E. and W. Reid, eds. 1981. *Models of Family Treatment*. New York: Columbia University Press.

Tracks, J. 1973. "Native American Non-Interference." *Social Work* 18:30-34.

Tseng, W. and J. McDermott. 1975. "Psychotherapy: Historical Roots, Universal Elements and Cultural Variations." *American Journal of Psychiatry* 132:378-384.

Ulibarri, H. 1970. "Social and Attitudinal Characteristics of Spanish Speaking Migrants and Ex-Migrant Workers in the Southwest." In *Mexican-Americans in the United States*, edited by J. Burma. Cambridge, MA: Schenkman.

Urban Associates. 1974. *A Study of Selected Socio-Economic Characteristics of Ethnic Minorities Based on the 1970 Census*. Vol. 2. *Asian Americans*. Washington, DC: Government Printing Office.

U.S. Bureau of the Census. 1977. *Marriage, Divorce, Widowhood and Remarriage*. Series p-20, no. 312. Washington, DC: Government Printing Office.

———1978. "Perspectives on American Husbands and Wives." *Current Population Reports*. Series p-23. No. 77. Washington, D.C.: Government Printing Office.

———1979. *The Social and Economic Status of the Black Population in the United States*. Series p-23, no. 80. Washington, DC: Government Printing Office.

———1980a. *Estimates of the Population of the United States by Age, Race, and Sex*. Series p-25, no. 870. Washington, DC: Government Printing Office.

———1980b. *Marital Status and Living Arrangements: March 1979*. Series p-20, no. 323. Washington, DC: Government Printing Office.

———1980c. *Statistical Abstract of the United States*. Washington, DC: Government Printing Office.

———1980d. *Subject Report: American Indians*. Washington, DC: Government Printing Office.

———1981. *Statistical Abstract of the United States*. Washington, DC: Government Printing Office.

U.S. Commission on Civil Rights, ed. 1980. *Civil Rights Issues of Asian and Pacific Americans: Myths and Realities*. Washington, DC: Government Printing Office.

U.S. Department of Labor, Bureau of Labor Statistics. 1980. *Employment and Earning* 25(1).

Vincent, F. 1967. "An Ecological Model for Assessing Psychological Difficulties in Children." *Child Welfare* 20:499-518.

Wachtel, S. 1982. "To Think About the Unthinkable." *Social Casework* 51:467-474.

Wahrhaftig, A. 1969. "The Folk Society on Type." In *The American Indian Reader*, edited by G. Wikerson. Albuquerque: National Indian Youth Council.

Watzlawick, P. 1976. *How Real is Real?* New York: Random House.

———S. Beavin, and D. Jackson. 1967. *Pragmatics of Human Communication*. New York: Norton.

Wax, R. 1970. *The Warrior Dropout*. New York: Aldine.

Weiss, R. 1975. *Marital Separation*. New York: Basic Books.

———1979. "Growing up a Little Faster: The Experience of Growing up in a Single-Parent Household." *Journal of Social Issue* 35:97-111.

William, J., and G. Morland. 1976. *Race, Color and the Young Child*. Chapel Hill: University of North Carolina Press.

Wintemute, G. and B. Messer, eds. 1982. *Social Work Practice with Native American Families*. Mitchell, SD: Dakota Wesleyan University.

Yang, C. 1959. *A Chinese Family in the Communist Revolution*. Boston: MIT Press.

Young, D. 1969. "The Socialization of Minority Peoples." In *Handbook of Socialization Theory and Research*, edited by D. Goslin. Chicago: Rand McNally.

Zintz, M. 1963. *Education Across Cultures*. Dubuque: William C. Brown.

About the Author

Man Keung Ho is Professor of Social Work at the University of Oklahoma. He is an Approved Supervisor and a clinical member of the American Association for Marriage and Family Therapy. He has served on the editorial board of *Practice Digest* and as an External Examiner for the Chinese University of Hong Kong. He has maintained an active practice in individual, marital, and family therapy, and is currently the director of Moore Transcultural Family Study Institute. His most recent book is *Building a Successful Intermarriage* (1984).